An Ottoman Century

SUNY Series in Medieval Middle East History
Edited by Jere Bacharach

An Ottoman Century

THE DISTRICT OF JERUSALEM IN THE 1600s

Dror Ze'evi

STATE UNIVERSITY OF NEW YORK PRESS

Published by
State University of New York Press, Albany

Printed in the United States of America

For information, address State University of New York Press,
State University Plaza, Albany, N.Y., 12246

Production by Cathleen Collins
Marketing by Dana Yanulavich

Library of Congress Cataloging in Publication Data

Ze'evi, Dror, 1953–
An Ottoman century : the district of Jerusalem in the 1600s / Dror Ze'evi.
p. cm. — (SUNY series in medieval Middle East history)
Originally presented as the author's thesis.
Includes bibliographical references and index.
ISBN 0-7914-2915-6 (alk. paper). — ISBN 0-7914-2916-4 (pbk. : alk. paper)
1. Jerusalem—History. 2. Turkey—History—Ottoman Empire, 1288–1918. I. Title. II. Series.
DS109.92.Z44 1996
956.94'4203—dc20 95-30362
CIP

10 9 8 7 6 5 4 3 2 1

To Amira, David, Lior and Omer

Contents

Note on Transliteration

People in the region of Jerusalem at the time of this study spoke two languages. The governing elite spoke Turkish, while the rest of the population were mostly Arabic speakers. Scribes at the *sharī'a* court in the city, which provided much of the source material for this study, moved at ease between Turkish and Arabic. Frequently one may find a Turkish expression or verb in a mainly Arabic document, or vice versa. Furthermore, there is almost no way of knowing what the pronunciation of many terms of Turkish or Arabic origin was. Were they pronounced as they are today in modern Turkish usage, or did they sound closer to Arabic speech? Sometimes it is even difficult to discern what language was spoken in court. Since the presiding judges usually came from Anatolia, and graduated from the State's colleges in Istanbul, most of them probably spoke Turkish better than they did Arabic. It would be reasonable to assume that few of them could have understood the colloquial speech of villagers, or even that of city dwellers. Translators played a very important part in this bilingual atmosphere. The records in court were probably first translated into Turkish for the qadi's sake, and then back into Arabic for the record.

For all these reasons it was difficult to decide what system of transliteration to use. Translating terms into Arabic would sometimes sound awkward, especially when some of the terms include Turkish or Persian syntax or morphology, as in ther terms *bad-ı hava*, or *beylerbeylik*. It would be no less awkward to render words spoken by an Arab *fallāḥ* in Turkish transliteration. I have decided, therefore, to use both systems of transliteration simultaneously. Terms used mainly by Turkish speakers; political, economic or military terminology prevalent in the imperial center; and direct translations from documents in Ottoman Turkish, were rendered in modern Turkish transliteration. All the rest, including terms originating in Turkish but commonly used by Arabic speakers, such as *sanjaq* (*sancak*, in Turkish) were rendered in Arabic. At times the decision had to be arbitrary.

In several cases, including place names like Hebron, Jaffa or Bethlehem, and familiar terms such as *sheikh* or *ulema*, the common form of the term was used.

Arabic transliteration follows the system of the *International Journal of Middle East Studies.*

Preface

Research for this book was done in several locations. The archives in Istanbul, Paris, Marseilles and London yielded important material. So did libraries at London, Jerusalem, Paris and Princeton.

The most important source for this work, however, was the *sharī'a* court in Jerusalem. Working there was a unique experience. Crammed into one small room we sat together—our guide and mentor, Sheikh As'ad al-Ḥusayni, three scribes, and two or three historians working on their research. We worked there for months, often holding the heavy volumes on our knees and doing our best to copy records into notebooks perched on the edge of a clerk's desk. At times we would all break into heated discussions of the political situation, or joke about the awkward conditions. Sheikh As'ad, a fountain of knowledge on questions of language, history and Islamic law, would lend a hand in decoding some of the more difficult texts.

But the most peculiar feature of working at the *sharī'a* court, was the fact that it was not an archive. We were working inside a functioning court of law. As we lifted our eyes from the ancient volumes, we could sometimes see similar cases unfolding before us. Couples came in to sign a marriage contract, a house owner would request a document of ownership, and sometimes a small delegation would come to solve a dispute. Though it belongs in another era, and I am aware of the differences, this experience has taught me more about my research than much of the material meticulously gathered there. I would like to thank all the qadis and officials at the Jerusalem *sharī'a* court who helped us so much, and above all Sheikh As'ad al-Imām al-Ḥusayni, and the director, Mr. Zayn al-Dīn al-'Alami.

My principal debt of gratitude is to Ehud Toledano, my advisor for the dissertation, who read the manuscript and provided a great deal of insight. His help and guidance were invaluable. I would also like to thank Amnon Cohen, who introduced me to the world of the *sijill* and helped me break the code; Halil Bey Inalcik, who discussed many subjects with me, read parts of the manuscript, and showed me where I got it wrong; and Michael Cook, who read several chapters and made me look at things more closely.

It is a pity that I cannot convey my thanks to Albert Hourani, a special person who devoted his time to guide and encourage me throughout my research. Albert also read the manuscript and offered many of his shrewd and observant insights.

Many friends contributed of their thoughts and knowledge. For their helpful remarks thanks are due to Iris Agmon, a constant intellectual stimulus; to Amy Singer and Itzik Reiter, my brothers-in-pen at court; to Nimrod Hurvitz, who had many sharp observations; and to Israel Gershoni and Haggay Erlich who saw me through the darker moments.

I wish to thank the staff of the *Başbakanlık Arşivi* in Istanbul and the staff of the American Research Institute in Turkey, as well as my colleague there, Fariba Zarinebaf-Shahr, for their help and hospitality.

The production staff of SUNY Press at Albany has invested much time and effort into publishing this book. I would like to thank them all for their wonderful work, and especially Christine Worden and Cathleen Collins, for their assistance and persistence in guiding me through the various stages of production.

I owe a debt of love and gratitude to my wife, Amira, and to my family, forced to follow me to London and Princeton, and to suffer my tribulations and long periods of absence visiting faraway archives. I am especially indebted to my son, David, who grew up to be my computer adviser, and saved me in those hours of panic, when the text suddenly disappeared somewhere in the bowels of the machine.

This work would not have been possible without the generous finanacial help of several institutions. I would like to thank my parents and my parents-in-law, the Rothschild foundation, the Yigal Alon fund, Tel-Aviv University, and Ben-Gurion University, for their help in various stages of this research. My sincere thanks to the staff of the department for Near East Studies at Princeton University for their assistance during my year of postdoctorate studies there.

Beer-Sheva
February 1995

Dror Ze'evi

Introduction

In 1512 a young new sultan arrived at the throne in Istanbul. Selim I, otherwise known as Selim *the grim,* reoriented the Ottoman empire to its eastern front, and challenged his two formidable rivals, the Safavid shah Isma'il, and the Mamluk sultan Qānṣuh al-Ghawri. Immediately following his accession to the throne Selim began to plan his campaign against the Safavids, and two years later, in early 1514, he left Istanbul at the head of his army, on his way to the eastern front. In August of that year the two armies met in the valley of Chaldiran (Çaldıran), north of Tabriz, the Safavid capital. the battle was won by Selim's army, but the approaching winter and the pressures of the janissaries forced the sultan to order a withdrawal to winter quarters in Anatolia.

Confrontation with the Safavids brought the Ottomans closer to the Mamluks. A defence treaty was signed between the Safavids and the Mamluks, and now it was only a question of time before Ottomans and Mamluks, contenders for leadership in Sunni Islam, would meet on the battlefield. Two years later, in 1516, Selim made preparations for yet another campaign in the East. It is not clear whether his initial plan was to return to his unfinished business with the Safavids, or to surprise the unsuspecting Mamluks, but as his army approached Syria, the Mamluk sultan, Qānṣuh, hastily arranged his army and marched north. Information about the advancing Mamluk army reached Selim, and a series of failed diplomatic contacts and half-hearted overtures turned down by both sides escalated the conflict until war was declared. On 24 August 1516, the Ottomans and the Mamluks faced each other on the plain of Marj Dābiq near Aleppo.

The Mamluks fought valiantly, but their old fashioned bows and arrows were no match for state-of-the-art Ottoman firearms. Waves of Mamluk cavalry attacks crashed against efficient Ottoman fire and at a critical moment an entire Mamluk flank, headed by the governor of Aleppo, Khā'ir (Hayır) Bey, crossed over to the Ottoman side. The battle ended in a crushing defeat for the Mamluks. The sultan, Qānṣuh, was killed, and the remains of his army retreated south. As Selim entered Damascus, delegations from all provinces of the sultanate came to pledge allegiance and to plead for amnesty and protection.[1]

The historian Ibn Ṭulūn, who recorded the events of the conquest, describes the Ottoman army's trip south to Egypt as short and uneventful, apart from short battles in the Jordan valley and at the village of Khān Yūnus, near Gaza. Small-scale uprisings in Safad, Ramla and Gaza were quickly and efficiently crushed, and on January 1517 the Ottoman army crossed the Sinai desert and prepared for another confrontation with the Mamluks. The ensuing battle, which took place in the field of Raydāniyya near Cairo, was an overwhelming defeat for the Mamluks, and the remains of the Mamluk army dispersed. The Ottomans had completed their conquest of the sultanate, and could now declare themselves uncontested leaders of the Islamic world, and keepers of its holy sanctuaries in Mecca, Medina and Jerusalem. Efficient bureaucrats set out to prepare the ground for establishing Ottoman order in the new territories.[2]

In the century following the Ottoman conquest, the district of Jerusalem still retained many characteristics of the vanquished Mamluk sultanate. Old social institutions, laws, cultural norms, and even surviving members of the ruling elite itself, were part of the new scene, and served as constant reminders of this slowly fading past. Not until the end of the sixteenth century did Ottoman rule emerge as a distinct type of Muslim government, leaving its special mark on culture and society.

In general terms the Ottomans accepted Mamluk administrative divisions, which saw Palestine as part of the Syrian province, but internally the partition of the area was changed. The province of Damascus (*eyalet* or *vilayet* in Turkish, *wilāya* in Arabic), was divided into new districts (*sancak* in Turkish, *sanjaq* or *liwā'* in Arabic) and subdistricts (*nahiye* in Turkish, *nāḥiya* in Arabic), but for several decades the new division retained Mamluk imprints such as the special status accorded to Safad and Gaza as the more important districts in the Palestinian provinces. Gaza was ruled by a governor with chances of promotion to the position of province governor (*vali, wāli*). The district of Jerusalem retained its Mamluk subdivision into three *nāḥiyas* (Jerusalem, Hebron and Banu ʿAmr) but in the course of the century the third subdistrict was abolished and only the first two remained.[3]

At the base of this new Ottoman administrative division stood the *timār* system. *Timārs* were landed fiefs of different size and income, distributed by the sultan to soldiers and officials, most of them officers of the famous *sipahi* cavalry units. An officer who was entrusted to a *timār* would receive his income from part of the fief's tax revenues, and in return would be required to keep the peace in his *timār,* and to arm and train several retainers for war. A district governor would in most cases be the commanding officer of a *sipahi* regiment, and the *vali*, the province governor, would also be commander-in-chief of all district governors.

Along with *timārs*, which officially remained part of the sultan's land, and in which cultivators had certain rights, systems of land tenure included *waqf* (Turkish: *vakıf*) land, dedicated by its owners to public welfare, religious purposes or private beneficiaries. In the district of Jerusalem *waqf* lands constituted a large part, perhaps even the largest category of cultivated land, estimated by some at around 60 percent. The Ottomans left Mamluk *waqf* institutions intact, and added many of their own during the sixteenth and seventeenth centuries. Beside *timārs* and *waqfs* there was some private land, mostly in and around towns and villages.

Improved security in towns and villages and for caravans on the road, a tighter system of administrative control, a more efficient bureaucracy and a pragmatic system of taxation which led to economic expansion, have all contributed to rapid population growth at the beginning of the sixteenth century. According to some researchers, the country's population at the time is estimated at two hundred thousand, most of them in villages. The population in each of the three biggest cities, Gaza, Safad and Jerusalem, was estimated at five to six thousand, and these numbers grew steadily until mid-century. Growth was also fueled by a renewal of maritime and regional trade, and by renewed settlement of Jews expelled from Spain, who found refuge in the Ottoman Empire. This trend was reversed later in the century, and the population continued to decline in the seventeenth century.[4]

As in many of their other conquests, the Ottomans left taxation principles more or less intact in the first decades of their rule. Taxes in Jerusalem, therefore, were collected according to a different system altogether than that prevailing in the Balkans or in Anatolia. But in their meticulous way the Ottomans carried out surveys of the conquered territories to determine production capacities and to define new rates of taxation. In the course of the century, taxes seem to have increased and revenues accruing from the province rose, even when the population began to decrease.[5]

Ottoman economic policy tended to compartmentalize the populace, and keep an eye over changes in occupation or status, but a flexible approach to applying laws and customs made it possible for people in the region to adapt to changing circumstances, and to initiate an economic boom in the sixteenth century. This same pragmatism had led the Ottomans to play down their control of local economy in the seventeenth century, and to allow the province and the district to conduct their own economic affairs. Jewish and Christian communities in Jerusalem, as in other districts of the empire, were integrated into the economic fabric. Ottoman attitudes to these minorities did not differ much from its treatment of Muslim populations. One indication is the degree of trust in which Christians and Jews held the new local *sharīʿa* court, and their willingness to apply for state justice even when they were not obliged to.[6]

Inside Jerusalem the conquest brought with it a change of emphasis. The Ottomans recognized the religious importance of Jerusalem, as their willingness to invest heavily in the city and its surroundings bears testimony. Instead of carrying on the Mamluk proclivity to invest in religious institutions, however, the new rulers chose to cut down spending on madrasas and mosques, of which the city already had its fair share, and to direct the flow of budget allocations, contributions and alms, to improving security, to providing water, to erecting a new covered market, and to enhancing the welfare of Jerusalem's population. Reconstruction of the city wall and the castle, some twenty years after the conquest, gave the inhabitants a sense of security which was lacking for so many years. Repairing and enlarging the water systems, including the building of a pipeline from the village of Arṭās south of Bethlehem to Jerusalem, helped provide water for the rapidly growing town. Rebuilding and renovating the markets, along with the establishment of a large size *waqf*—al-Khāṣikiyya, or Haseki Sultan—for the welfare of the inhabitants, gave a serious boost to the economy and to the city's standard of living. The awareness of social justice and proper administration brought by the Ottomans was enhanced by the establishment of a *sharīʿa* court, headed by a qadi appointed by decree from Istanbul to provide a counterweight to the governor and his retinue.

It took several decades, until the second half of the sixteenth century, for Ottoman patterns of administration and economy to set in. It took even longer for Ottoman culture and the new outlook of a world empire to become part of people's worldview. A mere century later, however, in the early 1700s, Palestine witnessed the beginning of Western encroachment on its economy and politics, and the rise to power of local potentates who defied Ottoman rule and rebelled against it. Intensive trade with Europe, mainly with France, brought with it glimpses of Western influence on local economic patterns, and at the same time helped alleviate some of the suspicion felt by inhabitants of this region toward the Christian West and its representatives. Through these chinks in the armor, some of Europe's culture found its way in. It is therefore just as difficult to discern in this later period which strands of local history are uniquely Ottoman, and which were the result of local power struggles or of outside influences.[7]

The truly Ottoman period in Jerusalem and in the other Arab provinces, therefore, is the one in between. The second century of Ottoman rule, forming the time frame for this study, is perhaps the clearest manifestation in this region of "the Ottoman way"—the distinct set of norms and methods that represents the empire's rule in all realms of life.

In Jerusalem the seventeenth century culminated in open rebellion in 1703, known as the naqīb al-ashraf revolt. Records of this event depict a society in turmoil, and cast a shadow over the whole period leading up to the rebellion. The book describes the district of Jerusalem in the century preceding these dramatic events, and analyzes their causes and circumstances.

At the outset of the book the stage is set, upon which the events of the century unfolded. Its first part portrays the countryside, agriculture and villages, as seen by contemporary Western travelers and pilgrims. Their reports are then contrasted with accounts from Arabic and Turkish sources, out of which other symbol-laden depictions of reality emerge. From the surrounding villages the description moves on to the city itself. In light of debates about the nature of cities in the Islamic world, one of the questions posed here is the extent of Jerusalem's urban character. Was there a municipal authority? Did the city's inhabitants feel a common bond uniting them as a community? Was it a clearly defined entity set apart from surrounding villages? Although Jerusalem, an ancient city, and the site of numerous conquests and cultures, cannot be taken as a model for all Islamic urban communities in the Ottoman period, its structure and function suggest the existence of a well-developed, typically Ottoman urban authority.

The city and the district are then examined in their political and social contexts. At the end of the sixteenth century, tensions were already apparent between local governors—sons and slaves of former senior officials, or Bedouin shaykhs in the area—and their colleagues appointed by the Ottoman government. This rivalry intensified during the seventeenth century as local governors formed governing households while strengthening their hold on the districts of Palestine. New source material found in Muslim court archives sheds light on the peculiar history and the downfall of these households.

For several decades local governing families managed to resist the center's pressures to appoint governors other than their own. Simultaneously, through intermarriage, business transactions and joint military ventures, they merged into one extended family, controlling most of Western Palestine. In the second half of the century, however, the imperial center retrieved some of its former power, and through a combination of covert action and political shrewdness succeeded in breaking the hold of these households. These were now replaced by other governors, appointed from Istanbul or from the provincial capital of Damascus. Chapter 2 traces the formation of local households, their consolidation as local ruling dynasties, the slow process of amalgamation into one combined force, and their dissolution at the end of the century.

First to notice these changing circumstances later in the century were the notables of Jerusalem. Following a period of readjustment in the wake of the Ottoman conquest, ulema (*'ulāmā'*), members of distinguished families, and wealthy merchants, gradually regained and reinforced their former status. Joining the same Sufi brotherhoods, participating in the same mystic ceremonies, the localizing governing elite and the emerging notable elite soon found common ground and created a basis for cooperation to the benefit of both sides. These ties enabled notables to acquire tax-free land and other assets, thereby strengthening their economic and social status. Later in the seventeenth century, having amassed considerable fortunes in city and village alike, notable families became aware of their cohesion as a group and of their social position, and strove to complement it with a measure of political power. The third chapter examines these processes and their tragic denouement in the 1703 revolt.

A main target of the revolt was the local military force. This establishment and in particular the very special role played by the bedouin in military affairs are not well known. Received wisdom describes the bedouin as diehard enemies of Ottoman rule and as a perennial menace to local governors. In the period surveyed in this study, however, bedouin tribes played a different role altogether. Following the decline of elite Ottoman troops—the *sipahi*s and the janissaries—bedouin warriors emerged as the main force capable of replacing them on the local scene. Governors hired them as militia forces in their service and employed them in a variety of security tasks. The unique formation of sedentary-nomad relations observed in this period, and the meaning these relations took on for the culture and economy of the district, were an early indication of bedouin involvement in Palestinian districts, which had become more widespread in later centuries.

Local economic life was dependent to a great extent on agriculture and systems of land tenure. Agrarian relations in the district were complex and tense. Here the lethargy of the center was evident. As the landbased cavalry and infantry became inefficient in the late sixteenth century, old mechanisms for distributing and managing fiefs lost their *raison d'être* and fell into disuse. *Timār* holders in the district of Jerusalem and its environs often preferred to lease their fiefs to the highest bidder in order to avoid the painstaking process of exacting taxes and overseeing the villagers. Local leasing of fiefs, later to become comprehensive government policy, caused considerable damage to the agriculture, and weakened rural areas. The imperial center chose to ignore these harmful tendencies, but other results, more beneficial for the local population, were equally ignored.

Periodic land surveys, an Ottoman bureaucratic practice used to register all land, population and expected yield, fell into disuse at the beginning of the seventeenth century. Replaced by a relatively lenient set of agrarian legal norms, it permitted peasants and other land holders to regard state land as freehold for all practical purposes, while upholding the principle of the sultan's ultimate ownership. Among those who stood to gain most from the government's leniency were once again the local notables. They managed to buy or rent large tracts of land and to increase their private holdings, using their high social profile and their government patrons as a shield against heavy taxation.

The century also witnessed rapid developments in the monetary and fiscal system, in local industry, and in internal and external commerce. In the sixteenth century, the economy was tightly controlled and centrally directed. Tax revenues were assessed through meticulous land surveys, the qadi's court published detailed price lists for basic commodities several times a year, and export of certain products and items to Europe was strictly forbidden. Beginning at the end of the century, these control mechanisms disappeared altogether. The fiscal system lost its guiding principles and the burden of arbitrary taxes became heavier. Local governors adopted a "laissez faire" attitude in internal trade, and external trade was also allowed to go on unhampered. Weaker central control and a disoriented tax system had immediate effects on local economic life, and on the integration of the area into the world economy.

Examining the place of women in the social system allows us to view such social and economic processes from a different perspective. Here, too, accepted stereotypes, originating in Western literature and projected backwards from later periods, are critically reevaluated. Local sources show clearly that women in Jerusalem lived and acted in a social and economic system separate to some extent from the dominant male establishment. Islamic law and local custom gave women a certain leeway in the realm of marriage and personal status, as well as in business and property rights. Many business transactions in the district were conducted by women who represented their own interests. What can all this tell us about discrimination of women, about their life in a male-dominated society, and about systems of social control?

It is my hope that examining all these perspectives together in such a small area over a period of time may afford us a more lucid understanding of Jerusalem as an Ottoman district in the seventeenth century, and perhaps shed some more light on the history of other Ottoman provinces and districts during the same period.

Chapter I

Zooming In

THE CITY AND ITS SURROUNDINGS

Historical research is always bound by time and space. This is the special context which the historian brings into his investigation of a culture or an event. Yet formal definitions of time and space can sometimes be misleading. The pace changes from one century to the next, and from one place to another. Likewise, the spatial borders that are believed by any human culture to surround it may change over time. These changes occur in the imagined space itself, and in the feared unknown beyond its borders.

Descriptions of the district (*sanjaq*; Turk. *sancak*) of Jerusalem in the seventeenth century may suggest the way in which this area was viewed by its inhabitants, by their rulers, and by travelers coming from abroad. It could serve as a basis for understanding local politics, culture and economy. The description starts at the district's borders, goes on to the villages and the city, and then on to the smaller neighborhoods and to the individual house itself.

THE DISTRICT OF JERUSALEM IN PILGRIMS' ACCOUNTS

The inhabitants of Jerusalem and its surroundings in the seventeenth century left few descriptions of their world. Local travel accounts, or chronicles written in the area by its Muslim inhabitants, are very rare. Most descriptions were written by Christian and Jewish travelers who visited the area in the course of the century. Apart from the distorting conventions of style and literary expectations in such accounts, many of the non-Muslim visitors were also torn between conflicting emotions. Their writing was conditioned by religious awe and longing for the biblical past; by misconceptions about the Orient, gleaned from generations of proto-Orientalist literature and Crusader myths; and by wide-eyed astonishment at its present-day rulers and inhabitants, so different, so strange and menacing.[1]

Historians trying to uncover the mysteries of this past era are very much like these travelers of old. They too weigh anchor in a distant port, carrying their own burden of memories and misconceptions, images of past glory, and notions of decline and corruption. They too find it hard to reconcile their images of gloom with depictions of reality that offer a different understanding. Following the travelers in their encounter with the new world that surrounds them may therefore introduce us to this faraway land, and guide us through our first hesitant steps. From these works of fiction that combine myth and reflections of reality, we may then proceed to another viewpoint, another reality—that of the local inhabitants.

At the beginning of the century an unknown English traveler described the Muslim inhabitants of Palestine as a barbarous crowd, fond of adultery, sodomy, rape and other beastly deeds. "There is no evil deed on this earth not performed by the inhabitants of this Terra Sancta or holy land, which hath the name and nothing else" he said.[2] Others, trapped in romantic biblical images, described a fertile land of milk and honey. One of them went as far as to describe the gigantic grapes he found in the "valley of Eshkol" south of Bethlehem, similar to those carried on a pole between two by Moses' spies.

Descriptions of both kinds abound in travelers' accounts. Some manage to combine both aspects, praising the countryside and its beauty, and denouncing its inhabitants at one and the same time. Many travelers copied descriptions from each other, perhaps in order to satisfy the readers' demand for accounts of holy sites which they have not been able to visit. Their descriptions are therefore not very reliable, and should be cross-checked. Still, several provide a more or less accurate description of areas they traveled through, and a close examination reveals consistent changes over time.

The first encounter with the Holy Land may have been the sight of a small port, where their journey at sea came to an end. After a perilous journey through a sea infested with pirates of almost every creed and nation, the ships arrived at Jaffa, Acre, Gaza or Haifa. The sight was grim and ominous. The coastal towns, destroyed by the Ayyubids and the Mamluks in the wake of the Crusades, in order to prevent another invasion and the reestablishment of a Crusader stronghold on the shore, were left in their ruin until the end of the seventeenth century. These were meager villages that could hardly supply the basic needs of traders and commerce.

Apart from Gaza, which had a small wharf, all provided nothing but natural anchorages, devoid of any docks or wave breakers. French merchants trading in wheat and cotton preferred the town of Ramle, some twenty kilometers inland, to the almost deserted port of Jaffa.[4]

Other travelers came by land, mainly from Egypt, in organized caravans transporting hundreds of people at the same time. At the slow pace of the caravan, it took some twenty days to travel from Cairo to Jerusalem. Many travelers complained about the delays along the way:

> [It was a] 20 days journey, which upon hors we could have come in 12, but the camels slow march and the Jews sabbathes whereupon the caravan rested did lengthen it to 20 which is the ordinary tyme that the caravan requires for that journey.[5]

Their first impressions of Palestine were, however, quite different. Having crossed the arid deserts of Sinai and the Negev, they were overjoyed at the sight of the stretches of fields and vineyards that welcomed them as they approached Gaza and the coastal plain.[6]

The road coming from Damascus was shorter and safer, but strangers still preferred to travel in company, usually with an armed escort. Highway robbers were not uncommon even along this main route, linking the capital of the province of Damascus with one of its major cities.[7]

Western Palestine, or the southwestern part of the province of Damascus, was divided at the time into four main districts (*sanjaqs*): Gaza, Lajjun (the northern valleys), Nabulus and Jerusalem. There were minor border changes in the course of the century, but as a rule this administrative and military division remained fairly stable from the Ottoman conquest until the eighteenth century. Travel and commerce between districts was unrestricted, and there was no visible demarcation of the borders. The district of Jerusalem, which the travelers now entered, extended from Ramallah in the north to Hebron in the south, and from Jaffa on the Mediterranean coast to Jericho and the Jordan valley to the east of the city.[8]

Two main roads crossed the district, one along the Judean-Samarian mountain range, running north to south, and the other, connecting the coastal plain in the west to the Jordan river valley in the east. The two mountain roads intersected in Jerusalem. Travelers coming from Jaffa followed the road east, along the plains to Ramle, to the valley of Ayalon, and then usually up the narrow creek of Bab al-Wad to the city. Those coming from Damascus, Acre and Haifa chose in most cases to travel south, through the plain of Esdraelon (Marj bani ʿAmr), Jenin and Nabulus, and the mountains of Samaria. Those coming from Cairo would choose either the road going north to Jaffa and hence east to Jerusalem, or the one leading northeast from Bayt Jibrin to Hebron, Bethlehem and finally Jerusalem.

Carried away by their biblical imagination, they were enchanted by the land's beauty and its natural fertility. At this period there were still vast areas of natural forest and grasslands. Roger, a Frenchman who visited Palestine in the 1630s, describes the many kinds of wildlife: lions, buffaloes, camels, leopards, boars, jackals and hyenas. A change in emphasis is apparent at the beginning of the eighteenth century, in the accounts of English travelers like Sandys and Maundrel. They describe an interim state where some areas are still intensively cultivated and abound in pasture, while others are depopulated and poor, overgrown or covered by marshes.[9]

In our century, however, travelers were still impressed by what they saw as their mules carried them inland. Those coming from Jaffa described the fields of cotton and vegetables, and noticed a change in the pattern of cultivation as olive trees and other fruit-bearing trees gradually dominated the landscape when they moved into the hills:

> The conntry ajacent [to Ramle] abounds in cotton which can be spun in very fine yarn they sell at 14 pence a pound. [. . .] We marched east and by south 6 myles through a vally pleasent and fertill [. . .Then] we marched SE [southeast] through a hilly country yet fruitful in cornes e ayle e more populous then the plaines of Gaffa[10]

Those coming from the north and south had the same impressions. John Sanderson, following the northern route at the beginning of the century, remarked that the meaning of the name Jenin in Arabic is paradise, and indeed "so pleasant is this place and cituation that well may it be cauled paradice."[11] Those coming from Hebron in the south were impressed by vineyards, fruit orchards and vegetables grown in the valleys and plains.[12]

Disappointment and fear replaced elation as they entered the more mountainous regions and climbed the steep valleys and hills. The wide and comfortable roads of the plains gave way to narrow and rocky paths. The northern road seemed more comfortable at first, but as it approached Jerusalem the surface became so uneven that even mules and asses found it hard to traverse.[13] Those coming from Jaffa and Ramle encountered an even more arduous journey. "We arrived at a very narrow valley, strewn with boulders and pebbles" writes Jean Doubdan. "These are the bad roads that will carry us almost as far as Jerusalem." This road was particularly difficult for the cumbersome caravans coming from Egypt, as one traveler remarks: "[The way was] very unsafe both for us and the camels which doe not agree to march upon hard stony and uneven ground."[14]

Many travelers felt they were entering a dangerous, wild forest. Some had visions of terrible beasts and wild half-naked barbarians. The tension and mystery they felt on the way, (doubtless embellished and exaggerated for the sake of their readers), heightened their expectations as they approached the holy city.[15]

As night descended, they looked for a safe shelter to sleep in. Along the roads there were several hostels, usually called *khān* by the locals, or *kale* (citadel) by the Ottoman government. Some were ancient, dating back to Crusader or Mamluk times, others were built or restored by the Ottomans with two purposes in mind. They were both fortresses manned by a small garrison, intended to secure the main routes, and inns for travelers, merchants and pilgrims. In the eyes of Western guests they were very uncomfortable, nothing more than a square court surrounded by stone walls. Travelers were not given rooms or food, and had to settle for the relative security afforded by the walls and the soldiers.[16]

From time to time along the road, the travelers had to set up camp in one of the villages. In larger ones they could sometimes find an Ottoman official or a Christian monastery that would take them in, but in most cases they relied, grudgingly at first, on the hospitality of villagers. D'Arvieux, a French nobleman who served the local governing family of Turabay in the district of Lajjun for several years, describes the system of village hospitality. In every village, he writes, there is one sheikh who is appointed by the governors as headman. This sheikh is ordered to erect a guesthouse, called a *manzil*. It is usually situated near the sheikh's house, and has two levels. Visitors are supposed to store their belongings and sleep on the higher level, and to tie up their mounts on the lower level. No charge is required for the lavish hospitality. In return these village headmen are exempted from certain taxes.[17]

As they would leave the village and return to the road, the travelers would once again be seized by fear and tension, no doubt fueled by the frequent appearance of armed horsemen demanding a sum of money as toll (*ghafār*, or "caphare.") Described in almost every traveler's account, often gesturing with their guns or spears, they had the appearance of desperate highway robbers. Descriptions of Palestine throughout the Ottoman period abound in stories about such adventures in which, miraculously, no one gets hurt. *Sijill* records, however, suggest a different explanation. An event recorded in 1680 may serve to elucidate this frequent misunderstanding:

> When visitors to the graves of the holy prophets, and to [the grave of] our lord *al-Kalīm*, may he rest in peace[18] ended their pilgrimage and intended to return to their homes, news had reached them that a quarrel broke out between the villagers of Bayt Iksa, and those of Bayt Liqya, both attached to the *waqf* of the *Khāsikiyya*.[19] The apparent reason for the quarrel was the allocation of *ghafār* payments. [The pilgrims were afraid that] if they returned [while this dispute was going on] they would be attacked by brigands. They [decided] that they cannot leave Jerusalem unless it was settled, since the road in

> question is favored by highwaymen and other menaces (*arbāb al-makhafāt wa-l-takhwīf.*)
>
> They asked the qadi, therefore, to summon both sides and solve this problem. First the qadi summoned a representative of the Khāṣikiyya *waqf,* and the supervisor (*mutawalli*) himself arrived. As the qadi instructed him, he brought to court the headmen (*al-mashāyikh wa-l-mutakallimīn*) of both villages. To the qadi's questions they replied that in the past both villages guarded the road, and divided the tolls equally among those accustomed to receive them. The dispute arose when a certain person from Bayt Liqya decided that he should take all gains and was not prepared to share them with others in his own village, or with the villagers of Bayt Iksa.
>
> Having heard the evidence, the qadi instructed both sides to return to the old arrangement, and to protect travelers from robbers along the stretch of road passing through their villages. If anyone traveling on this road is robbed or harmed in any way, the qadi warned, he would hold them responsible, and order those in charge of the village to punish them.[20] In view of this decision both sides declared a truce, and decided to divide the *ghafār* money equally between the two villages. If anyone travelling on that road will lose anything, they promised, they will either return it or reimburse him.[21]

Integrating villagers and bedouins into the road defence system in return for a fee they had the right to collect from travelers on the road was apparently an official Ottoman (or at least local) government policy. Sometimes these villagers demanded more than they were allowed to, and from time to time real robbers masqueraded as road guards, but in most cases *ghafār* was legal payment for services rendered, and even imposed as a duty by the authorities. But seeing the unruly villagers, their authoritative manner, and the lack of any direct communication, gave rise to a myth of insecurity, violence and robbery on the way to Jerusalem, repeated endlessly in travelers' accounts.

A bit shaken, but usually safe and sound, the travelers could finally see Jerusalem from the hilltops surrounding it. They were struck by its stone walls, and by the many domes, turrets and minarets. Excited and relieved they knelt and prayed, and then hurried down to the city's imposing gates.

PHYSICAL WALLS, MENTAL WALLS

Any attempt to describe the city itself presents some of the questions debated for many years under the general heading of "the Islamic city"—

questions related to the specific character of Islamic cities as opposed to non-Islamic ones. A possible starting point for this debate is Max Weber's book, *The City*, where he sets the "Western city" in opposition to other types of cities. In Western and central Europe, he writes, cities emerged as a result of political and economic forces. The outcome was the creation of a social structure—the urban community—which is unique to the West, and almost unknown in other cultures. Among the conditions leading to the creation of an urban community were a predominance of trade and commercial relations, the existence of a citadel or ramparts, a marketplace, courts of law possessing a degree of autonomous jurisdiction, and at least partial political autonomy.[22]

In the Orient many of these conditions existed, says Weber, but in most cases cities had no administrative autonomy and lacked the ability to form urban associations: "The city as corporate *per se* was unknown."[23] This fact finds expression in the physical layouts of Oriental cities. Communal associations in the Islamic world were always on a narrower basis—guilds or neighborhoods. Control was always in the hands of a monarch, through ministers or slaves, and never transferred to notables or elders in the city. Even in the modern era, when the Ottoman Empire reformed the municipal administration of Mecca, it created some sort of balance between several authorities, but not a corporate unity of the city itself. In the urban centers of the Orient, he concludes, the urban community never existed as a framework.

From a relatively early stage, observers of Islamic cultures focused on three issues suggested by Weber's formulation. One questioned the existence of a municipal authority in the city. Another applied itself to corporate action, or to questions pertaining to the emergence of an urban community in Muslim cities. A third examined the layout of the city itself, and the way it reflects the social realities of the city. Most observers did not distinguish between the three issues in their research. Von Grünebaum, for instance, following the French historian Marçais, concludes that Islamic cities had no municipal authority to guide them, and that this was reflected in their appearance as a haphazard collection of ethnic or religious neighborhoods. Since no frameworks existed for corporate action on the municipal scale, this helter-skelter city design is typical of the Islamic world.[24]

This attitude finds full expression in the writings of Ira Lapidus on Muslim cities in the late Middle Ages. Looking at Cairo, Damascus and Aleppo in the Mamluk period, Lapidus draws the conclusion that in these cities guilds and Sufi brotherhoods were loosely knit organizations that did not provide a basis for communal cooperation. Other types of organization, on a larger scale, were practically nonexistent. In his opinion, any kind of corporate feeling must have centered around the ulema (*'ulama'*,) and since the religion regarded politics as part of its responsibilities, the ulema considered day-too-day administration in the city part of their duties. The ulema were the only cohesive element inside the city, and conducted its affairs through various networks of patronage and clientship. According to Lapidus the most efficient networks were those that united people according to their adherence to any one of four Islamic schools of jurisprudence (*madhhab*s.) If any sort of organization can be found in these cities, it is therefore bound to be along the lines of these networks.[25]

In a later article Lapidus reaffirms his views on the Muslim city, and defines it as a geographic location of social groups whose members and activities were either greater or smaller in scope than the pale of the city itself. Cities were physical entities, but not social bodies unified by typical Islamic qualities.[26]

In a recent article, Janet Abu-Lughod criticized this attitude. In books on the Islamic city, she writes, one can find chains of transmission, like the ancient *isnād*s attesting to the authenticity of hadith statements. Most research works on Islamic cities were based on a study of one case, or very few cases, in the same region, Usually it does not examine the whole range of cities in the Islamic cultural sphere. Many of these works, like those of von Grünebaum and Marçais, draw on a distinct corpus of research—a North-African paradigm that dates back to the period of French colonial rule of the Magreb. Another "chain of transmission" which includes, among others, the works of Lapidus, focuses on the cities of Egypt and the Fertile Crescent. These two distorted views of the Islamic city have created false images, and described situations particular to one area as total truths pertaining to the totality of Islamic culture.[27]

According to Abu-Lughod, the first doubts concerning these examples were raised in a study by Hourani and Stern which undertook to examine the concept of Islamic cities. In this work, which serves as a basis for her own conclusions, Hourani and Stern pointed out the specificity of these earlier examples, and mentioned several other Islamic cities that do not fit the structures suggested by former researchers. Another critique of this reigning paradigm appears in an essay by the anthropologist Dale Eickelman, suggesting that instead of a sole Islamic model, there should be several different ones.[28]

Abu Lughod's own work focuses on the physical structure of the city. Cities and quarters in which Muslims reside are easy to identify even in faraway countries and in cultures that differ greatly from each other, she claims. This should lead to the conclusion that Islam *does* have certain common features, different from those that characterize other cultures. A city's structure is influenced by its topography, the building materials used, means of transportation, social organization and municipal legal codes. Since topography, means of transportation and building materials are different in every location, the domains relevant to an investigation of specifically Islamic influences are social organization, and relevant Islamic legal systems.[29]

Three dominant traits of Islamic cities stand out in these domains: separation of religious communities, gender-oriented prohibitions, and the legal system bearing on property. All Islamic cities therefore display a space laden with semiotic meaning. The city's streets and houses are warning signs and instructions, advising the stranger on the proper way to act.[30]

Cultural conditions separating between Muslims and other "people of the Book" (mostly Christians and Jews, but later also Hindus, Buddhists, etc.) did not evolve as a direct result of Islamic teachings, but rather as an outcome of long periods of war and strife. It may therefore be categorized as an historical, not an "Islamic," cultural phenomenon. Still, it is typical of almost all Islamic cities. The second trait—gender prohibitions—is indeed uniquely Islamic in its extent. Islam lays down strict rules of separation that minimize the possibility of invading women's privacy even by sight, not just by physical or verbal contact. The structure of the house, the location and shape of doors and windows, the distance between houses, all these stem to a certain extent from the laws and norms of separation.

The third trait—Islamic property laws—defines the priorities and rights in urban planning. In the Islamic legal system, the owner himself has first priority in designating urban space. His neighbors also have certain rights, mainly concerning their own privacy, while the authorities have almost no rights at all. When, at times, this distinct set of property laws was enforced by a weak government, or a negligent administrative system, the obvious result was some disorder: concealed approaches leading to the house became more important than the main road itself, and the resulting chaos blurred what remained of the original plan.

Abu Lughod concludes that the debate should be focused not on the typical structure of "the Islamic city" but rather on the specific Islamic framework in which such cities were established and governed, and which contributed to their special character. Islamic cities vary a great deal, as regards their structure, and the relationship between various functions within them, but the shared historical and cultural heritage did create a measure of resemblance, which unites all Islamic urban settlements.

Suraya Faroqhi adds another dimension to the debate. The importance attributed to religion in defining the structure of the city is exaggerated, she claims. It certainly has a role in defining the shape and structure of buildings and cities, but ascribing so much importance to religion implies that there are no real changes over time in moral and social normative systems. Such an assumption renders all social history meaningless. There is no doubt that significant changes have occurred in relation to morality and society throughout Islamic history. These changes were reflected in the structure and administration of cities, and even of single houses. Modern research should examine these changes, and lay aside the discussion of perennial aspects of religion and culture.[31]

In order to put these contrasting views in focus, let us now turn to a description of Jerusalem as one example of an Islamic city. It is true that the city itself was not founded in the Islamic era. Its general layout was determined many years before it was conquered by Islam. During the long period of Islamic rule Jews and Christians were a significant part of the population, and influenced the city's form and its functions. The centers of meaning and gravity inside the city were dictated to a certain extent by its topography. Still, Jerusalem was (and is) a holy Islamic city, and many of its inhabitants were Muslim ulema and clerics committed to upholding the tenets of Islamic religion and culture. In light of the data gathered about the city, we can begin to address the questions posed by modern research concerning the Islamic city—did its physical structure reflect its Islamic character? Was it an "urban community" as defined by Weber, or just a conglomerate of streets and houses, a geographical accident that did not correspond to any social body, as Lapidus describes it? Did the Ottoman government maintain some sort of a municipal administrative system, or was the city run by its inhabitants according to patronage lines? Following the city's description, we may resume the thread of the debate and try to answer some of these questions.

Rebuilt by Kanuni Sultan Süleyman (the Magnificent) in the mid-sixteenth century, the walls around the city of Jerusalem still stood high and imposing a century later. From descriptions made by travelers and from local documents, it appears that the wall was still seen as an efficient means of defending the city and its inhabitants. One traveler, later thrown into jail on suspicion of being a spy, describes the fortifications around the city:

> Upon the south side of Jerusalem there is a great iron gate whereon are planted seventeen pieces of Brass Cannon and is as large as the West gate of the Tower of London, the walls being very thick and fifty eight or sixty foot high. The North wall is not so strong and hath been often surprised but the South nearer on the East is impregnable, the bow of the hill on which the wall standeth being five times higher than it; on the North wall are 25 pieces of brass

> cannon near the gate which is also of iron; the East gate, a little without which St. Stephen was stoned, is to this day called by his name; there are five pieces of Cannon planted between the ruines of Port Aurea, or the Golden Gate, and the West Gate through which I first entred and where I saw fifteen pieces of Cannon more to secure it, which are iron as the rest. To conclude, Jerusalem is the strongest City that I saw in all my travels from Grand Cairo hither.[32]

The big gates were locked and bolted at sunset, and gate-keepers were placed at every entrance to make sure no one entered without inspection. Even during daytime entrance to the city was controlled. Christian and Jewish pilgrims were not allowed to enter by themselves. They had to unbuckle their swords and hold them in their hands, and to await formal escort. Sometimes they were received and escorted by the city's police officer, the *sūbāshi*.[33] In other cases the heads of their congregations were allowed to welcome the guests and accompany them on their way into the city. Visitors belonging to sects who had no representation in the city sometimes identified themselves as members of other sects and requested their protection. The defence expert mentioned above, a ship's captain by trade, was thrown in jail when, too proud to pretend, declared he was an Englishman, "for the Turks absolutely denied that they had ever heard either of my prince or my country, or that they paid any tribute."[34]

Unknown Muslims also had to go through some identification process before they were allowed to enter. *Dhimmī*s (non-Muslims living in Islamic lands) and *ḥarbī*s (non-Muslims from non-Muslim lands) had to pay entrance fees. Complaints were sometimes sent to the Sublime Porte in Istanbul, requesting a diminution of the fee.[35]

Both the Ottoman central government and the local administration saw the maintenance and defence of the wall as an important task. At the beginning of the century several firmans (Imperial decrees) were sent to the local governor, instructing him to rebuild parts of the wall. In the city itself the qadi made sure the wall was maintained as the city's main defence. It seems that the inhabitants themselves appreciated the importance of the wall and the measure of security it afforded:

> On the 20th of Rabīʿ al-awwal 1033 (24 Jan. 1624) several people, including the governor Muḥammad Pasha, the *mufti* (jurisconsult) Zakariyya *efendi*, the *khaṭīb* (preacher) in al-Aqsa, the *miʿmār bāshi* (chief architect) in the city,[36] and many others, came to court, and reported to the qadi that several Christians in the city built their houses contiguous to the wall. They claimed that these structures may undermine the city's security. Having checked the implications, the qadi instructed all inhabitants of the city to build their houses

at a distance of four *dhirāʿ* (yards[37]) from the wall. Houses touching the wall will be destroyed, he warned, and their owners will be flogged seventy times.[38]

A month later, however, several people returned to court, among them *sheikh al-sūq* (head of the market) and several soldiers in the local citadel. They reported that Gregor, the Armenian archbishop (*muṭrān*), was among the people whose houses were adjacent to the wall, and as a result of the former decree part of his house was destroyed. Since then, they said, thieves and bandits have picked the narrow passage near archbishop Gregor's house as their favorite spot. They lurk there day and night, and attack innocent passers-by. The qadi therefore issued another decree, permitting the Armenian dignitary to rebuild his house at that spot. There may have been other reasons for the new decision. Perhaps it was bought with Armenian money, But the exception demonstrates only that as a rule these new regulations were enforced, houses were demolished, and the testimony of Muslim witnesses was a necessary prerequisite to changing the former decision.[39]

What was it that motivated the Ottoman government, the city's local rulers, and the rest of the population, to be so adamant about the wall? Why did they invest so much time and money to maintain and rebuild it? One possible answer is the fear of bedouin attacks on the city. The Ottoman government saw Jerusalem as a city on the desert's edge, in need of protection from nomadic assaults. But such assaults did not occur in seventeenth-century Jerusalem, and local authorities were usually on good terms with the bedouins. Another possible motivation, and one that seems closer to the truth, is the fear of a resurgence of the Crusades, or of a premeditated Christian attack on the city.

A major cause for concern in the eyes of the Ottoman government at the beginning of the century was the aspiring young Lebanese amīr, Fakhr al-Dīn al-Maʿnī (the Second). A letter sent by Pindar, the English ambassador in Istanbul, in 1614 echoes this Ottoman concern. At that time Ottoman agents reported that the rebellious amīr, who found shelter in the court of Tuscany in Italy, prepares to gather a fleet and return to the Lebanon, where he will recruit an army, and set out to conquer Palestine and Jerusalem. Such apprehensions were augmented by news of the establishment of a new religious-military order in Tuscany, specifically intended to lead the new crusade. The Ottoman fleet, writes ambassador Pindar, is deployed along the Lebanese coastline to prevent a landing, but if such a landing were to take place in spite of these efforts, instructions were sent to the pasha of Damascus. He is to go to Jerusalem and expel all monks and priests residing there, apparently to prevent their acting as a fifth column to help the rebel's forces when they reach the city:

> They are in great jealousie of some intendment by the Christians to assist the Emir of Sydon and therefore they have well guarded those seacosts to prevent his landing, and the cheife imployment of the Captan Bassaw (the Ottoman admiral) is to withstand anie sea forces may be sent with him, which is causing of his goeing out two monthes sooner then was accustomed. And in the meane time for fear of anie practice by the Christian princes about the Hollie land (as this conceipt is raysed because of the Emir of Sydon, if he weare established againe in his conntry) the Bassa (governor) of Damascus hath order to goe to Jerusalem and to turn out all the friars and Christians, and to prohibitt all secoors hether of pilgrims or other.[40]

Threats posed by the recalcitrant Lebanese amīr continued to bother the Ottoman government in Istanbul, Damascus and Jerusalem for several decades. In 1623 Fakhr al-Din did in fact invade the Palestinian coastal plain, and was stopped only by a coalition of local forces on the banks of the Yarkon ('Ujja) river, not far from Jaffa. Even in the thirties, until his defeat, and finally his execution in 1635, the amīr and his armies posed a threat to the Ottoman center. The authorities and the local population in Jerusalem, as in many other parts of the empire, were united by fear of a renewed crusade led by the amīr, aimed at the reestablishment of Christendom in Jerusalem.

Local rulers—the governors of Jerusalem—were aware of this clear and present danger. The tribulations suffered by a French consul who arrived in the city in 1623 attest to this pervasive fear and suspicion. Jean Lempereur had obtained his nomination as consul in Jerusalem after a protracted series of negotiations by the French ambassador to the Porte. Bearing a royal Ottoman decree he proceeded to the city with an impressive entourage, and finally presented his credentials to a haughty and reserved local qadi. He was allowed to reside in the Christian neighborhood, provided he would pay at some later date a sum of money promised in the decree.[41]

Before long the new consul found himself at odds with the governor and the qadi. Lempereur thought the reason was the governor's greed and his own insistence on the rights of French merchants in Ramle. But in a letter he sent to the king of France on the 20th of November 1624 he claimed that the governor undermines his position, alleging that he is cooperating with the amīr Fakhr al-Dīn, and that he intends to deliver the city of Jerusalem into his hands. The governor, writes Lempereur, managed to convince his superiors in the provincial capital. They in turn sent a contingent of twenty horsemen to detain the consul and fetch him to Damascus, where he was made to pay a large ransom. It seems, then, that this new crusade created real, tangible fears, that could be manipulated by the local governor. It may also have been, of course, the real reason for the consul's deportation, and there might have been an element of truth in the allegations.[42]

Fear of a renewed crusade was pervasive in the Muslim community of Jerusalem throughout the century. Doubdan, who visited the city many years later, describes a riot sparked by restoration work in the convent of the Holy Saviour (St. Sauveur) in 1652. In the course of repairs local Muslim construction workers began to excavate under the convent. Several ancient rooms were discovered, and soon rumors began to circulate. The inhabitants of the city, already suspicious of the monks who "were building a castle in order to destroy the city, and by this means would soon become our masters" told stories of a long tunnel being dug by the Christians. Through these tunnels, the rumor persisted, Christian armies will invade the city. Some said these tunnels led to Jaffa, and others thought they may lead to Malta, to the fortress of the knights of St. John, their formidable enemies.[43]

Alongside the physical walls of the city, then, another set of walls was erected—mental walls that blocked out other cultures, other ideas. The Muslim population of Jerusalem saw in every Christian action a hidden meaning, in every Western idea a Trojan horse carrying the avant-garde of a new crusade. The Christian population of Jerusalem was suspected of being a potential fifth column, waiting for an opportunity to betray the city. These suspicions competed with the traditional Muslim attitude of tolerance towards the "people of the Book", set higher sectarian walls, and hampered interconfessional relations. Each community led its own life, integrating with all others in trade and the labor market, but shunning intellectual contact.[44]

Events that left a deep impression on one community—the miracles and wonders of the Sufi sheikh Muḥammad al-ʿAlami, the mystic Lurian Kabbala developed in the Jewish communities of Safad and Jerusalem, the rise and fall of the false messiah Shabbetai Zevi, the original reform ideas of Cyril Lukaris debated by the Greek-Orthodox church in Jerusalem—echoes of all these hardly penetrated the walls of suspicion, and failed to leave a lasting impression on the culture and life of neighboring communities. In this state of affairs the physical separation of these communities was accentuated, and each community preferred to enclose itself in its own perimeter.

THE CITY AND ITS INTERNAL DIVISION

The territory demarcated by the walls in the seventeenth century is almost identical to the area of today's walled city of Jerusalem. Only minor changes in the gates and walls were carried out since the restoration of the walls by Sultan Süleyman, apparently as part of his millennarian campaign.[45] The city's population was relatively small. On the basis of demographic data from the previous century, it can be assumed that the population did not exceed ten thousand inhabitants throughout the century. Maps drawn by travelers and pilgrims, though inaccurate, convey a sense of large open spaces, and no density of population anywhere in the city.

In a research based on sixteenth century Ottoman tax surveys,[46] Amnon Cohen and Bernard Lewis have found that whereas in the Mamluk period the city's quarters had some homogeneous character based on ethnic communities or social distinctions, this state of affairs gave way to a much more heterogeneous mix, both socially and ethnically, at the beginning of the Ottoman period. They attribute this mainly to the influx of immigrants from other parts of the empire. This situation began to change a century or so after the conquest. Quarter perimeters were still not clearly defined, the area was not yet divided into the four distinct quarters characteristic of today's walled city, but some sort of division along ethnic and religious, as well as social lines, did emerge.[47]

Confessional neighborhoods evolved around the religious centers of meaning in the city. The Muslim population gathered around the Haram (Temple mount), mainly in the northeastern areas. The Christians tended to buy and build their houses around the Holy Sepulcher convent, and when the Franciscan convent moved from Mount Zion to this area in the mid-sixteenth century, another center of meaning drew Christians together. Armenian Christians preferred the vicinity of their own convent in the southwestern part of the city. The Jews found themselves, whether by default or because they chose to reside near the Wailing wall, in the southern neighborhoods: al-Sharaf, al-Maslakh and al-Risha.

This division, though recognized by all inhabitants, was not strictly adhered to, or imposed. Muslims resided (or at least bought and rented houses) in all quarters. The *sijill* contains numerous sales deeds in which Jews and Muslims, including some wealthy notables of the local elite, buy houses in Jewish neighborhoods, either from Jews or from other Muslims. No limitation was imposed on Christians or Jews wishing to buy houses in Muslim neighborhoods, but most preferred the safety of their own communities. As a result of growing tensions, the process of sectarian separation was apparently in one of its active stages.[48]

As in the city of Aleppo a century later, people had close ties with their neighbors, cooperating in law suits against "immoral" residents of the quarter or corrupt officials, but in contrast to the seemingly structured Aleppine quarter, in Jerusalem this communal action did not correspond to any administrative unit. It appeared to be a spontaneous reaction to circumstances, shared between several neighbors, who decided to take action on their own initiative.[49]

It is harder to determine whether neighborhoods reflected social or economic differences. Did all members of the elite prefer to reside in the same areas? Were some areas considered more aristocratic than others? At first sight the *sijill* seems to suggest that people of every economic and social background, including villagers, bought houses everywhere, but in this respect evidence in the *sijill* might be misleading. Buying a house, or part of one, was sometimes a mere investment, motivated by economic considerations, and did not always reflect people's preferences in choosing their home. Local notables saw immovables as a relatively safe investment, and bought houses and courtyards in quantity. The *sharīʿa*'s partnership laws also made it possible for people to invest in tiny fragments of such property. Townspeople, as well as villagers and even total strangers, could, for example, buy one *qirāṭ*—one part in twenty-four—of a luxurious, well-situated house, which would then be rented out, providing a steady income. These purchases reflected neither the buyer's status, nor his choice of residence.

Still, there are indications of alignment along economic and social lines, at least in the Muslim community. This can be gleaned both from the recorded inheritance of deceased inhabitants of the city, and from large auctions of property, usually offered for sale by wives and daughters who inherited houses and wished to sell them. In some cases it is clear from lists of furniture and personal belongings attached to the record, that the house being sold was indeed the main residence of the family. This can also supply further evidence about its economic and social status.

The considerable diversity of such records implies that neighborhoods in themselves in fact had no homogeneity, and that their borders did not define social or economic strata. Rich and poor, high and low, lived in the same areas. On the other hand, they indicate some sort of socio-economic differentiation within certain neighborhoods, in relation to the area's proximity to centers of meaning. Wealthier people tended to live closer to their sacred shrines. In predominantly Muslim areas, a house closer to the Haram was apparently preferred. The farther away from the Haram, the less attractive, and probably the less wealthy the neighborhood.

Rich and influential notables bought houses near the gates leading to al-Aqsa and to the Dome of the Rock. Others resided in houses looking into the Haram. Thus, the wealthy ʿAsali family bought a house "straddling the Gate of the Chain" (Bāb al-Silsila) close to the Kaitbay madrasa. Another notable endowed as *waqf* a house in the same area which was formerly the private residence of Musa Pasha ibn Ridwan, a governor of Gaza and Jerusalem. Many notables lived in Bab Hutta, close to the northern gates of the Haram, while others chose the eastern parts of Bab al-ʿAmud, along the alleys leading to the mosques.[50]

URBAN CONTROL AND THE PUBLIC DOMAIN

City life flowed around several religious and administrative centers. Separate sectarian cohesion was maintained and reproduced in religious institutions—mosques, Sufi lodges, churches, convents and synagogues. These were not just places of worship and prayer. In many cases they hosted a whole spectrum of community life. In a short treatise written by Abu al-Fath al-Dajjāni, a seventeenth-century scholar, about the deplorable state of al-Aqsa and other mosques, the purist Sunni author describes the ḥaram as a place of worldly pursuits and enjoyment, condemning women's gossip, petition writing, singing and dancing, selling and buying. The *ḥaram* has even become a playground for little children and a meadow for grazing sheep, he complains.[51] The same was true, to a smaller extent, in regard to the Holy Sepulcher, and to other convents and synagogues, where Jewish or Christian congregations met to discuss religious, as well as worldly matters, and to celebrate holidays, holy days and festivals.

The "secular" life of the city revolved around a different set of institutions.[52] These institutions, though representing Muslim rule and superiority, tended to be more tolerant towards other religions, and allowed a greater deal of social and economic interaction between the communities. First and foremost among them was the *sharīʿa* court (*majlis al-sharʿ al-sharīf*, literally: "the council of the noble law"). This establishment, at the entrance to the Ḥaram, near the gate of the chain (Bāb al-Silsila) contained the qadi's court. The range of its activities and responsibilities, however, transcended that of any Western equivalent. In fact the district qadi was also acting mayor in charge of municipal planning, maintenance, social welfare and hygiene; chief notary; police commissioner; and part-time purser for the Ottoman government. A description by the Ottoman traveler Evliya Çelebi, may reflect some of the *sharīʿa* court's responsibilities:

> Twenty *ağas*[53] serve by Imperial decree under the molla of Jerusalem.[54] The first is the *muhzir başi* who was appointed by the Sultan in an

> official ceremony. He is in charge of keeping the gates at night, and is aided in his duties by Imperial forces. The second *ağa* is the *su nazırı*, (supervisor of water supply). The third *ağa is the mimar başı*, in charge of construction and repairs. The fourth is the *mühendisbaşı* chief engineer). The fifth is the *mu'temedbaşı* (chief purser). The sixth is the *sarrafbaşı*, head of the money changers, who pays the ulema their yearly Sultanic grant. The seventh *ağa* is the *veznedarbaşı* (treasurer). The eighth is the *subaşı* (in charge of public order). The ninth is the *bazarbaşı* (market supervisor). The tenth is the *şehir Kethüdası* (city deputy) and the eleventh is the *bezazıstan kethüdası* (deputy in charge of the inner market). Finally, every day all heads of merchant guilds (*esnafın şeyhleri*) present themselves at the council to perform their duties.[55]

It is well known that Evliya's writing tends to exaggerate and embellish, and cannot be considered an accurate description. Furthermore, few of the officers he mentioned appear in any capacity in the period's *sijills*, but as an overview of the *sharī'a* court, Evliya's description is not totally inaccurate. *Sijill* records describe the court's involvement in almost all spheres of activity mentioned: the qadi used to send his chief architect to examine requests for building, restoration and demolition, and granted authorizations on the basis of his reports. The city's economic activity was coordinated by his court with the head of the market (*shaykh al-sūq*), the market supervisor (*muḥtasib*),[56] the scales supervisor (*kayyāl bāshi*) and the head of the merchants (*shaykh al-tujjār*), who represented all merchants and artisans. Special teams of investigation, made up of the local police officer (*subāshi*), the court summons officer (*muḥḍir bāshi*) and court scribes, were sent to investigate crimes and filed reports. The court served as purser and treasurer for the government in some matters of tax collection, and in payments made by the central government to officials and notables in the city.[57]

Other affairs were conducted in the court building itself. Court cases ranged from theft and murder, to requests for welfare charity and child custody. Contracts and sales deeds were signed in the presence of the qadi and his aides, Marriage agreements were recorded, and divorce cases settled. Representatives of the population came to court to protest against corruption and misrule, and local governors chose the same establishment to convene notables and plebs. Villagers came there to pay their taxes, and *dhimmis* (Christians and Jews) followed suit to pay the poll tax (*jizya*) imposed on them.[58]

It is evident, therefore, that defining *majlis al-shar' al-sharif* as a mere court of law, does not take into account the immense range of public and municipal activities conducted there in the Ottoman period (at least until the mid-nineteenth century). Although this institution will be referred to as the "*sharīʿa* court," it must be borne in mind that this was the city's main social establishment, and that it wielded considerable political influence within and beyond the city's walls.

Another institution of central economic and social importance was the market or bazaar. The marketplace in Jerusalem, as in most other Ottoman cities, was a well-organized, ordered exchange, supervised by the authorities. The market directed and defined the economic life of Christians, Muslims and Jews, who were sometimes members of joint commercial or artisanal unions. Slaves and servants traded there alongside members of local and governing elites. Janissary soldiers shared their meals with humble artisans. The market was a source for contagious rumors and a testing ground for economic policies.

The marketplace was therefore a stage set for confrontations of different social groups, where brawls and riots broke out. It was also the means for many to cross the social divide and move upwards. Making money through trade or manufacture was almost a prerequisite for social mobility. The market provided shelter for runaway slaves, unemployed soldiers, or villagers escaping exploitation by their landlords. The market was one of the main links between the city and its surrounding villages and bedouin tribes. Yet this was also a clearly structured and hierarchical institution, where villager, townsman and bedouin each had their place and function, where each recognized his role in an ancient order.[59]

A leading social welfare role was fulfilled by the Khāsikiyya *waqf*. This was in fact a complex of institutions: large soup kitchens, stores, schools, hostels and mosques, dedicated in 1552 by Khaseki Hürrem Sultan, wife of Sultan Süleyman the Magnificent. The Khasikiyya, aimed at providing welfare for the inhabitants of Jerusalem, was the largest *waqf* ever established in Palestine. Scores of villages, in the vicinity of the city and even as far north as the *vilayet* of Tripoly (Tarablus al-Sham) in Lebanon, paid their taxes directly to the *waqf*'s officials. Many of the city's poorer inhabitants, alongside some of the not-so-poor *ʿulamā*, received a daily plate of food from the *waqf*'s kitchens (*ʿimāra*.) Determining the right to such a daily portion (*ṭāsa min al-ṭaʿām*) was part of the qadi's duties.[60]

In addition to its social role, the *waqf* also played an important part in the city's economy. Its supervisors operated flourmills, olive and sesame oil presses, and bakeries. Many guilds sold most of their produce to the *waqf*. These supervisors and comptrollers determined the city's economy to a large extent. The sheer numbers of ledgers, letters and firmans concerning the *waqf* in the *sijill* and in Istanbul's archives attest to its importance in the eyes of the Ottoman authorities. Although the institution seems to have declined at the end of the seventeenth century, a Damascene visitor to Jerusalem at the end of the century describes it as a thriving and dynamic institution:

> Then we passed by the *Khāsiki Takīya*,[61] famous in and around Jerusalem. We have found it full of goods and good deeds, its flourmill spinning on its hinge, and all its stores standing proud, brimming with charity and mercy.[62]

Like the local market, the Khasikiyya *waqf* institutionalized the relations between the city and its rural hinterland. Khasikiyya officials bought large quantities of food and firewood from neighboring villages. Other villagers were paid to collect and purchase commodities for the *waqf*. Villagers were suppliers, either by law or by concession, but never eligible for welfare support themselves. This was reserved for townspeople. Like the market, therefore, the *waqf* functioned as both an intersection of city and village, and as a clear demarcation of the boundaries between them.

A lesser-known establishment was the hospital, al-*bimāristān al-Ṣalāḥi*, named after its founder, Ṣalāḥ al-Dīn al-Ayyūbi (Saladin).[63] Travelers and pilgrims do not mention the hospital, perhaps because the Christian and Jewish communities had other, smaller facilities. Information about it in Muslim sources is also scant, and in our period it might have declined. But several records in the *sijill* indicate that towards mid-century there was at least one attempt to restore the hospital and renew its function:

> On the 6th of Shaʿbān 1045 (15 January 1636) sheikh ʿUmar ibn ʿAbd al-Samad, the supervisor of waqf *al-bimāristān al-Ṣalāḥi*, arrived in court, and informed the qadi that parts of the hospital are ruined, and urgently in need of repair. At his request the qadi appointed a team, including a surveyor (*nā'ib al-kashf*) and the chief architect, to examine the building.
>
> The team found out that new gates are needed for the staircase, and restoration work is necessary in *bayt al-marḍa* (the sick bay) and *bayt al-majānīn* (the mental institution.) Partial restoration is needed in *bayt al-mughtasal* (the laundry/ bath) and *bayt al-kaḥḥālīn* (the eye clinic). Four *iwāns* (recess-like sitting rooms) have partially disintegrated, and so have the stone benches at the entrance. Other rooms are filled with dirt and garbage. The *muʿallim* (master builder) ʿAbd al-Muḥsin was brought over, and estimated the overall cost at 552 *ghurūsh*.[64] [Prices are listed for each item on the list].
>
> In view of this report the qadi allowed the *mutawalli* to carry on with the restoration, and to pay the necessary costs from the *waqf*'s funds as a first priority.[65]

The principles guiding this institution, the social groups admitted or treated, are unknown, but the *bimāristān* had been part of the Muslim urban community in Jerusalem for quite some time, providing medical care for a variety of physical and mental problems.

The main public social pastime in male society was coffee drinking, which had caught on at the end of the sixteenth century, in defiance of *fatwa*s and imperial decrees banning or denouncing the new custom. The *sijill* records many apparently prosperous coffee houses, where tobacco and hashish soon became part of the scene. The sources do not provide any information on the clientele of these establishments, but owners seem to have come from several social groups: ulema, officers and government officials, artisans and merchants. In light of Ralph Hattox's research on coffee and coffee houses in the Ottoman Empire, it can be assumed that here too the coffee house served as a meeting place for all levels of urban society, at least in the Muslim community, and functioned as part-time literary salon and local news network.[66]

PRIVATE HOMES, THEIR STRUCTURE AND CONTENTS

The Muslim house in seventeenth-century Jerusalem retained its traditional style, uninfluenced by Western building traditions. The house itself, its furniture, housewares and ornaments, were part of a coherent social culture, influenced by Islam and by other ancient Near Eastern and Mediterranean traditions.

Most of the houses in Jerusalem and in neighboring towns were built of stone, coated with plaster on the inside. In this respect local masonry was well developed and advanced in comparison to other cultures where, as Braudel notices, cheaper and less durable wooden houses were erected.[67] Poorer people, however, lived in very small houses, usually in one room. Travelers often had the impression that buildings were unstable, and on the verge of collapse. *Sijill* documents frequently refer to such small houses or rooms, usually called *bayt*, to set them apart from the bigger house, the *dār* which sometimes included several *buyūt* of different sizes.

Affluent houses included many rooms, balconies, kitchens and lavatories. They were often built in two stories, the first sometimes serving as a stable for horses and mules. Rich houses would include a cellar or storeroom to keep stocks of food and other commodities, as well as water reservoirs and storage tanks for oil in their courtyards. Some houses had patios and rose gardens, and even ornate water-fountains. Yet even these upper-class houses were not built in pompous style, or as Morison comments, referring to the governor's mansion: "A French bourgeois would consider himself badly lodged" (un bourgeois de France s'estimerait mal logé).

In large houses roofs were constructed as domes of stone, while in smaller ones flat roofs were built, leaning on several wooden beams. In many houses a short parapet was constructed on the roof, where people stored things, worked, and sometimes slept in summer. Most roofs were slightly pitched to allow rainwater to flow into underground reservoirs.

Inside, houses were divided by a partition, preferably a wall or a patio, but in poorer houses by a drape or a sheet, into an external sphere—the *salāmlik* (*selamlık* in Turkish) and an internal one—the *ḥarīm*, or *ḥaramlik* (*haremlik* in Turkish).[68] This division into two well-defined spheres is sometimes described as separating the male/public and the female/private areas of the house, but as Leslie Peirce has shown in her work on the imperial harem, this division is somewhat misleading, and conventional Western notions of public and private are not necessarily congruent with division by gender.[69] In governing households the *ḥaramlik* was usually the center of public administration, and both domains were at one and the same time forbidden to some, open to others, and under legal and moral public scrutiny.

In wealthier houses, shared by several mature women—with their husbands and sons—each would have separate quarters, sometimes joined together by a courtyard, where women would meet to work or discuss things. Movement between the *ḥaramlik* and the *salāmlik* in the presence of male visitors was strictly forbidden to anyone but the husband or father and small children. When no male visitors were around, everyone apparently moved freely inside the house.

Travelers coming to Jerusalem described the terrible revenge of husbands against strangers who dared cross the sacred line. [70] Yet, oddly enough, there is little mention of such cases in the *sijill*, and most of those mentioned occur in villages outside the city. In some cases the investigators chose not to indict the possible perpetrator, possibly because the motive was justified at least by norm and custom, if not by law. But an investigation of some sort was always carried out in cases of death caused by unnatural causes, even when believed to have been an accident. Apparently stories about the frequent slaying of wives and suspected male lovers was more a myth perpetuated as a means of socialization than an actual practice, at least in the city.

The strict demand for boundary definitions separating external and internal found expression in entrances and doorways. These were often located in alleys and cul-de-sacs branching off from the main road. Windows had no panes in most cases, and those located in women's quarters had screens of wood (*mashrabiyya*) to hide them from view, and yet allow the women themselves to look outside. Alleged sightlines of indecent views from windows and roofs were often cause for a lawsuit or a complaint to the qadi. When winter came, inhabitants of the city filled their windows with wood and sawdust to keep out the cold. Heating in most cases was provided by earthenware bowls of coal placed in the middle of the room.

Furniture did not vary greatly between rich and poor, but there were some differences between Muslims on the one hand, and Christians and Jews on the other. Muslim homes displayed relatively few items of wooden or metal furniture. Records of inheritance in the *sijill* do not mention wooden or metal beds, tables or chairs. In some Christian and Jewish houses, however, tables and chairs were part of the furniture. These items did not become part of the Muslim house until the nineteenth century.[72]

Braudel, who discusses this basic difference, stresses the existence of two different cultures that merge only seldom. In fact, the only place where the two furnishing styles coexisted was China, which apparently adopted desks and chairs in the sixth century, but chose to use them for separate functions and to retain the old "Oriental"-style furniture. In Jerusalem, where both styles remained side by side for centuries and did not merge, the existence of an entrenched cultural attitude is manifest.[73] Braudel does not provide an explanation for the apparent inability of these two different styles to coexist. In the local context, however, one reason may be a distinct Muslim problem. Dividing the house into two distinct parts, *ḥaramlik* and *salāmlik*, and sometimes having to accommodate several women, meant that each room would have to serve for numerous functions. The use of traditional "soft" furniture allowed for swift changes in room functions: eating, entertaining, sleeping, and so on. Introduction of "hard" wooden or metal furniture would have meant assigning one major function to each room, and hence reducing the already limited flexibility of the house. Jews and Christians, who were not subject to such strict norms of gender separation, and many of whom had strong cultural contacts with Europe, adopted such styles more readily.

Most Muslim houses—whether belonging to janissary officers, ulema, governing families or *ra'āya* (*reaya* in Turkish: all those of nonelite status)—included mainly items of cloth and wool. Carpets, stuffed pillows, sheets and blankets. The rich would sleep on mattresses laid out on stone benches. During the day, ornate silk, velvet or cotton pillows would be placed on these benches. Wooden or metal chests, sometimes bound in leather, contained clothes, books, cutlery and other expensive items.[74] China plates, bowls and cups were common in rich houses, earthenware in others. In most cases no forks and few spoons are mentioned in inheritance cases. Several knives, mostly silver, were used to prepare food before it was served. Pots and pans were made of copper or clay. Several records indicate that it was fashionable to use plates elevated on a "heel" to serve food. Many houses contained elaborate tobacco-smoking implements and candleholders. Foodstuffs were usually kept in large clay pots, sometimes covered by ash to preserve their contents.[75]

Books and manuscripts were relatively rare. They appear in several inheritance records, mainly in houses of ulema and governors. All the books mentioned were religious, mostly having to do with Islamic jurisprudence (*fiqh*). This may reflect the small numbers of literate people in society, although taking into account the high prices of manuscripts few people could afford them even when they knew how to read and write. Governors and members of the ruling elite were also mostly literate, and some displayed a keen interest in poetry.[76]

ISLAM AND THE CITY

Picking up the thread of debate about the nature of Islamic cities, we should now try to see how Jerusalem's structure and layout conform to these ideas and whether they contribute to our understanding of the "Islamic city."

In the three major issues debated—the city's management, the existence of an urban community, and the physical layout—different, sometimes contradictory answers emerge. The city's layout was influenced to a considerable extent by Islamic cultural and social norms. The structure of houses, the location of doorways and windows, the spatial relations between houses, the creation of semiprivate alleys, the process of separation into distinct quarters—all these were determined by cultural and legal norms, and by historical processes influenced by these norms. They lent the city a distinct Islamic character, leaving its clear imprint on the ancient Roman-Byzantine layout.

The Muslim majority in the city undoubtedly felt a bond to an urban community, distinct from the villages around it, and stronger even than small-scale corporate entities like guilds or madhhabs. It was founded upon the city's status as a holy shrine, symbolized by the wall engulfing the city and separating it from its surroundings. It fed on a recurring fear of Christian crusade. These common bonds gave rise to corporate urban activities—complaints to the qadi about the state of the wall, protest against Western consuls, and finally, a sense of solidarity demonstrated in the Naqīb al-Ashrāf revolt at the beginning of the eighteenth century. The revolt, an uprising against the governor appointed by the central government, united the inhabitants of the city. They bolted the gates, and endured the hardship of siege and starvation for two years.[77]

To what extent did this urban community include Jews and Christians? In most cases, it seems, they looked on as bystanders, sometimes in fear, sometimes identifying themselves with their neighbors. Their bond to the predominantly Muslim urban community was probably weaker than their attachment to their own religious communities. They were discriminated against, had to pay extra taxes, and sometimes despised and ridiculed by the Muslim population. The shadow of a crusade, hovering above, did not permit any detente. Yet there are indications that Christians and Jews did see themselves as part of the urban community. They frequented the qadi's court, and did not hesitate to file complaints against members of their own community, or even against Muslims. They were members of guilds, and sometimes even elected to head them. Finally, during the revolt, there are indications that Christians sided with the rebels and helped them fight the governor's forces.

On the third question—the existence of municipal administration—the evidence is unequivocal. Seventeenth-century Jerusalem is characterized by an impressive array of municipal services, orchestrated by the qadi and his aides. The *sharīʿa* court dealt with all municipal problems: construction and demolition, hygiene, waste disposal, taxation, security, public order, market supervision, maintenance of water supply and social welfare. Other institutions, among them a charity *waqf* and a public hospital, cooperated in this urban project. Finally, frequent complaints by notables and others recorded in the *sijill* suggest that a measure of feedback and accountability existed between the urban community and the authorities.

We may conclude that Jerusalem was indeed peculiarly Islamic in many respects, and that its design and organization do reflect the existence of a coherent urban community, at least as far as the Muslim majority was concerned. Although the period under consideration was a time of contraction, it appears that in other centuries this urban community expanded to include minorities as well. Inasmuch as it reflects the Islamic influence on urban centers as a whole, Jerusalem indicates that Islamic civilizations did manage to shape their own special kind of city, and their own type of urban community.

Chapter 2

The Rise and Fall of Local Dynasties

When Jerusalem was conquered in 1517, the Ottoman Empire was a highly centralized bureaucratic state. Its power emanated from the sultan and his household, and filtered down to governors, administrators and military commanders throughout the realm. In the province of Damascus, as in all other provinces, the Ottoman center played a major role in regulating subjects' lives, their economy, security, public order, religion and social welfare. In the course of the first century of Ottoman rule, however, this state of affairs changed radically. A series of disruptions known collectively as the "Celali revolts," and the insurrections of mutinous pashas in eastern Anatolia, from around 1590 to the middle of the following century, made communications between the Anatolian center and the Arab provinces much more difficult.[1] Coupled with changes of emphasis in the government itself, these developments encouraged centrifugal tendencies, and centralized government gave way to a much more decentralized system. One of the main consequences was the seizure of actual control of the provinces by local governing families, known in the Ottoman political language of the time as *hanedans*.

This chapter considers the formation of one such local Ottoman elite made up of governing families in the highest rungs of local provincial government from the late 1600s, and its dissolution at the end of the seventeenth century. Provincial government, it should be stressed, was dependent upon many more officials, officers and soldiers at the lower echelons of the governing elite. Subsequent chapters will focus on these groups and on their transformation.

Soon after the conquest, Ottoman bureaucrats set out to demarcate provinces (*eyalet* or *beylerbeylik* in Turkish) and districts (*sanjaq*) in the newly conquered lands. Surveyors commissioned by the state combed towns and villages, registering every household's estimated income and tax yield. The new districts were then divided into even smaller surplus yielding units, generally called *timars*. *Sipahi*s, the soldiers and officers of an elite cavalry force trained in the capital, were brought over and settled in these *timār*s. Some of the taxes gathered by the state with the help of *timār* holders were used to pay for their salaries, and, relative to the estate's annual income, for additional soldiers under the *sipahi*'s command. Provincial administration was structured as a cavalry unit. Every group of *sipahi*s had a commanding officer, a *bölük başı*, usually granted a larger estate, and himself an adjudant of the district's governor. In the eyes of the Ottoman government, the district governor (*sanjaq bey*) was first and foremost a cavalry battalion commander. The governor of a province (*vali, beylerbey*) was, in addition to his other duties, a regiment commander in the *sipahi* corps. When called to the flag, a governor and his *sipahi*s were expected to join the march of the imperial army and wage war against the empire's enemies.

Until the mid-sixteenth century, two main sources supplied the empire's military and administrative manpower. One was the *devşirme* (literally, "gathering"). Every few years the sultan dispatched his troops to Christian villages in the Balkans and in Anatolia, to look for promising youths who would constitute the empire's future elite. The boys thus gathered would then formally become the sultan's slaves. Most were sent to farmers in Anatolia, where they would convert to Islam, learn the language and acquire other skills. Those would usually become soldiers and officers in the imperial army. A hand-picked group of boys would be brought to the inner service (*enderun*) in the royal palace, where they were to begin a long and rigorous process of education. Through the years a series of tests and selections determined who would leave to join the *sipahi*s or janissaries, who would be appointed personal valet to the sultan, and who would serve his master as an architect or a historian. Those earmarked for promotion had their careers planned, and in due course were given senior appointments in the provinces. Successful governors became state ministers.

Another source of manpower was the households of governors and ministers themselves. At their request, their sons and clients were sent to the provinces as middle rank administrators. Those who showed greater talent and ability were sometimes appointed to higher, better-paying positions in the provincial government, and some eventually became district and province governors. In theory there was a third source. Subjects of non-elite status (*reaya*) who volunteered to fight in a war and showed exceptional valor would sometimes be granted a *timār*. But the only way to reach the battlefield and fight a war would be to join the household of a governor or a high-ranking officer and become his client. In any case, those of *reaya* status who were granted *timars* seldom advanced beyond this stage in the first generation.[2]

In research based on Ottoman governor appointment registers, Metin Kunt examined the structure and status of provincial administration from the mid-sixteenth century to the mid-seventeenth century. Such appointment registers were kept and updated on a regular basis in the Ottoman capital, in order to allow the sultan and his aides to keep track of governors in each of the empire's myriad districts and provinces. The registers included details on the appointee himself, his origin, known relatives or patrons, and his present income. Having analyzed these ledgers statistically, Kunt concluded that the system of governor appointments changed a great deal during this period.[3]

The main conclusion of Kunt's research is the considerable devaluation in the importance of the district, and a parallel increase in the centrality of the province in internal Ottoman politics. The *sipahi* cavalry, with its reliance on bows and javelins and its inefficient handling of firearms, faded into obsolesence towards the end of the sixteenth century. As their military importance diminished, so did the administrative-economic system which served as a basis for their organization and structure. The district governor, whose main duty was to command a *sipahi* battalion and lead it into battle, was no longer a pivotal functionary. By contrast, the province governor, who had a much wider range of duties and responsibilities, gained in importance.

There were other changes. Towards the end of the sixteenth century governors and high-ranking officials, usually referred to as *ümera* (Arabic *umarā'*—lords, princes), insisted that their sons and clients be considered for senior government positions. This rapidly became the main source for provincial administrators. *Ümera*, who were formerly incorporated into the provincial system as timariots, or at most as holders of a *zeamet* (larger *timar* estate and a somewhat bigger contingent to command) were now appointed directly as district governors. Increased demands by the *ümera* for allocation of jobs to their protegés resulted in an inflation of governors. One immediate consequence was the abolition of the *devşirme* system. Instead of boys gathered from Christian villages, the inner service of the sultan's palace now admitted and trained the sons and clients of *ümera*. One of the only channels for social mobility for non-Muslim subjects was thus blocked.

Yet another consequence was shorter terms in office for governors and other high officials. *Ümera* eligible for governor status now had to play a game of musical chairs within a limited, and ever shrinking number of districts and provinces. The term of office as district governor became shorter, and in the seventeenth century governors were often appointed only for a year or two. Many senior officials found themselves with no district to govern, and were forced to take long vacations from office. In order to allow them to maintain a household in keeping with their status, the government bestowed on many governors estates with life-long tenure (*ber vech-i çiftlik*). These estates were sometimes very distant from the center, and the unemployed governor usually administered them from afar. This undermined the position of district governors even further. Large parts of their dominions were now taken away and given to other, higher ranking officials. The area actually under the governor's jurisdiction had shrunk considerably, even within his appointed district.[4]

As the system's internal logic slowly faded away, any position in government centers or in the provinces could serve as a springboard to the position of district governor. Whereas in the past every candidate had to present a record of service in junior government positions, now a prospective governor was not required to show any previous experience. Inexperienced sons of *ümera*, and those related to patrons in the imperial center, were given governorships in major districts.

While this tendency continued, says Kunt, the central government became increasingly worried about governors becoming too entrenched in their districts, forging an alliance with local elites to defy Ottoman rule. On the other hand, however, governors still needed to have some knowledge of specific problems and conditions in their region. The emerging pattern therefore dictated frequent transfers of governors from one district to another, but usually within the same province.

Kunt's sources have the advantage of a view from the center, and the ability to analyze statistically large numbers of districts in a vast area over a long period of time. But registers of appointment may also have a built-in drawback. A distant and formal point of view, of the kind usually found in Ottoman bureaucratic registers, may sometimes obfuscate the political nuances of appointments in the districts and provinces of the Ottoman Empire. This is where a smaller-scale study, concentrated in the district of Jerusalem and its neighboring districts, may view Kunt's conclusions against the background of local politics and society and provide some important insights.

Ottoman conquests brought about numerous changes in administration and in the structure of local government. Jerusalem, as well as the neighboring districts of Nabulus, Gaza and Lajjun, were placed under the jurisdiction of Damascus. Former Mamluk governors were deposed. A new system of taxation was worked out. District governors, qadis, *sipahis* and janissaries were sent by the government to rule its new possessions. The new administrative units in Palestine, however, retained some earlier Mamluk traits. In several districts a familiar administrative system, reminiscent of the Mamluk household, emerged at a relatively early stage. Several governing families appointed by the Ottomans managed to secure their rule in the area and transfer power within the family for more than a century. This system of hereditary rule in the *sanjaq*, was to influence other regions of the empire in the next century.

Three *ümera* households, *hanedans*, rose to power in the southwestern districts of the province of Damascus. The houses of Riḍwān (Turk. Rizvan), Ṭurabāy and Farrūkh (Turk. Ferruh) were to rule these districts until the late seventeenth century. While the latter two were the subject of several studies, no research has been done on the Riḍwāns, an important and influential family which held sway over most of Palestine for many years.[6]

These studies fail to recognize the full extent of dynasty rule over the districts of Palestine in the seventeenth century. The Farrūkhs, Riḍwāns and Ṭurabāys governed the districts of Jerusalem, Nabulus, Gaza and Lajjun almost until the end of the seventeenth century. During that time their relations gradually developed through marriage, political alliances and economic transactions. In the second half of the century, they became one extended dynasty. This chapter describes the local dynasties, their relations with each other and with the Ottoman center, their culture, and their final dissolution in the 1670s. Their disappearance towards the end of the century had a lasting effect on society and politics in the region.

THE RISE OF LOCAL DYNASTIES

The Riḍwāns

The house of Riḍwān was the most prestigious and influential of all dynasties in the southwestern districts of the province of Damascus. Its members regarded themselves, with some justification, as leaders of the region and to some extent as patrons of other households. The founder of the dynasty was Kara Shahin Muṣṭafa Pasha, a "slave of the gate" (*kapı kul*), a product of Sultan Süleyman's *devşirme* system who was educated in the inner service of the palace and reached a very high position in the Ottoman government. In 951 (1544–45) Muṣṭafa was appointed governor of Erzerum, and in 955 was made governor of the province of Diyarbekir. When his term of office ended he became personal tutor (*lala*) of prince Bayezit, the sultan's son.

Later on, apparently as an interim appointment, Mustafa received the governorship of Gaza, which, though a mere *sanjaq*, retained some of its former Mamluk grandeur. In 970 (1562–63) he was appointed governor of Egypt, a post he was deposed from three years later, in 973 (1565–66), perhaps because his patron Sultan Süleyman had died, and the new sovereign, Selim II, was reluctant to put his trust in the former tutor of Bayezit, his brother and rival. Mustafa Pasha died a short while later. His son, Riḍwān Pasha, who gave his name to the dynasty, was made treasurer (*defterdar*) of Yemen, and later governor of Gaza, during his father's lifetime. In 972 (1564–65) he became governor of the province of Yemen, and was deposed two years later. His deposition may have had something to do with that of his father at the same time, though no explanation is provided by the sources. He returned to the governorship of Gaza, and was later made *vali* of Ethiopia (Habeş), Basra and Diyarbekir, in succession. In 987 he led a military contingent in the war against the Safavids, and, as a token of gratitude for his distinction, was awarded the province of Anatolia in the Ottoman heartland, where he died in 993 (April 1585).

Riḍwān's brother, Bahrām Pasha, also became a high-ranking official in the Ottoman provincial administration. Starting out as governor of Nabulus, he was later appointed *Beylerbey* of Damascus and leader of the Hajj caravan from Damascus to Mecca (*amīr al-ḥajj al-shāmi*). Bahrām was the owner and patron of a Circassian *mamlūk* named Farrūkh, who was to become governor of Jerusalem and founder of the Farrūkh dynasty. Bahrām's sons and *mamlūk*s continued to rule the district of Nabulus alongside their Farrūkh allies well into the second half of the seventeenth century. Another of the family's *mamlūk*s, Kiwān, was sent to Damascus, where he distinguished himself in the service of the governor. Kiwān's son was to become governor and *amīr al-hajj* in the 1670s.[8]

Though no explanation is provided in biographies of the dynasty's ancestors, it is evident that they chose to make the city of Gaza their home and castle. Riḍwān's son, Ahmad Pasha, governed the district of Gaza, sometimes incorporating Jerusalem and Nabulus, for over thirty years and was frequently appointed *amīr al-hajj*. Unlike his predecessors, Ahmad had to fight for promotion to *beylerbey*, and grew old before he was given a province to rule in 1009 (1600–01) having sent gifts and large sums of money to countless vezirs and bureaucrats in Istanbul. He died in 1015 (1606–07).[9]

The next in line, Ḥasan Pasha ibn Aḥmad, was nicknamed "Arap" (the bedouin), probably because by that time the family came to be identified with the efficient control and intimate knowledge of the Bedouin. He justified his nickname time and again in the prolonged war against Fakhr al-Dīn of Lebanon, when his bedouin units proved most efficient and defeated Fakhr al-Dīn's army. Arap Ḥasan also managed to climb up in the ranks and was appointed governor of Tripoly (Ṭarāblus al-Shām), only to be deposed several years later, in 1054 (1644). Muḥibbi, who wrote his biography, mocks him, saying he was addicted to worldly pleasures. According to this biographer, Ḥasan had many wives and concubines, who bore him eighty-five sons, most of whom he did not recognize by name. When one of his sons died he was unable to remember who he was until his advisers described the son and his mother. "In short, Ḥasan Pasha had fun in this world," says Muḥibbi ominously. His style of living had not only brought him punishment in the next world, as Muḥibbi implies, it had also burdened the family with a heavy debt.[10]

Arap Ḥasan's son, Ḥusayn Pasha, was apparently a better administrator than his father, and managed to resuscitate the family's economic fortunes. In his father's lifetime he was appointed governor of Jerusalem and Nabulus, and *amīr al-ḥajj*. When Arap Ḥasan died, he inherited the impoverished governorship of Gaza. Ḥusayn's period in office was prosperous and peaceful. His reputation reached the bedouins and strife between the settled and nomad populations decreased considerably. When his son Ibrahīm came of age, Ḥusayn appointed him governor of Jerusalem, and later on gave him the family's stronghold, the district of Gaza, while he himself chose to govern the district of Nabulus and lead the *ḥajj* caravan from Damascus. A few years later, in 1070 (1660–61), Ibrahīm was killed in a punitive expedition against the Druze in Lebanon, and his father resumed control of Gaza.

Anonymous petitions sent to Istanbul—complaining about his failure to lead the *ḥajj* caravan and secure safe passage for the pilgrims to Mecca—served as an excuse for the Ottoman government to depose him. He was arrested in the castle of Muzayrīb on the *ḥajj* route and brought to Damascus, where he was imprisoned, and his assets were confiscated. A short time later he was transferred to Istanbul, and died there in prison, in 1073 (1662–63).[11] After Ḥusayn's death his brother Musa governed the district of Gaza for a short period. His name is mentioned in Jerusalem's *sijill* records in 1081 (1670). It is difficult to establish the exact date his rule ended, but soon afterwards Gaza was taken over and Ottoman officials were appointed governors. The Riḍwān period was probably the last golden age of the city of Gaza. From this point on, the once magnificent city declined, to become little more than a village in the nineteenth century.[12]

The Ṭurabāys

Members of the Ṭurabāy family, a clan of the Banu Hāritha bedouin tribe, may have held the title of *amīr al-darbayn* (*amir* of the two roads), even in Mamluk times, before the Ottoman conquest, though the Ṭurabāy mentioned by Mamlūk sources seems to have been a Mamlūk bey unrelated to the bedouin Ṭurabāy clan.[13] As Sultan Selim's armies progressed south to Egypt after their victory over the Mamluks at Marj Dabik, the Ṭurabāys offered them assistance as guides and scouts. When the last of the Mamluks were uprooted and the sultan returned to Istanbul, the family was rewarded for its services. It was given the territory known as Lajjūn, later to become a formal *sanjaq* comprising mainly the valley of Esdraelon (Marj Bani ʿAmr), the northern hills of Samaria, and the lower Galilee. Under the Ottomans, the Ṭurabāys continued to perform their traditional tasks, and they retained their title of *Amīr al-Darbayn*.

Soon they were given another task—leading the pilgrims from Damascus to Mecca, or, more often, watching over the district of Gaza while the Riḍwāns were away leading the *ḥajj* caravan. From time to time the sultan issued commands instructing the Ṭurabāys to transfer contingents, and sometimes even to take over the administration of Gaza until its governors returned from their mission. The Ṭurabāys fulfilled these obligations to the letter, gaining the praise and trust of the Riḍwāns.[14]

The first member of the family to be mentioned by name in Ottoman sources is Qaraja ibn Ṭurabāy, who offered his help to the advancing imperial army. His son, Ṭurabāy ibn Qaraja, remained loyal to the Ottomans during the famous revolt of Janbirdi al-Ghazali, a former Mamluk *bey* who was appointed governor of Damascus by the Ottomans, and rose against them in 1520. When the revolt was suppressed, Ṭurabāy gained favor in the eyes of his Ottoman masters, and was given more land.[15]

After a short period in which the Ṭurabāys themselves were in a state of rebellion for unknown reasons, things were straightened out, and ʿAli ibn Ṭurabāy was appointed governor of Lajjun in 1559. Another son, ʿAssāf, mentioned by the sources in 1571, ruled the district for over a decade, and extended his power and influence to other regions, including the district of Nabulus. In 1583 he was deposed and banished to the island of Rhodes, only to reappear six years later, demanding to be reinstated in his territory. He was granted a pardon and allowed to settle in Lajjun, but meanwhile another ʿAssāf, apparently an impostor, seized the *sanjaq*. This impostor, "ʿAssāf the Liar" (*al-kadhdhāb*) as he was later known, decided to go to Damascus and confirm his appointment. Upon arrival he was seized and executed. Although the real ʿAssāf was not reinstated in his district, Lajjūn remained in Ṭurabāy hands for many years to come.[16]

The next ruler in the dynasty was Ṭurabāy ibn ʿAli, of whom little is known. He died in 1010 (1601) and was succeeded by his son Aḥmad, who ruled the district of Lajjūn for forty-seven years, until his death in 1057 (1647). Aḥmad was famous for his courage and hospitality. He helped the Ottomans defeat the rebel Janbulād, gave shelter to Janbulād's rival, Yusuf Sayfa, and later played a major role in the prolonged series of battles fought against Fakhr al-Din II, in cooperation with Muḥammad ibn Farrūkh and Ḥasan ibn Aḥmad ibn Riḍwān.[17] A grateful Ottoman administration repaid him by expanding his fief, but this spirit of goodwill did not last very long. A register of provincial appointments from the mid-seventeenth century, records Aḥmad ibn Ṭurabāy's appointment as governor, confirmed in Rajab 1042 (January 1633). A later note, however, states that "when extent of the insurgency on the part of this district governor (*mutaṣarrif*) became apparent, the said district was bestowed, in return for a certain sum, upon Mūsa, the former *bey* of [. . .], on 11 Muḥarram 1050 (3 May 1640)." Later in the same year another note in the register states that Aḥmad Ṭurabāy was reinstated as governor of Lajjūn.

When Aḥmad died, his son Zayn assumed control of the district and governed it wisely until 1660. Upon his death he was replaced by his brother Muḥammad, who, though well-meaning and broad-minded, was weak and addicted to opium, according to d'Arvieux, his French secretary and friend. At this point Turabāy rule in the *sanjaq* of Lajjūn began to wane. In 1082 (1671) Muḥammad passed away and other members of the family ruled the *sanjaq* until in 1088 (1677) "the government abandoned them" as Muḥibbi writes, and the Turabāys were replaced by an Ottoman officer.[19]

The Farrūkhs

Former studies of the house of Farrūkh end with the death of Muḥammad ibn Farrūkh, but as new sources reveal, the Farrūkh dynasty went on to rule the districts of Jerusalem and Nabulus for several more decades.[20]

The Circassian *amīr* Farrūkh began his career as a military slave (*mamlūk*) in the service of Bahrām Pasha, brother of Riḍwān Pasha of Gaza. In 1596, under the aegis of his master, he was appointed to the post of *subashi* (officer in charge of public order) in Jerusalem. When Bahrām died young Farrūkh embarked on an independent career, first as governor of Jerusalem, where he received his first appointment in 1603, and later on in Nabulus, where his rule began in 1609. Nabulus was to become a haven for the Farrūkhs for many years to come. In the following years his governorship alternated between these two districts, sometimes governing both of them at the same time. His Nabulus governorship brought him the lucrative title of *amīr al-ḥajj*, which at the time became almost synonymous with an appointment in Nabulus. Death found him in 1030 (1621), while leading the *ḥajj* caravan, a task he performed with great skill and courage.[21]

Muḥammad ibn Farrūkh, who replaced his father as governor of Jerusalem and Nabulus, inherited his father's courage, but was also remarkably cruel and ruthless. It was rumored that he had a hand in his father's death. Jews and Christians in the city sent long letters to their brethren abroad, describing the plight of the local population. Muslims sent petitions to the sultan's palace, pleading for protection. Fearing his cruelty, his many enemies in the city did their best to convince the governor of Damascus and the sultan's vezirs to replace him. His loyalty and expertise in leading the *ḥajj* caravan were, however, indispensable, and the government decided to turn a blind eye to his cruelty. As a result, he ruled Jerusalem only intermittently, for short periods of time. He was allowed to remain in Nabulus, and was even permitted to add the *sanjaq* of Karak-Shawbak in Trans-Jordan to his fiefs. He died in 1638 and left two sons, ʿAli and ʿAssāf.[22]

Very little is known about the first son, ʿAli. Muḥibbi mentions him in his father's biography, saying he was appointed *amīr al-ḥajj* once. ʿAssāf, the second son, is also mentioned only in Muḥammad's biography. According to Muḥibbi he was appointed *amīr al-ḥajj* several times, and died in Konya (Anatolia) in 1081 (1670). Rafeq adds that ʿAssāf fulfilled his duties as *amīr al-ḥajj* in the years 1665-69, and a local chronicler, Iḥsān al-Nimr suggests that he was replaced in this capacity by one of al-Nimr's ancestors, Mūsa Pasha al-Nimr. His fateful trip to Anatolia in 1670 was intended to regain the sultan's favor.[23]

The *sijill* registers of Jerusalem and Nabulus are an invaluable source of information about ʿAssāf Farrūkh and his family in the years following his father's death. The only register surviving in Nabulus from the mid-seventeenth century was compiled at a time when ʿAssāf Bey (later Pasha) was governor of Nabulus and *amīr al-ḥajj*. This register covers the period from 1655 to 1657. Apparently ʿAssāf's rule in Nabulus continued before and after this period. *Sijill* records tend to praise contemporary governors, while allowing some criticism of former ones. The Nabulus *sijill* is no exception, but if the register is anything to go by, ʿAssāf's reign was considerably milder than his father's.[24]

Later documents from the *sijills* of Jerusalem in the years 1078–80 (1668–70) mention ʿAssāf as "*amīr al-umarā*ʾ ʿAssāf Pasha, governor of Nabulus and Jerusalem and *amīr al-ḥajj*." A register covering 1081 (1670) records his death in Anatolia. A list of his assets recorded in this register for inheritance purposes, mentions a wife, two young sons and a young daughter. For some unknown reason, all documents pertaining to his death and inheritance are erased by pen strokes (although they are still readable). After his death no other members of the family were appointed, although the family's descendents remained part of the local elite in Damascus, Nabulus and Jerusalem well into the eighteenth century.[25]

TOWARDS A UNIFIED DYNASTY

The three dynasties which controlled Gaza, Jerusalem, Nabulus and Lajjūn had common interests from the outset. Documents from the late sixteenth century reveal a series of contacts between the Riḍwāns and the Turabāys concerning the yearly pilgrimage. The Farrūkh-Riḍwān relationship began when young Farrūkh was brought as a slave from Circassia into the household of Bahrām Pasha. In military slavery tradition relations between the *mamlūk* and his master resembled a father-son relationship, and this bond remained firm even when the *mamlūk* was given his freedom. This factor, as well as Farrūkh's competence and loyalty, convinced Bahrām and Riḍwan Pasha to make him *subashi* of Jerusalem, and later on to support his bid for the governorship of Jerusalem.[26]

Relations between the Farrūkhs and the Turabāys were also based on the need to protect roads, fight common enemies and lead the *ḥajj* caravan. These relations were forged in the early 1600's, and were greatly strengthened when Farrūkh's son, Muḥammad, took over and found a trusted ally in Aḥmad ibn Turabāy.[27] In the course of the seventeenth century this common basis was expanded, and ties between the three families were further reinforced until the Farrūkhs, Riḍwāns and Ṭurabāys became one extended family. Their relations were based on multiple marriage links, strategic interests in the province of Damascus, and even joint business transactions.

FAMILY TIES

Biographical dictionaries, provincial appointment registers and travel accounts do not tell us much about marriage and family ties between governing families. Most Western travelers, of course, were far removed from local politics, and had very little background to build their understanding on. Local inhabitants knew much more about these ties, but, being private matters which involved women, they were not discussed in public. Even the Ottoman authorities did not deem it proper to remark on these family ties in appointment registers, and were satisfied with hints (transparent to them, almost impervious to us) about patrons and benefactors. It is through documents in the *sijill* that we can begin to reconstruct the local political scene, in particular family ties between the local dynasties.

Mannāʿ notes that Muḥammad ibn Farrūkh married ibn Ṭurabāy's granddaughter in order to seal the alliance between them on the eve of their great battle against Fakhr al-Din in 1623. One of the sons born of this marriage may well have been ʿAssāf Pasha ibn Muḥammad, named for his great grandfather ʿAssāf, an ancestor of the Ṭurabāy clan.[28]

Marriage ties between the Riḍwāns and the Farrūkhs also began at an early stage. A segmented record in the Nabulus *sijill*, discussing a change in custody over orphaned children, alludes to one such marriage:

> [The court appoints] his excellency Ḥusayn Pasha, governor of Gaza, as *shar'i* custodian (*waṣiyy*) over his sister's son, the minor *amīr*, Farrūkh ibn [. . .] ibn Muḥammad Pasha ibn Farrūkh Pasha, [and authorizes him to take charge of] the orphan's property received from his deceased mother, the honorable lady [. . .], daughter of the deceased *amīr al-'umarā'* [. . .]. [The authorization includes the right] to buy and sell, negotiate, and conduct other transactions, the profits thereof accruing to the orphan, amīr Farrūkh. In this capacity he replaces the boy's uncle, his father's brother, his excellency 'Assāf Bey, since the latter has shown willingness to be relieved as custodian from this date onwards. Copied on 10 Rajab 1066 (4 May 1656).[29]

Husayn Pasha Riḍwān, we learn from the record, was a maternal uncle (*khāl*) of the orphaned *amīr*, whose mother and father have both died. According to the record the boy's paternal uncle (*'amm*) was 'Assāf Bey Farrūkh. If we accept Muḥibbi's testimony that Muḥammad ibn Farrūkh had only two sons, 'Ali and 'Assāf, then young Farrūkh must have been 'Ali's son. The relationship may therefore be reconstructed as follows: Husayn Pasha's sister (daughter of Ḥasan Pasha) married 'Ali, son of Muḥammad ibn Farrūkh. 'Ali and his wife died in unknown circumstances, and the uncle was asked to take custody of his nephew.

The question of appointing a custodian emerges once more in a later series of records in the Jerusalem *sijill*. This time the orphans are two sons and a daughter of 'Assāf Farrūkh himself (who meanwhile became a Pasha):

> Since *amīr al-ḥajj, amīr al-umarā'* 'Assāf Pasha died, may his soul rest in peace, and has left small children—Muḥammad Bey, 'Ali Bey and Mahmanūd *khānım* [Turkish *hanım*, title of a lady]—all of whom are minors, the need has arisen to appoint a custodian who will take charge of all that was bequeathed by their father, and manage everything in accordance with interest and fate, in matters of buying and selling, negotiations, and other transactions, profits of which would benefit the heirs. Our master the qadi has consulted Allah, exalted be he, and chose *amīr al-'umarā'* Mūsa Pasha, the current governor of Gaza, to be legal custodian over Muḥammad Bey, 'Ali Bey and Mahmanūd Khanım, and to take possession of the inheritance [. . .]. All this was decided when it was brought to the qadi's attention that Mūsa Pasha is the maternal uncle of the minors and is concerned about their well-being.[30]

Another segment, describing the deceased ʻAssāf Pasha's estate, provides another clue to the complex family relations between the Farrūkhs and the Riḍwāns:

> This is a register recording the estimated value of the property belonging to the departed *amīr al-ḥajj, amīr al-umara* ʻAssāf Pasha. Those entitled to inherit him are his two minor sons, Muḥammad Bey and ʻAli Bey, his minor daughter Mahmanud Khātūn (another title for a lady), and his wife, pride of the modest Shaqra Khātūn, daughter of the deceased *amīr al-umarā'* Husayn Pasha, former governor of Gaza. All this was recorded in the knowledge of Mūsa Pasha, current governor of Gaza, who was appointed legal custodian over the said orphans.[31]

Reading the two records together allows us to disentangle more of the complex family ties between the two clans. It appears that Shaqra Khātūn, ʻAssāf Pasha's only (living) wife and the mother of his children, was a daughter of Ḥusayn Pasha Riḍwān. As in the former Nabulus records, here too a relative from the Riḍwān side of the family—Mūsa Pasha, Husayn's brother—is called on to take charge of the bereaved family and act as legal custodian. Preference for the Riḍwāns as custodians responsible for both children and property seems to be no coincidence. It indicates their dominant status in the emerging unified dynasty, as well as the intimate family relations between the Riḍwāns and the Farrūkhs. These were not mere political marriages. They carried with them a long-range commitment and a continuity that generated common economic and cultural interests.

Such evidence of family ties in the *sijill*, though by no means exhaustive, demonstrates clearly that until their destruction in the 1670s local clans went through a process of unification which forged them into one extended dynasty. This dynasty regarded all *sanjaq*s of Western Palestine (and sometimes those in Trans-Jordan as well) as common fiefs. In times of trouble they would all gather into one or two *sanjaq*s and await a chance to remove their rivals and reclaim the others. Throughout the seventeenth century there were several such circles of expansion and contraction.

The family ties of ʻAssāf Farrūkh could serve to demonstrate this integration of the three clans. His mother was probably, Aḥmad ibn Ṭurabāy's granddaughter. His wife was the daughter of Husayn Pasha Riḍwān, and his sister-in-law, his brother's wife, was Husayn Pasha's sister. When ʻAssāf's brother died, Husayn Pasha became his orphans' legal custodian, and when ʻAssāf himself passed away, Husayn's brother, Mūsa, was appointed his children's custodian until they reached maturity. But with

'Assāf and his generation this process also reached its peak, and a few years later the extended dynasty was destroyed.

Fig. 2.1. Ties Between the Households of Riḍwān, Ṭurābāy and Farrūkh

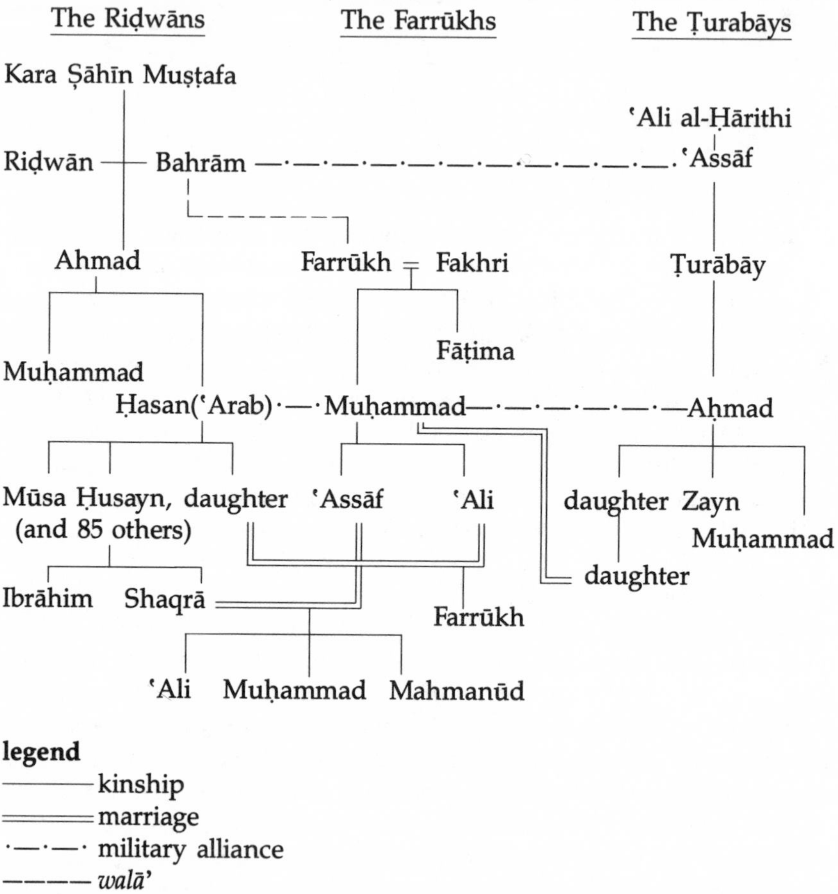

WAR AND BUSINESS

Marriages were not the only ties to connect the governing families. Common property, and the lingering memory of battles fought together against common enemies, were day-to-day bridges of communication, myths sustaining unity.

The beginning of military cooperation between the clans had its roots in the yearly *ḥajj* caravan, which required that the governor chosen to be that year's *amīr al-ḥajj* abandon his *sanjaq* for prolonged periods of time and appoint a trusted neighboring governor to take care of his *sanjaq* until he returned. Governors had to make sure no one would raid the *sanjaq*, reap off taxes, or cause damage to their own private property. Good relations between governors were a prerequisite for a successful pilgrimage, and the Ottoman authorities, for whom success in the *ḥajj* was a major political interest, encouraged such friendships.

The Riḍwāns allowed the Ṭurabāy *amīrs* to replace them as governors while they led the *ḥajj* caravan, creating a relationship of trust and budding cooperation which grew as the years wore on. A firman of 1589 declares that the amīr Riḍwān has commended ʿAssāf ibn Ṭurabāy for his valor and assistance, and that the Ottoman authorities have taken this into account in their future dealings with the Ṭurabāys.[32]

But mutual trust became real alliance once Fakhr al-Dīn's growing power and influence threatened to engulf the whole region and destroy the foundations of their strength. In 1613, in the wake of a series of skirmishes with local forces, Fakhr al-Dīn's army defeated forces sent by the governor of Damascus. A large contingent of the imperial army was dispatched against him from Istanbul, and the *amīr* was forced to flee and seek shelter in Europe. He finally arrived in Milan, at the court of the princes of Tuscany, who were to become his future allies and protectors.

In 1618 Fakhr al-Dīn contacted the new grand vezir in Istanbul, and managed to placate him and return to Syria. Four years later, in 1622, he regained his old title, and took control of the districts of Safad and ʿAjlun. In the same year he was appointed governor of Nabulus and tax collector in Gaza, threatening the continued rule of the Riḍwāns and the Farrūkhs in the district. Unmoved by Ottoman efforts to restrain him, Fakhr al-Din then collected his forces and descended to the coastal plain, heading south towards Jerusalem and southern Palestine.

Encouraged by the Ottoman authorities, who were more apprehensive now of Fakhr al-Dīn's growing strength, the three clans allied themselves, and pledged to stop Fakhr al-Din's march south. The alliance, headed by "Arab" Ḥasan Riḍwān, Muḥammad Farrūkh and Aḥmad Ṭurabāy, checked Fakhr's advance and finally routed his army on the banks of the Yarqon (ʿAwja) river in 1623. Fighting against a strong, well-equipped enemy backed by one of Christendom's richest royal houses, the three families had to share their resources in order to buy arms and stores, acquire estates in Trans-Jordan for other allies, and pay bedouin sheikhs who joined the Riḍwān-Farrūkh-Ṭurabāy alliance.[33]

Not once throughout the seventeenth century was this alliance compromised by any of the three families. Disputes among them were in most cases resolved by mutual agreement, and only rarely by Ottoman arbitration. Joint economic ventures created a new, long-term raison d'être for the alliance and renewed interests.

Some of these ventures began as a simple bequest of property to a daughter or a sister married to an allied family. According to Islamic law and local custom, women inherited a substantial portion of their deceased kin's possessions (usually half the amount inherited by a male in the same kinship relation to the deceased). Quite a few of these assets were parts, or shares, of an orchard, a shop or a house, other parts of which were held by the wife's family. In many cases women chose to keep their property and administer it by themselves, but in the course of a marriage assets would sometimes be combined with those of the husband. In the second and third generation, sons and daughters held portions of both properties. The assets of the Riḍwāns, Farrūkhs and Ṭurabāys thus became inextricably bound together.[34]

Alongside these assets, the allies had other common business. At times they would join forces to extract more money from the defenseless rural population, or even to raid and rob entire villages, as in the case of Aḥmad Ṭurabāy and Muḥammad Farrūkh, who united their armies to ravage and plunder several villages in the region of Ramallah. There is also mention in the *sijill* of business deals involving the Farrūkhs and the Riḍwāns. The governors, it seems, made use of their ties and their special status to conduct shady business deals:

> His excellency 'Assāf Pasha, governor of Nabulus and *amīr al-ḥajj*, leases from Mustafa ağa ibn Sulayman Tuqlīzade, with his own money, on his own behalf, what the latter had himself leased from the exalted *amīr al-umara* Husayn Pasha, the governor of Gaza. This same property was leased by Husayn Pasha from the famous *'ālim*, Jārallah, the *mufti* of the *Ḥanafi*s in Jerusalem, who is also supervisor and comptroller of the *waqf* of the Jawhari *madrasa* and the 'Uthmani *madrasa* in Jerusalem. [The first rental contract] was signed in accordance with a legal ruling in the court of Gaza on 26 Rabī' al-Thāni of the year mentioned below (21 Feb. 1656).
>
> The property rented is a tract of land named "al-Maqsam" measuring 42.5 out of a total area of 60 *faddān*, in the lands of the village of Tul Karm. The area is known by all concerned, and recognized [by the inhabitants], which renders its exact description here unnecessary. The lessee is permitted to use the land for winter and summer crops, and for all other accepted uses, for a period of one

> year, beginning on 26 Rabīʿ al-Thāni 1066. The rental is 250 *ghurūsh*, paid directly to the lessor. The present lessee acknowledged having received the property. All this was proved and certified at the qadi's court, after all *sharʿi* aspects of the matter were taken into account. Recorded on 15 Rajab 1066 (9 May 1656).[35]

This record, so imbued with *sharʿi* legalistic jargon, raises some interesting questions: Why was such a long chain of lessors needed? Why did ʿAssāf Pasha, a governor famous in Jerusalem as well as Nabulus, need the mediation of his father-in-law, and of another Ottoman officer, to rent a tract of land from a *waqf* in Jerusalem? Why is there such an emphasis on the legality of the deal? In any case, it is clear from this and other records that the Farrūkhs and the Riḍwāns were involved in a long series of joint business ventures, not all of them in accordance with *sharʿi* law or Ottoman *kānūn*. Other transactions recorded include the rental and purchase of houses, flour mills and tracts of land.

In the several decades of their alliance the governing families of the four *sanjaqs* acquired a vast amount of property. Some indication of their riches may be reconstructed from ʿAssāf's inheritance documents. When ʿAssāf Pasha died on the way to Istanbul in 1670, doubts were raised concerning his holdings in Nabulus and in the little town of Ramla. A document was then drafted by the court, listing his assets in the two towns, and acknowledging the right of Mūsa Pasha, his children's legal custodian, to administer this property:

> In the town of Nabulus: A big house in town—600 *ghurush*; the *wikāla* (a local hostel and caravanseray) and half the coffee house—600 gh.; half a soap factory (*maṣbana*)—300 gh; a bakery—60 gh; a soap factory courtyard and a room—60 gh; 3 orchards—300 gh; two shops and their taxes—25 gh; two houses bought in the city—50 gh; two separate houses—30 gh; a flour mill—80 gh; water operated flour mills—100 gh; half an Olive grove—40 gh.
>
> In the town of Ramla: Flour mills on the ʿAwja river—600 gh; a bathhouse in Ramla—300 gh; a coffee house—50 gh; a large house—250 gh; a small house—30 gh; small living rooms—30 gh; a small room—15 gh; an orange grove and an orchard (leased)—150 gh; a new vineyard—20 gh.[36]

In total, the deceased governor's estate in Nabulus and Ramla is estimated at 3,690 *ghurush*. This was only part, perhaps a small part, of the pasha's possessions. The document does not list other forms of property beside immovables—debts, coins, jewellery and other valuable items. We know from other documents in the Nabulus and Jerusalem *sijills* that

ʿAssāf rented the taxes of several villages in the vicinity from *waqfs* and from *timar* holders, and had received a considerable income from this activity. The Farrūkhs also had other important assets in Jerusalem and Damascus which were not listed in this document.[37]

Funds gathered in this fashion did not only serve to maintain a high standard of living. A governor in the Ottoman Empire was expected to establish a household in keeping with his rank and income. Since funds provided by the state were always insufficient, the governor of Nabulus, an almost permanent *amīr al-ḥajj*, needed large sums of money every year to prepare and stock up for the expected pilgrimage. Finally, money paid in Istanbul and Damascus made sure that the local dynasties would remain in their districts and disrupted attempts to appoint other governors. The economic alliance between the dynasties guaranteed that all three families would be able to meet these heavy requirements and succeed in their tasks.

COURT CULTURE AND FAMILY LIFE

We know very little about daily life in the households and courts of Palestine's governing dynasties. There are few testimonies about their way of life, their cultural pursuits, their belief systems or their ideologies. In this respect there may be some difference between the Ṭurabāys and the other two families. The Ṭurabāys, bedouin by origin and culture, preserved their desert Arab heritage and went on raising camels and horses. They retained their old nomadic tents, although by the seventeenth century they were already established in the towns of Lajjūn and Jenin. The heritage of the Farrūkhs and the Riḍwāns, in contrast, had its roots in the Mamluk-Ottoman world of slave soldiers and court etiquette.[38]

The founders of both Farrūkh and Riḍwān dynasties traced their origins to slavery. Kara Shahin Mustafa Pasha, Riḍwān's father, was a product of the *devşirme* system at its peak, in the days of Sultan Süleyman. Brought by the janissaries to Istanbul, he was officially enslaved and entered the sultan's service, a military slave whose acquired status would lead him into the Ottoman elite as a soldier, an officer, a governor or a state minister. Mustafa had in fact traversed the whole distance, becoming a vezir, and the sultan's trusted aide.[39]

Farrūkh was a slave too, albeit of a different kind. He was bought or captured in Circassia, and brought into the household of Bahrām Pasha, Kara Shahin Mustafa's son. Like other slaves in the service of the Riḍwān family, Farrūkh was educated and prepared for a career in the governing elite of the Ottoman Empire. This trajectory, which Kunt calls "the slaves' slaves" (*kulların kulları*) was the established pattern of socialization and career path of the *ümera*. It competed with the *devşirme* for a while, and finally led to its disappearance at the turn of the sixteenth century.[40]

Ottoman governing elite culture always emphasized the importance of both book and sword—knowledge of fencing, archery, tactics and strategy, along with an acquaintance with religion, music, poetry, the visual arts and science. The education of a boy in the *devşirme* system integrated all these into a common cultural system, which characterized this elite and set it apart from the old Ottoman Muslim aristocracy, whose bastion was the religious professions. In this respect, as in many others, the sultan's palace served as a model, copied on a smaller scale by governors and vezirs of the realm. Alumni of this prestigious palace school fashioned their own households to resemble the sultan's palace, and tried to give their own *mamlūks* the sort of education they received themselves. As a result, the governing elite, which included both the sultan's slaves and the slaves' slaves, shared the same cultural values.

The Riḍwāns and the Farrūkhs considered themselves part of this Ottoman elite. In their biographies they are usually portrayed as competent, courageous warriors, and at the same time as patrons of art and culture. This description is so prevalent in Muḥibbi's descriptions as to suggest the existence of a topos, a literary stylistic device. According to his biography, Aḥmad ibn Riḍwān was a man of great courage and valor, as well as a brilliant scholar, with a profound understanding of history and science. Poets of his era, says Muḥibbi, wrote songs praising his encyclopedic knowledge. Aḥmad loved to talk about religious knowledge (*'ilm*) and always consulted the ulema on matters of state. During his reign Gaza became a cultural center, influenced by the governor's attitude, and by the fame of his great friend and protegé, Khayr al-Dīn al-Ramli.[42]

Aḥmad's son Ḥasan was so notorious a spendthrift and hedonist that nothing in his biography could match his exploits, but Husayn Pasha is described by Muḥibbi as the paragon of perfection. He was a handsome, noble, cultured man, yet a man of deeds whose reputation preceded him. Though for some reason he could not read or write, he knew many books of poetry and prose by heart. He was also a resolute leader in politics and war who forced the bedouin to submit and cooperate.[43]

Farrūkh and his son Muḥammad are described in the same vein. Farrūkh is the "distinguished hero, of fearless heart" famous for his generosity, courage and nobility. His son, remembered by local Jewish and Christian sources mainly for his cruelty and greed, is portrayed by Muḥibbi as "one of the world's most famous heros and renowned noblemen" who had left an indelible impression on the bedouin. When bedouin wished to frighten a fellow tribesman, recounts the biographer, they would shout "Here comes ibn Farrūkh!" In his spare time ibn Farrūkh loved reading, music, and other cultural pursuits. He memorized many stories, including al-Ḥariri's long poems (*maqāmāt*), and loved to sing.[44]

It seems that the writer sympathized with the local Farrūkh and Riḍwān governors, who in his days were already removed from power. His sarcastic description of Ḥasan Pasha Riḍwān suggests that he was, at least to some extent, impartial and free from government pressure or censorship, and that he could have written straightforward biographies of local governors. Yet, even if Muḥibbi's descriptions are exaggerated, reflecting a petrified literary type that does not correspond to reality, and even if some of the songs of praise quoted in these biographies were commissioned by the governors themselves, they also reflected a will on the part of these local governors to portray themselves as successful products of the Ottoman governing elite's socialization system, a cultural complex whose values were dictated by the educational system of the sultan's slaves in the center. This was undoubtedly the normative reference system sought by the local dynasties.

In his book *Bureaucratic Reform in the Ottoman Empire,* Carter Findley refers to the almost unavoidable transformation from a household based on slaves to an extended family as the social and economic basis of the governing elite. Many of the governors and senior officials in the Ottoman Empire were torn away from their original families and recruited as slaves. Eventually they were set free and expected to build a household of their own, commensurate with their rank and income. In the first and second generations these households had to rely mainly on male and female slaves, but in later generations, as family ties were extended and new children were born, a real family gradually replaced the artificial one. This process was usually built upon a series of political alliances and marriages. Other means of extending the family were the adoption of young slaves as children, and the emerging system of patron-client relationships. In Findley's view this was an organizational form which imitated the sultan's household, and itself evolved into a model replicated on many levels of society and the administration.[45]

The series of political marriages, economic transactions and political alliances described above fits in with this assumption. In the early stages, governors' households were based mainly on military slaves (*mamlūks*). Trained to become officials and governors, they often reached the highest positions in provincial government. Other household slaves were bought as status symbols, intended to maintain the governor's obligations towards the Ottoman dynasty, to emulate the imperial household, and to imply a further measure of legitimacy. In later years, however, the governors themselves married, and pledged their children in marriage, in order to establish their political credentials, but also in order to create real families of their own.

Most of the marriage ties were exogamous, the partners coming from outside the family, though in most cases from the same social strata. Along with marriage ties between the dynasties, there were also several weddings arranged with other notable families—bedouin sheikhs, Damascene aristocracy, or prestigious local men of religion.[46] Endogamous marriages, inside the family itself, were rare, although as the years wore on and intermarriage between the three dynasties remained frequent, the three in fact became one extended family, and what were once exogamous marriages became endogamous.[47]

The number of legal wives and children can in most cases be arrived at by checking inheritance documents in the *sijill*. If these are any indication, polygamy was not rare, but in most cases one or two legal wives were deemed sufficient, although there is no way of knowing the number of concubines whose sons were disavowed by their fathers, as permitted by the *sharī'a*. Ḥasan Pasha's eighty-five sons were definitely an exception.

It is hard to determine the average age of marriage for men and women in this group. Since in most cases women survived their husbands, it can be assumed that women were married at a relatively young age to older men. After their husbands' deaths wives usually kept a substantial part of the property, often using it to go on conducting business on their own. In the *sharī'a* court, widows of former governors were always treated deferentially, commanding respect and keeping their titles and high status.[48]

The governor's household, fashioned after the imperial palace model, displayed other symbolic elements which included battle standards and a military band that accompanied the governor on his way to the battlefield. Fallen into enemy hands, the captive banners and band became symbols of failure and defeat. All these symbols of official power were complemented by an extravagant affluent dress, and an indulgence in aristocratic sports and leisure pursuits.[49]

It is harder to determine what language members of the local dynasties spoke among themselves and with the local Arabic-speaking inhabitants of the region. Years of cooperation between the three dynasties, as well as close contacts with other bedouin tribes, must have left their mark on the culture of all dynasties, creating a new hybrid Bedouin-Ottoman culture. This local culture was evident in court life, dress and probably language as well.

Their close relations with the bedouin and the local notables, their command of Arabic literature and poetry, the nickname "Arab," referring to Ḥasan Pasha Riḍwān, all indicate that they were versed in Arabic language and culture. Arabic was certainly the language spoken by the Ṭurabāys, who needed a translator for their correspondence with the Sublime Porte in Istanbul.[50] But evidence as to the language preferred by the Farrūkhs and Riḍwāns is inconclusive. Their Caucasian origins, their Ottoman gentlemen's education, and the attempt to reproduce the imperial household on a smaller scale, suggest a strong Turkish influence. Some corroboration can be seen in the frequent use of titles like *hanım* and *khatun*, reserved for Ottoman ladies, in court records referring to their women. Although most names were Arabicized, sometimes Turkish personal names would appear, as in the case of Mahmanud, daughter of ʿAssāf Pasha.

Court records were always written in Arabic, except when official state decrees were copied into the *sijill*. There is never any mention of a translator or Arabic-speaking representative when a member of these dynasties is present. However, since the qadi himself was almost always a Turkish speaker sent over from the imperial center, probably no translation was needed, and the trial's record was perhaps later translated into Arabic.

All this does not provide us with a firm basis to decide whether the language and culture preferred were Turkish or Arabic. Most governors of local descent spoke both languages quite well. It may be assumed that as their rule went on, and ties with local notable families were strengthened, Arabic was used more frequently.

AN OTTOMAN THRUST TO ELIMINATE THE DYNASTIES

Throughout the second half of the seventeenth century a clandestine struggle for control of the Palestinian districts took place between the alliance of local dynasties on the one hand, and the central government on the other. Ever since the destruction of Fakhr al-Din's power, and the elimination of this immediate threat to its security, the center tried to appoint its own candidates—high-ranking officers, governors of other districts, sons of the Center's elite—as district governors in the western parts of the province of Damascus, and to curb the power of local forces.

In the *sanjaq* of Gaza, the Riḍwān stronghold, the effort had little chance of success. This was also the case in Lajjūn, where the Ṭurabāys held sway and hampered any attempt to appoint other governors. Now and then the Ṭurabāys were removed from power for short periods, but they soon managed to regain their control. The Farrūkhs managed to hold the fort in Nabulus most of the time, but the joint Riḍwān-Farrūkh rule in Jerusalem was not very stable. Several times during this period other *sanjaqbeys* were appointed by the imperial center, frequently leading to drawn-out disputes over the right to govern the area, and to many bribes being handed out in Damascus and Istanbul.

Ottoman jubilation over the victory of the southern alliance opposing Fakhr al-Din soon abated, as the Ottoman center found itself facing the same alliance, which controlled the Palestinian *sanjaq*s and regarded them as a private fief. Careful not to cross the line of open rebellion, these local dynasties nevertheless resisted the center's attempts to weaken their hold over Jerusalem, Nabulus, Lajjūn and Gaza. From the center's point of view, perhaps the most important aspect of this problem was diminished revenues and the loss of control over the pilgrimage route from Damascus to Mecca. Attempts to replace the local dynasties as *umarā' al-ḥajj*, which began in the 1740s, subsequently failed. At a time of confusion and disarray in the center, the expertise offered by the Farrūkhs and Riḍwāns, their combined military strength and their good relations with the bedouin made them invaluable to the government.[51]

In the second half of the century, when the Köprülü vezirs had embarked on a costly campaign to recentralize the Ottoman Empire, more drastic measures were decided upon to end the rule of local dynasties, and to increase the center's influence. Such a decision was probably not recorded and is nowhere to be found. But indications of this campaign, though largely circumstancial and based on conjecture, are apparent in both local and external sources. These measures bore the traditional earmarks of Ottoman power politics—use of secret agents and elaborate political tactics. The authorities tried to fabricate proof of misrule and corruption on the part of the local dynasties, and especially the Riḍwāns, who were rightly considered the most important local force on the scene. An early attempt to remove the Riḍwāns from power is echoed in this enigmatic, badly preserved record in the Nabulus *sijill*, from May 1656. Around that time Ḥusayn Pasha Riḍwān, the governor of Gaza, suddenly arrived in the city of Nabulus and paid a visit to his son-in-law 'Assāf Pasha. The *sijill* records several transactions in which Ḥusayn Pasha participated at the time. Then, one day, a group of people appeared in court:

> Several people from the village of [. . .] in the southern regions of the Nabulus district arrived at the *sharī'a* court. Among them were Naṣrallah ibn 'Ayyāsh, Da'ūd ibn Shaḥāda the *faqīh*,[52] ḥājj 'Awda ibn Aḥmad and Muṣliḥ ibn 'Ali.
>
> Eight days prior to this date, [they told the qadi,] two people came to their village: the exalted sultan's messenger (*ulak*), along with a man called Ibn Sa'd from the village of Jabaliyya in the district of Gaza. According to their testimony this Ibn Sa'd told them that "I and a group of other people from the village of Jabaliyya made up our minds to travel to the threshold of felicity [the Sultan's palace]

> and complain against [. . .]. But Isma'īl Pasha incited us to file a complaint against his excellency *amīr al-umarā* Ḥusayn Pasha, the current governor of Gaza, instead. We did send a petition complaining about him, but this complaint had no basis, and was made under pressure of the above-mentioned Isma'īl Pasha."
>
> [Ibn Sa'd] ran away from the said messenger who was sent to escort him to Istanbul. All facts were thus duly recorded in the *sijill* on the 8th of Rajab 1066 (2 May 1656).[53]

Was this a determined Ottoman effort to destroy Ḥusayn Pasha, or a private attempt by a political rival to incriminate the governor and take over his district? Was there any connection between this chain of events and the sudden appearance of Ḥusayn Pasha in Nabulus at the same date? Did the event take place as described in the document, or did the villagers receive some encouragement to emphasize certain aspects of the incident from 'Assāf Bey, Ḥusayn Pasha's friend and son-in-law? The *sijill*'s laconic description leaves many of these questions unanswered, but, as indicated by the arrest and trial of Ḥusayn Pasha several years later, the authorities did not hesitate to resort to such tactics in their campaign against the local ruling dynasties.

Muḥibbi, mourning the death of Ḥusayn Pasha, whom he considered one of the most righteous rulers of the time, recounts that he was denounced to the Ottoman authorities, accused of negligence in conducting the pilgrims and the *ḥajj* caravan to Mecca, arrested, manacled, and brought to the citadel in Damascus. He remained there for a while, and was then sent on to Istanbul, where he was murdered in jail in 1073 (1662–63). A poem written to commemorate his death by his contemporary 'Abd al-Sammān al-Dimashqi, suggests the real motive for his imprisonment and execution: "He committed no crime, But these are days of envy's rule. Chained inside a dungeon cell they feared him, as one would fear a sword in its scabbard."[54]

The Ottomans must have assumed that by killing Ḥusayn Pasha they would remove the keystone of the alliance, and would eventually be able to destroy the remnants of the extended dynasty. If this was their assumption, it proved right. After his death the district of Gaza was governed by his brother Mūsa Pasha, a weak, unimpressive governor who was manipulated into relinquishing rule of the district, and was summarily replaced by officials appointed from the center.

Next in line was 'Assāf Farrūkh. 'Assāf died in Konya, on the way to Istanbul, in 1081 (1670–71). The circumstances of his death were very mysterious. Muḥibbi's short statement conceals more than it reveals. What did he die of? was he sick? murdered? killed in an accident? Perhaps his death was too close for comfort to Muḥibbi's writing date, and the biographer did not allow himself to hint about it as he did in the case of Ḥusayn Pasha. *Sijill* records pertaining to his death, present another enigma. All these documents are crossed out, as if to say that they are no longer valid. This may be an indication that the imperial treasury intended to confiscate his property, or to deny any knowledge of his death. Be that as it may, ʻAssāf was promptly replaced by an ex-*Beylerbey*, brought from a distant province. Although Farrūkhs went on living as part of the elite in Jerusalem, Nabulus and Damascus, their era in government was over.

The Ṭurabāys followed suit. In 1677, a few years after the death of ʻAssāf Farrūkh, a window of opportunity presented itself to the patient Ottoman central government. As their mainstay, the tribe of al-Ḥāritha, moved eastward to the area of ʻAjlun, the Ṭurabāys, who had already lost the support of their allies and relatives, had to give in to Ottoman pressure. The last, incompetent Ṭurabāy ruler was replaced by an Ottoman officer, who was later given several other Palestinian *sanjaq*s.

Vezirs of the *divan* in Istanbul, led by the Köprülüs, estimated that destruction of the local dynasties and their replacement by the government's men, was likely to assist the process of centralization, and would eventually strengthen the government's control and increase its income. But logical though it may have seemed, their hopes were quickly thwarted, and their centralization efforts faltered almost from the start. From the center's point of view, local dynasties should have had several serious advantages. Despite the wider margins of autonomy they demanded, despite their disregard for imperial decrees and their frequent refusal to join the army in times of war, locally based governors were, in most cases, quite efficient rulers. Apart from their expertise in leading the *ḥajj* caravan, and their special relationship with the bedouin tribes in the area, they forged an alliance with the local notables based on mutual interest, and enlisted their support in dealings with the population at large. Their era was not devoid of hardship, dissent or insurrection, but the local dynasties were well acquainted with the territory under their control, and its production capabilities. They knew how to walk the narrow line separating a heavy yoke from overexploitation which might eventually lead to rebellion or to the abandonment of villages.

In the local dynasty era valuable information flowed back and forth between the rulers and the ruled. Direct channels of communication built in the long years of dynasty rule were reinforced by local notables. Increased coordination between the governors and the populace allowed for a rather smooth and uninterrupted operation of state machinery, tax collection and production control. In return for this relatively coherent socioeconomic system, which went on operating smoothly even as the *timar* system began to degenerate, the Ottoman authorities had to pay by giving up total control and relinquishing some of their economic gains.

With the destruction of local dynasties, and the appointment of new governors, this state of affairs changed radically. The new governors regarded their appointments as a mere source of income. They gave up the crucial alliance with the notables, and the latter, stripped of their many privileges, joined forces with the rapidly expanding group of the exploited. The new governors did not try to curb the powers of *timar* holders, janissaries and *subāshi*s, who exploited the rural and urban population, plundered them at will, and showed their contempt by defiling mosques and holy sites, discarding any semblance of just rule. Townspeople lost their property. Villagers deserted their homes. In the Mühimme ledgers in Istanbul complaints piled up about exploitation of villagers, janissaries wreaking havoc in the holy ḥaram, and the dispossession of ulema. Petitions were sent by Muslims, Christians and Jews, signed jointly by ulema and *reaya*, imploring the "threshold of felicity" to restrain governors and their henchmen.[55]

It is not surprising therefore, that when the populace could bear no more, and when opportunity presented itself, the inhabitants of Jerusalem rebelled against their governor. Led by the city's senior notables and headed by Mustafa al-Ḥusayni, head of the prestigious *ashrāf* families (*naqīb al-ashrāf*), the revolt broke out following a long period of unrest. The rebels attacked and pillaged the qadi's house, and executed his translator (*tercüman*), a corrupt man who symbolized the decay of all systems of rule and justice. Soon they took over the whole town, and, supported by a majority of the inhabitants, began to administer the city's quarters and its economy by themselves.[56]

The central government in Istanbul, busy at the time putting out another fire closer to home—the army insurrection known as the "Edirne Vakası" (the Edirne incident)—allowed the revolt in Jerusalem to go on for some time before making the first serious attempt to suppress it. In the meantime internal animosities split the rebel camp into two warring factions. A weakened *naqīb al-ashrāf* now faced the government forces commanded by a new governor, who besieged the city. After a few weeks of siege a compromise was reached: the citadel was surrendered and the taxes paid. In return the siege was lifted, and the new governor and his army remained outside the walls. The city remained in rebel hands for a time, until pressure from without and dissent from within forced the *naqīb* and his men to flee in October 1705, and the revolt ended.[57]

The initial failure of its thrust for centralization, and the revolt that followed, made the reestablishment of Ottoman rule in Jerusalem a difficult task. In the wake of this turbulent period substantial military units were stationed in the city, encumbering both the government and the populace, weakening the local economy and decreasing the empire's real revenue. Finally, the rise of local potentates like Ẓāhir al-'Umar and Aḥmad Pasha al-Jazzār, a second cycle of local dynastic rule several decades later, suggests that these attempts at centralization were inadequate in the long run as well.

THE IMPERIAL CENTER AND PROVINCIAL ADMINISTRATION

The emerging outline of Ottoman provincial administration in the first half of the seventeenth century corroborates many of Kunt's conclusions. Most of the local governors were indeed members of the *ümera* class. A few of them were raised and educated in the sultan's palace, but beginning in the late sixteenth century several *ümera* dynasties took control of ruling positions in the districts of Palestine, and applied pressure on the center to pass these positions on to their clients and sons. As a consequence a special amalgam emerged: an elite that was Ottoman in its politics and its self-perception, yet deeply rooted in the province as concerns its family ties, its assets and its peculiar cultural style. This emerging local-Ottoman elite recognized Istanbul as the legitimate source of political power, and did not try to break away completely from its hold, but at the same time created a local power base and attempted to increase the measure of its autonomy. At first, when the alliance of southern governors fought and defeated the rebel Fakhr al-Din, this tendency to localize government coincided with the center's political aims. Later on, however, the central government tried to introduce its own representatives, without giving up the expertise and experience of the locals.

Kunt's assumption that the Ottoman government tended to move district governors from one position to the next within the same general area in order to retain their knowledge of the region, while limiting their period in office so as not to allow them time to build a power base, sums up this ambivalent Ottoman attitude. The Farrūkhs, for instance, were frequently transferred from Jerusalem to Nabulus, and at times just barely managed to retain the title of *amīr al-ḥajj*. These tendencies were evident all around the Ottoman Empire, but focusing on the case of Jerusalem and its ajacent districts provides us with some insights into the workings of the system. Two subsystems vied for power in the empire. The first, the imperial administration, based its claim on its authority, on its legitimacy, and on the center's military power, usually effective enough as a vague threat. The second, a local one, opted to carve out a piece of the imperial cake for itself, building its own power on accumulated riches, on a set of alliances and on the invaluable experience gained through years of control. Governor appointments, therefore, were not simply decided by the sultan and his aides. They were the result of a complex series of pressures and needs in which the *ümera* had a lot to say. The kind of ties described here between neighboring governing lineages, the creation of extended families and the fact that we find members of the extended family moving about between the same few districts, suggest that the limited movement of district governors at the period was as much a result of their own pressure as it was a result of the center's policy. Even when governors were transferred from one district to another, they usually exerted much pressure to remain in the extended family's realm and augment its power.

In his research on the Edirne incident, the 1703 revolt in Istanbul, Rifaat Abou al-Haj suggests that a similar process has taken place in Istanbul itself: Pashas and vezirs in the center took over the recruitment of manpower for government service, striving to block the sultan's own recruitment agencies. The real struggle, therefore, may have involved these two groups: (1) the "central *ümera*"—vezirs and senior officials in the imperial center and their clients, and (2) the provincial *ümera* dynasties.[58]

Kunt's work ends in the middle of the seventeenth century. The years that followed constitute an important new phase in the history of Ottoman provincial administration. In the course of the 1670s the Farrūkh-Riḍwān-Ṭurabāy *ümera* complex was destroyed. Local dynasties were replaced by governors appointed from Istanbul. Command of the *ḥajj* caravan was taken from their hands and conferred on the governor of Damascus. The immediate reasons for these steps are not recorded. It may have been another phase in the struggle between the center and the provinces, or a concerted attempt of the Köprülü administration to recentralize control of the provinces. In any case, the Ottoman success in destroying the local-Ottoman elite was not followed by a strong, efficient centralized administration, and therefore did not bear the expected fruit. Instead of reinforcing government control, the disappearance of local dynasties brought about more disorder and weakened Ottoman control.[59]

Chapter 3

The Sufi Connection

JERUSALEM NOTABLES IN THE SEVENTEENTH CENTURY

As the seventeenth century drew to a close, and the central government faced the harsh realities of a defeat in Vienna and the Karlowitz treaty, Ottoman statesmen had to shift the focus of their attention inward. The following century began ominously, rebellion breaking out almost everywhere. A considerable effort was needed to quell these rebellions, and to restore a somewhat diluted version of Ottoman law and order.

The most famous incident, known as the *Edirne vakası*, broke out in Istanbul—the heart of the empire—in 1703, and resulted in the deposition of the sultan, and the rise to power of his younger brother, Ahmed III. Revolts and incidents on a smaller scale broke out in Damascus (in 1695, 1706 and 1725), in Cairo (in 1711) and in Jerusalem (in 1703). These revolts apparently had very little in common. They occurred in different locations. They were not simultaneous or sequential. Sometimes years elapsed between one incident and the next, and in each case the social groups taking part, the government's approach to the problem, and the outcome for the parties concerned were different. Sometimes the rebels achieved part of their goals, sometimes they lost their heads.[1]

These occurences are usually seen as a violent response to centralization efforts, or as resistance to corrupt and oppressive Ottoman rule. But while this may explain the reasons, it does not provide a full understanding of the social forces initiating the revolt, or those participating in it. Some works, such as Rifaat Abou el-Haj's research on the 1703 revolt in Istanbul, refer to the connection between the circumstances of the revolt itself, and the social and political aspirations of social strata in the Ottoman elite. Abou El-Haj does not define the *Edirne vakası* as a revolt of one social group against the sultan, but points out the fact that the instigators behind the actual rebels were part of an emerging social stratum. Descriptions of other revolts in the same period tend to suggest that they too were initiated and led by people of high social standing and considerable political power, usually referred to as "notables."[2]

The importance of notables in Ottoman political history is well known, and needs but a short introduction. The term was first used by Uzunçarşılı, followed by Gibb and Bowen in their book *Islamic Society and the West*. Gibb and Bowen assumed that these notables—referred to as *ayan* (*aʿyān* in Arabic)—were people distinguished by their considerable landed property, and chosen by the public to represent its interests. In the eighteenth century they took over the administration in most major cities, and considerably weakened the qadi's power.[3]

A more accurate definition was suggested by Albert Hourani. Inspired by Max Weber's definition of the "patriciate" in Western cities, Hourani poses three main conditions for the development of a type of politics that includes notables. First of all, direct and personal links of patronage exist between a group of influential patrons in the city and other subjects, with many in the villages working and producing for this group. Second, patrons reside in the city and control much of its administrative and economic structure. Third, the patrons or notables enjoy considerable political leeway, either as a result of the city's independence, or when the city is governed by a distant or indifferent monarchy (more often the case in the Islamic world).[4] In order to be influential, the notables must have some political clout, and yet be viewed by the government and the people as representatives of the population. The special position of the notables is based on their being a mediating stratum between the government and its subjects. They must therefore be careful in their dealings with both sides. They must be sufficiently independent not to be identified with the government, and yet be wary of actions which could be interpreted as acts of rebellion against it.[5]

This role has been assumed by various city-based groups. In Ottoman towns and cities three such groups can be found. The first is that of the ulema, whose power emanated from their high standing as upholders of the *sharīʿa* and from their central importance in the day-to-day management of the empire, as well as from the fact that they usually came from well-established prestigious families. Over time these families managed to acquire certain wealth through control of *waqf* foundations and through commerce. The religious institutions' role as a channel for social mobility also lent it a great deal of prestige.[6]

Commanders and officers of military units stationed in the city constitute the second such group. Their power stemmed from their control of local garrisons, which more often than not developed an independent esprit de corps loyal to its own commanders. The officers were usually under the imperial center's command, and sometimes opposed the local governor. Strong ties developed between these military units and local merchants, allowing them to intervene in local politics and economy. A third group was made up of "secular notables"—families who attained their status and power through past connections to the military or political establishments, from their famous ancestry, or from the stronger cohesion (*ʿasabiyya*), of certain families, controlling large waqf foundations.[7]

Hourani does not give an exact periodization for the rise of notables in the Ottoman Empire, but through his examples and contexts, it becomes apparent that the formation process of the "notable estate" takes place mainly in the eighteenth century, reaching its apex at the beginning of the nineteenth century. In every part of the empire different groupings rose to power. In Egypt they comprised mainly military commanders of Mamluk households, and the same phenomenon can be discerned in Ẓahir al-Umar's and Jazzār Pasha's Acre, as well as in the Mamluk households in Baghdad. In Mosul the ulema incorporated rich merchant families into the local notable group, while in the towns and cities of Syria the leading part was assumed by the ancient and prestigious bourgeoisie, headed by the *ashrāf*. This formation was so dominant that it absorbed the descendants of mamluk households and other military elites.[8]

A series of revolts in the middle of the nineteenth century marks a turning point in the history of the notables, as they tried to rebel against authoritarian and centralizing governments in Istanbul and Cairo. But after a short period of decline, they reappeared as leaders of national resistance movements.[9]

Halil Inalcik examines the notables in the specific context of the Ottoman Empire from a different angle—their bid for political power, and their ambivalent relations with the central government. This is presented as a complex equation: on the one hand, the stronger the central government, the weaker the notables. On the other hand, there is mutual attraction, as the notables seek to be incorporated into the governing elite. Inalcik sees wealth as the main criterion for notable status, and the Ottoman agrarian systems of *iltizām* and *mukataa* (*muqāṭaʿ*), as the means for self enrichment most often pursued. There were two main groups of notables—the military, who had *askeri* (*ʿaskari*) status and therefore belonged to the governing elite, and local ulema and merchants of the unpriviledged *reaya*, who were not officially recognized as state officials. In the second half of the seventeenth century, notables of *reaya* status started to infiltrate government positions, mainly as representatives of governors, usually called *mutasallim* (*mütesellim*), *voyvoda* or *subaşı*. Only in the eighteenth century did the notables manage to get incorporated into the state's service, and win the titles of *bey* and *paşa*. As such titles were conferred on them, they can no longer be called notables (or *ayan*), and must be perceived as part of the Ottoman establishment.[11]

In the eighteenth century, at the height of their power, the notables effectively controlled entire provinces. In many districts general councils evolved, comprising qadis, notables and military commanders. Already in 1680 the Ottoman government proclaimed a set of rules for the election of a *reis-i ayan*, or head of the notables, from among his peers, and at the beginning of the eighteenth century a formal appointment letter was sent to the holder of the post. But at the same time the central government felt the need to curb the power of the *ayan*, and to force them to abide by its laws and regulations. A series of steps taken by the government in that direction heralded the beginning of nineteenth century centralization efforts.[12]

Karl Barbir, examining Ottoman rule in Damascus in the eighteenth century, takes into account both Inalcik's and Hourani's views on the notables. Barbir suggests a clearer definition of the notables as social groups whose power stemmed mainly from mediating between the government and the population. This definition excludes groups like the lords of the valleys (*derebeys*) in Anatolia, locally based governors in Syrian districts, or Mamluk households in Egypt. Although not officially a part of government, these latter groups did in fact constitute part of the ruling institution, or at least tried to replace it. Furthermore, Barbir suggests that *aʿyān* in the Arab provinces were mostly of the first kind—ulema and their affiliates—and that *aʿyān* of the second and third kinds—namely military commanders and "secular" families—were more common in the European provinces. This definition allows us to distinguish between local governing elites, and local notables who, at that period, seldom governed by themselves.[13]

Research done by Inalcik, Hourani, Barbir and others focuses on the eighteenth century as the crux of notable politics. They all agree that its roots are to be found in the previous century, and perhaps even before that. Their research, however, does not provide us with a clear picture of this evolution in the sixteenth and seventeenth century. When did notables start to see themselves as a distinct group? When did they start taking an interest in local politics, and, finally, were the widespread incidents at the beginning of the eighteenth century part of this general process?

The eruption of revolt in Jerusalem at the beginning of the eighteenth century, led by a group of ulema and *ashrāf,* raises similar questions in the local context: whether such a group of notables emerged in the city at the time, what its social and cultural characteristics were, and what its aspirations were. Another relevant question pertains to the depth of the group's penetration into local politics, and the aims of the revolt.

A QUESTION OF TERMINOLOGY

The main source for the frequent use of the term *aʿyān* as a synonym for "notables" is probably the many firmans addressed to the *aʿyān* (usually in the Turkish form: *ayan-ı vilayet ve iş erleri*—"the *aʿyān* of the province, and men of affairs"). This term has been used extensively, but, as many sources from the period itself reveal, "*aʿyān*" was a general term, describing men of the elite, or men in elevated positions, and was not meant to distinguish between local notables and Ottoman governors, or their entourages.[14] In fact, the *sijill* uses this term as an honorific title for dignitaries of the governing elite, many of whom were foreign or localized foreigners, while local notables had other titles bestowed on them, as can be gathered from this list of people assembled in court in 1652:

> After sheikh ʿAbd al-Karim al-Ṣāmit was arrested, many notables arrived in court, including ʿUmar *efendi* the *mufti* of the shāfiʿis, Shams al-Dīn *efendi, naqīb al-āshrāf* sheikh Aḥmad al-Ḥāmidi, the *mufti* of the *Mālikis*, the model of teachers (*qudwat al-mudarrisin*) sheikh Sharaf al-Dın al-Dayri, the model of *imāms* sheikh Sulaymān al-Daʿūdi, *nāẓir al-nuẓẓār,* the pride of righteous men sheikh ʿAbd al-Raḥmān. . .the paragon of *amīrs* (*qudwat al-umarā'*) Mustafa bey, *the pride of the aʿyān* (*fakhr al-aʿyān*) ʿAli the *alaybey* [commander of the *sipahis*] in Jerusalem, *pride of the elevated and aʿyān*, Aḥmad al-Khawzaʿi, *pride of the aʿyān* Ḥusayn ağa, the *mutasallim* of Jerusalem, *The pride of the elevated and the aʿyān* Muḥammad ağa the commander of the citadel, and the head merchant (*sheikh al-tujjār*) ʿAbd al-Jawwād.[15]

Those referred to as *aʿyān* in this document, as in many others, are the military commander of the *sipahi* cavalry, the governor's deputy, and the commander of the citadel. All held official Ottoman positions and titles, and did not see themselves as part of the local notable elite. The ulema-based local notables are given a plethora of names and titles—"the model of teachers," "the pride of the righteous," and so on—but none are referred to as *aʿyān*. It appears then that the term *aʿyān* was not used by people in the period under discussion to denote the local notable elite. It is possible, although this would require further research, that at a later period, in which it was used by the notables themselves, the term expressed a sense of cohesion and identity not yet achieved in the early period. For lack of a more suitable name, therefore, this group shall be defined as "the local notable elite," or "the notables" in order to set it apart from the other distinct group, which should perhaps be termed "the local-Ottoman governing elite," or simply the "governing elite," described in the previous chapter.[16]

THE ROLE OF SUFI FRATERNITIES

The two elite groups evolved side by side in Jerusalem from the time of the Ottoman conquest. Both groups—the governing elite, based mainly on Ottoman *ümera* and on local, pre-Ottoman military units, and the notable elite, comprised almost entirely of ulema and *ashrāf*—experienced many ups and downs throughout the first two hundred years of Ottoman rule. But until the beginning of the eighteenth century, these two distinct groups did not merge into one elite, and did not control the local government and the religious institutions jointly. They were set apart by their cultural discourse and identity, and usually by their ethnic origins, as well as by the positions and titles conferred on them by the Ottoman government.

There was also a third group, descended for the most part from Mamluk or Ottoman military groups. These apparently formed a cohesive small elite of their own. Looked down at by the local ulema-based notability, and by the new local-Ottoman governing elite, they perceived of themselves as part of the higher echelons of society, enjoying some of the benefits of former rank and commission, but very little actual political power. The Mamluk pattern of socialization also expressed itself in the courts of local governors, such as the Farrūkhs, Riḍwāns and Ṭurabāys, where several generations of lesser officers were raised and bound by links of patronage to the governing elite. Only in rare cases did the local notability merge with these groups, when daughters of officers married local notables, in which case the family would be assimilated into the local notable group, leaving few traces of its "military" past.[17]

For quite some time close ties existed between the local notables and their governing peers. These ties were based mainly on a common cultural world which was created by and found expression in Sufi brotherhoods. In the city of Jerusalem, the connection between Sunni orthodoxy and the sufi fraternities or *ṭarīqa*s (literally, a road or path to true knowledge of God) was unusually vigorous. Suspicion and aversion, which characterized such relations at other times and in other places, were replaced by a great affinity and impressive cooperation. One of the reasons may by the prestige of two famous Sufi families, al-ʿAlami and al-Dajjāni, residing in the city. These families influenced Jerusalem's character as a religious and cultural center, and attracted many sufi visitors.

ʿAbd al-Ghani al-Nābulsi, a well known Sufi and *ʿālim* from Damascus, visited the city several times in the late seventeenth century and wrote about its cultural and religious life.[18] Al-Nabulsi describes a proliferation of sufi fraternities in the city and around it. As he approached the city walls, he recounts, a group of Sufis of the Adhamiyya brotherhood welcomed him and accompanied him through the Damascus gate. Strolling along the streets and around the mosque of al-Aqṣa and the Dome of the Rock, he noticed many active sufi meeting places—*zāwiyas* (*zaviye*) and *takiyyas* (*tekye*). Among others he mentions the names of the Mawlawis (Mevlevis), the Shādhilis (ṣazılıs) and the Kalandaris (Kalenderis), in addition to the famous *ṭarīqa* of the Dajjānis and the ʿAlami Asʿadiyya, which was a branch of the Shādhili order. Other Sufi prayer sites were inside the sprawling Khasikiyya *waqf* complex and in several of the better-known madrasas and colleges in town. The remarkable series of receptions held in the houses of local notables and officials in honor of the famous Sufi visitor is further evidence of the high esteem in which the local orthodox establishment viewed the sufis.

Evliya Çelebi also describes Jerusalem as an important Sufi center. Always prone to exaggeration, Evliya claims to have seen seventy different Sufi fraternities in the city, all with their own places of worship. He mentions the Aḥmadiyya, the Rifāʿiyya and the Mawlawiyya, whose mosque is close to Damascus gate. All these establishments, recounts Evliya, are spacious and well built, and all enjoy the prosperity of rich *waqf* endowments.[19]

Biographies of ulema and other Jerusalem notables transmitted by al-Muḥibbi, shed some light on the unwritten covenant between the ulema and the Ṣufi orders. It appears from these biographies that al-Azhar in Cairo was the main center of learning for Jerusalem ulema. Many sent their sons there in order to study juisprudence (fiqh), hadith and other *sharīa* sciences. In Cairo's colleges young ulema received their degrees, and sometimes replaced their original schools of legal doctrine (*madhhabs*) by new ones. Few chose (or could afford) to study in the great madrasas of Istanbul, despite the obvious career paths such an education offered.[20]

Al-Azhar was considered a strict orthodox college, where Ṣufi tendencies were frowned upon. Most of the ulema did not "receive their *ṭarīqas*" there, not even outside the standard curriculum. Still, in most of the biographies described by al-Muḥibbi, Palestinian ulema completed this part of their education when they came home. Here, mainly in Jerusalem, the connection between orthodox religion and Ṣufi brotherhoods was natural and almost automatic. Many of the ulema found their way into the Ottoman administration, while holding on to their Ṣufi beliefs.[21]

One such scholar was ʿAbd al-Ghaffār ibn Yūsuf al-Qudsi "al-ʿajami" (d. 1647), who studied hadith and fiqh in Cairo. Upon his return he was appointed ḥanafi mufti of Jerusalem. At the same time he studied the principles of the Naqshbandiyya, a well-known orthodox *ṭarīqa,* from Muḥammad al-Naqshbandi, and the ʿUlwāniyya from sheikh Muḥammad al-Dajjāni, and joined both *ṭarīqas*. So did Muḥammad ibn Aḥmad al-Khurayshi, the ḥanbali mufti at the end of the previous century (d. 1592), whose Sufi beliefs led him to preach asceticism, thereby crossing the vague line between accepted and heretic Sufi doctrine. A well-known shāfiʿi scholar, ʿAbd al-Qādir ibn Aḥmad al-Ghazzi (d. 1676), became a holy man (*walīy*), following in the footsteps of his famous mentor, Muḥammad al-ʿAlami. Sons of *ashrāf* families, headed by the Wafā'is, better known later on as the Ḥusaynis, were also part of the Sufi circle.[22]

People who came from prominent Sufi families were members of high standing in the orthodox establishment. Thus, Muḥammad ibn Ahmad al-Dajjāni (d. 1617), a "possessed" (*majdhūb*) Sufi, became *mufti* of the *shāfiʿiyya,* and the ʿAlamis themselves, heads of the rifāʿi *ṭarīqa,* are frequently described as ulema of great distinction in fiqh and hadıth.[23] The French priest Roger, who stayed in Jerusalem for some time, was impressed by the Sufis, and by their social standing. Roger sees them as Muslim monks, very much like their Christian counterparts—separated from the rest of the people, perhaps celibate, and devoted to God. Their monasteries, he says, are clean and well kept. They grow flowers in their gardens, and play music, which constitutes an important part of their liturgy. Upon arrival in Jerusalem, many of them attend mass at the convent of the Holy Saviour, and are enchanted by its music. They are respected by the people, many of whom bequeath their property to Sufi orders. They are also held in high esteem by the governor and his entourage, who join in their ceremonies and pray with them.[24] "Lords, Pashas and governors usually have one of these Sufis by their side, and when they go away, they set them up in their own tents and pavillions"[25]

The *sijill* adds its own layer of description to the world of Sufis and ulema in Jerusalem, and traces the process whereby *ṭariqas* allied themselves with the local-Ottoman governing elite. Several of Jerusalem's governors in the first half of the century were either active members, or at least enthusiastic supporters of Sufi *ṭariqas*. They may have been influenced in this tendency by friends and allies in Istanbul or Damascus, other strongholds of Sufi doctrines. Governors provided financial support for their favorite orders, and under their patronage Sufi sheikhs accumulated great wealth.[26]

Along with property bequeathed or dedicated to Sufi orders by ulema, the *sijill* records several formal dedications of *waqfs* by governors or other high officials to their favorite Sufi *ṭarīqa*. A *waqf* dedicated by a governor of Jerusalem to the order of the Mawlawiyya is discussed in a series of records in the *sijill*. According to the first record, on 5 Rabīʿ al-Thāni 1033 (27 December 1623), a large *ḥākūra* (orchard, garden) in the quarter of bāb al-ʿAmūd was bought by Muḥammad Pasha, governor of Jerusalem, from the lady ʿĀ'ida *khatūn*. The orchard, an inheritance from the lady's husband, Khosh Khabar Ağa, a janissary in Jerusalem, included fig trees, other fruit-bearing trees and rose bushes.[27]

On the morrow, Muḥammad Pasha reappeared in the *majlis* (the *sharīʿa* court) and in the presence of several witnesses declared his will to dedicate the orchard as a *waqf*. Those entitled to enjoy its fruit, he stipulated, shall be, first and foremost, the Mawlawi Sufis. If they, for some reason, become extinct at some future date, the income should be divided among the other Sufis in Jerusalem. He further stipulated that the *waqf*'s mutawalli (supervisor) should be Ahmad *efendi*, sheikh of the Mawlawiyya.[28]

Documents in the *sijill* concerning debts and credit provide an indication of the wealth of Mawlawi Sufis. At the end of Jumāda al-thāni 1100 (April 1689), the sheikh of the Mawlawis was summoned to the qadi to present his establishments balance sheets. The balance, copied into the *sijill*, shows that during the year in question the *ṭarīqa*'s income was 2,050.75 *ghurūsh*, a very substantial sum. The *ṭarīqa* controlled a series of *waqfs*, made up mostly of shops and houses in the city, some of which were dedicated by members of the governing elite. Other *ṭarīqas*, including the Rifāʿiyya overseen by the ʿAlami family, also managed to accumulate wealth and to exert a great deal of influence as owners of land and property.[29]

The two spheres of contact—the one shared by Sufis and orthodox ulema, the other between governors and Sufis, were reinforced by a third sphere, comprising considerable parts of both—that which included local ulema and members of the governing elite. Since most ulema were members of Sufi groups, and since Sufi brotherhoods acted as cultural and religious centers of meaning for governors and their entourages as well, it was only natural for the two elites to find a common world of discourse.

This discourse was complemented by other ties between the two groups. Al-Muḥibbi mentions the special relationship between the great jurisconsult Khayr al-Dīn al-Ramli, and Aḥmad Pasha ibn Riḍwān, a famous governor of Gaza and Jerusalem and a patron of ulema. Aḥmad Pasha's grandson, Ḥusayn Pasha, is also remembered for his patronage of many ulema. Several other men of religion whose biographies are recorded by Muḥibbi were employed in the courts of such governors. Close relations were made possible by the fact that during the first seventy years of the century, governors were very often part of a local dynasty, or appointed for longer periods.[30]

Supported and encouraged by the governing elite, the emerging group of local notables accumulated considerable wealth and increased its influence among the rest of the population. Later on, when centralization efforts threatened their achievements, an influential notability enlisted the support of many inside and outside the city. This process, which led to the emergence of the notables as a cohesive and determined group, can best be described by following in the footsteps of three such families throughout the seventeenth century.

THE MAKING OF NOTABLE FAMILIES

The ʿAlamis

The ʿAlami family, which was most prominent in Jerusalem's Sufi establishment, traced its ancestry to the Maghribi Sufi ʿAlam al-Din Sulaymān (d. 1388) and to the famous saint (*walīy*) Ibn Mashīsh. The founders of the Jerusalem branch of the family probably arrived in the city in the fourteenth century. Two prominent members of the family were appointed city governors (*na'ib al-salṭana*) and comptrollers of the holy mosques (*nāẓir al-ḥaramayn*) in the Mamluk period.[31]

Following the Ottoman conquest in 1516, the ʿAlamis lost some of their former political power, but were quick to regain it. At the end of the sixteenth century rumors began to spread about the miracles and supernatural powers of Muḥammad al-ʿAlami. Soon his reputation reached far and wide, and added to the family's prestige. Aided by sheikh Asʿad ibn Ḥasan, the grand *mufti* of Istanbul, Muḥammad al-ʿAlami had a mosque built for his *ṭarīqa* on the Mount of Olives. When he died, in 1038/1628, his family buried him in the mosque, which later became a place of pilgrimage.[32] The *sijill* records the dedication of a *waqf* by the grand *mufti* in Istanbul, Sheikh Asʿad Abu Saʿīd. The *waqf*'s property included several houses, a flour mill and a bakery. Its profits were to be given to the Sufis of the Asʿadiyya mosque (*al-khānkāh al-Asʿadiyya*) headed by sheikh Muḥammad al-ʿAlami. It is further stipulated that Sheikh Muḥammad will be the *waqf*'s comptroller, and will appoint all its employees. All profits accruing to the *waqf* and not dispensed will be passed on to Sheikh Muḥammad and his descendants.[33]

This *waqf*, as well as other, smaller ones dedicated to the sheikh or given to him as presents, served as a basis for the family's enrichment in later years. The sheikh's son, ʿAbd al-Qādir al-ʿAlami (d. 1079/1668)—mentioned by al-Muḥibbi as a well-known and honest *'alim*—masterminded the economic moves made by the family. 'Abd al-Qādir invested mainly in land and property. He bought houses in the city, rented bath houses and workshops, got concessions from the qadi to use rainwater in the Holy Sepulcher's reservoir, and administered the many bakeries and flour mills already in the family's possession. Later on, he acquired the right to collect village taxes, and bought land in several regions.[34]

'Abd al-Qādir also enjoyed the privileges shared by other ulema and Sufis in the city. He received small grants from Istanbul and was exempt from most taxes imposed on the rest of the population. His name, along with that of his son, appears on the list of recipients of *kharāj* (*harac*) payments, and on lists of ulema receiving *ṣurra* (*sürre*)—annual grants of money from Istanbul. Iḥsān al-Nimr, a twentieth century local historian, mentions an 'Abd al-Qādir al-'Alami as qadi in Nabulus in the middle of the seventeenth century, indicating perhaps his main occupation and another source of wealth.[35]

Other members of the family also dealt in commerce and apparently amassed a considerable fortune. The Dajjānis, a rival Sufi family, followed a similar path. Members of both families would sometimes fight in court over property, debts or trade rights. At the end of the century the 'Alamis portrayed in the *sijill* are a rich family, famous for their religious and Sufi knowledge, with a widening sphere of political influence in the city and around it. A later biographer, al-Muradi, writing in the eighteenth century, describes another member of the family, Abu al-Wafā' al-'Alami, as a great sheikh, perhaps the leader of Sufi sheikhs in town (*shaykh al-shuyūkh bi-l-quds al-sharīf*) and recounts that the 'Alamis were one of the most famous families in the city. This is corroborated by the Sufi writer al-Nābulsi, who became Abu al-Wafā's close friend.[36]

The Ḥusaynis (Wafā'is)

Records of formal requests by people to be considered *ashrāf* attest to the considerable benefits to be gained by joining this privileged group. At times, as in the following record, a special inquiry was needed to establish the applicants' credentials before allowing them to wear the green turban and enjoy this most coveted status:

> Sayyid Ḥamūda ibn Ṣalāḥ al-Majdali arrived in the *majlis* today, and presented a document (*tadhkara, tezkere*) signed by the *naqīb al-ashrāf* in Jerusalem, glory of all *sādāt* (*ashrāf*) Mustafa *efendi*. According to the document, on the date shown the *naqīb* received a delegation made up of Sayyid Aḥmad al-Jindāsi, Sayyid Ṣāliḥ al-majdali, and

> Sayyid Mūsa ibn Ṣaliḥ. All testified that Ḥamūda is a *sharīf* on his mother's side, her mother being a scion of the *walīy*, Sheikh ʿAwaḍ. When all this was proven to his satisfaction, the *naqīb* allowed the above mentioned Ḥamūda to place on his head the green turban worn by all his colleagues the *sādāt*, and thus command the honor and consideration that his position entitles him to.
>
> Sayyid Ḥamuda requested that this document be registered in the *sijill*. His request was accepted, and the document was duly authenticated and copied, on the 22 Rabīʿ al-Awwal 1086 (16 July 1675).[37]

Later known as the Ḥusaynis, the Wafā'is are mentioned, as early as the mid-fifteenth century, as one of Jerusalem's influential families, and as *nuqabā al-ashrāf*. Later, in a 1615 record, ʿAbd al-Qādir al-Husayni is mentioned as "*sayyid al-sādāt*," or head of the *ashrāf* in the city. In another record ʿAbd al-Qādir is summoned to the *majlis*, and asked to testify that an order given by the pasha in Damascus to the governor of Jerusalem, commanding him to rebuild and fortify several castles on the road to Mecca, cannot be fulfilled. The governor claimed that he was unable to carry out the order for several reasons, while ʿAbd al-Qādir testified to the effect that this request was unprecedented and therefore bordered on the illegal. The summons may have been issued because the *naqīb*, being part of an old, established family, had a long memory of things past.[38]

An appointment as *naqīb al-ashrāf* carried with it certain duties as an arbitrator, as a representative of certain *waqfs*, and as an objective witness in matters involving local elite groups. These duties are recorded in the *sijill*:

> Half of the taxes levied from the village of Qaryat al-ʿInab (west of Jerusalem) belong to *waqf* al-Dawla al-Ḥasana. The other half should be divided equally between the two *timars*, that of the *sipahi* called ʿAjam zade, and that of Sulaymān ibn ʿAbdalla, a dependent (*tābiʿ*) of Shams ağa. On Muḥarram of 1033 (November 1623) several villagers from the said village arrived in court with 4 *qintārs* of pure [olive] oil, to be divided among those entitled to it. The weighing and division were attended by the *naqīb*, Sayyid ʿAbd al-Qādir al-Wafa'i.[39]

That same year ʿAbd al-Qādir is also mentioned as *shaykh ḥaram al-quds* (sheikh of the Jerusalem holy sanctuary), and as a debtor demanding payment from villagers in the vicinity. The records imply that the debt in question was in fact village taxes rented by the Ḥusaynis.[40]

During the somber years of Muḥammad ibn Farrūkh's reign, the Ḥusayni family went on building its fortune, and was apparently on good terms with the notorious governor. In the 1630s ʻAbd al-Qādir was replaced by his son, Shams al-Dīn. Like his ʻAlami contemporary, Shams bought land and property, making use of the vast *waqf* properties at his disposal. In 1635 he is mentioned, alongside ʻAbd al-Qādir al-ʻAlami, as a recipient of the *kharāj*. Like his father he often appears as arbitrator or witness in the *sharīʻa* court. On special occasions recorded in the *sijill*, his name is the first to appear on the list of local notables attending, further proof of his elevated status.[41]

At the turn of the century the title was held by Muṣṭafa al-Ḥusayni. Muṣṭafa's son, Muḥammad, who inherited the title from his father in February of 1700, was a prominent leader of the emerging notable elite, and the main force behind the uprising known today as "the Naqīb al-ashrāf revolt," in 1702–3. The uprising's eventual failure brought about the downfall of the Ḥusaynis and their replacement in the role of *nuqabā' al-ashrāf* by a lesser known family—al-Ghuḍayya. In the middle of the eighteenth century the Ghuḍayyas changed their name to al-Ḥusayni, reviving the name of their predecessors.[42]

The ʻAsalis

The seventeenth century witnessed the rise of several rich merchant families. Prominent among them were the ʻAsalis and their peers and rivals, the Mirliz family. At the beginning of the century, members of the ʻAsali clan are mentioned in *sijill* records of purchase contracts concerning workshops and small businesses. Khawāja (in that period, a common title for merchants) Muḥammad al-ʻAsali is mentioned in 1013/1605 as *shaykh al-tujjār* (*bazar başi*, head of the merchants) in the city, and it seems that the title passed on in the family for several generations.[43]

Later on another son of the family is mentioned, one that would lead the family for most of the century—Sheikh ʻAbd al-Jawwād al-ʻAsali. As a prominent figure among the city's merchants, he was frequently summoned to court to testify or to provide an expert opinion on a variety of business and production issues. His title also placed him a step above the rest of the merchants on the social ladder. In public gatherings at the *majlis*, ʻAbd al-Jawwād's name and title were mentioned frequently at the end of the list of notables, as a sort of barrier between the names of the elite and the nameless description (*jamāʻa min al-muslimīn*) of the rest of the people attending.[44]

ʻAbd al-Jawwād held the same position during the 1660s and 1670s, accumulating property and social status. Marriage records in the *sijill* show that he paid very high sums as bride-price for his sons. One of his sons married into the rival merchant family, Mirliz, but the other two married upwards and traversed the social divide. Kamal al-Dīn married Zāhira bint Sharaf al-Dīn Efendi, daughter of a famous and distinguished scholar. The *mahr* (dower) paid was 600 *ghurūsh*, an unprecedented sum in Jerusalem at the time. Another son, Sulaymān, married into a military family and apparently managed to buy himself a formal title. In records of commercial transactions, he is referred to as "the paragon of grand and noble (*qudwat al-amājid wa-l-a'yān*) Sulayman Bey ibn 'Abd al-Jawwād."[45]

For his fourth son, Ṣalih, 'Abd al-Jawwād chose the religious profession. Ṣalih was taught in the best schools, and upon graduation was given the privileged post of reading the Qur'an in al-Aqsa mosque. This position placed him on the lists of those receiving salaries and moneyed gifts from Istanbul. It also allowed him to engage in commerce without paying taxes, and soon he became one of the richest people in the city. In his book, al-Nābulsi describes a visit to Sheikh Ṣālih's house in 1690. Although a resident of Damascus, the provincial capital, al-Nābulsi was impressed by the opulence of "the pride of mighty and noble, the essence of generosity in our time, Sheikh Ṣālih al-'Asali." He depicts in detail the marvelous house, the fountains in the drawing room, and the delicious food served to the many guests.[46]

The 'Asalis had made it to a secure niche in the higher echelons of the notable elite. In later years they bought other titles, local janissary commissions and government positions. More than any other family, the 'Asalis made good use of the meager possibilities for social mobility and elite integration inherent in the social system.

INTEGRATION OF GOVERNING AND NOTABLE ELITES

Rich and influential local notable families tried to ally themselves with the local Ottoman governing elite. In an article about the integration of Turkish-speaking Ottomans into Damascene society, Barbir argues that relatively large groups of Turkish speakers settled in the city during this period. These groups included Sekban[47] fleeing from Anatolia, former janissaries and some ulema. They developed a subculture different from that of the governing elite, and in the seventeenth century began to merge with parts of the local society, changing its culture in the process. Mixed marriages were very popular, and proved to be the best means for quick integration.[48]

In Jerusalem this phenomenon was not as common. This may be attributed to the provincial character of the city and to its remoteness from the main arteries of transportation. Another variety of integration was apparent here—a tendency of the governing elite itself, especially its second generations, to assimilate into the local notability, and a parallel tendency of nonmilitary groups to buy their way into the military. As in Damascus, marriage proved to be the most efficient integrator, as the following record, referring to Sulaymān al-'Asali's transactions, demonstrates:

> On the 8th Ramaḍān 1100 (26 June 1689), the former *mīr alāy* (commander of *sipahis*) in Jerusalem, Iṣḥāq bey ibn Muṣṭafa bey, bought a coffee house in the quarter of bāb al-ʿAmūd [the exact location is specified in the record]. The sellers were Bihān Fakhr, daughter of Aḥmad *al-shurbaji* (*çorbacı*—janissary officer) and wife of ʿAbd al-Karīm al-Shurbaji, and Sulaymān bey al-ʿAsali, representing his wife ʿĀida khatun bint ʿAbd al-Karīm al-Shurbaji. [Other members of ʿAbd al-Karīm's family are also mentioned as sellers.][49]

This sales deed of a deceased janissary officer's coffee house, transferred to his sons and daughters as part of the inheritance, reveals a family well entrenched in Jerusalem, with complex family connections and property in the city. One of his daughters married Sulaymān bey al-ʿAsali, a member of the rich local merchant family on the rise. This was Sulaymān al-ʿAsali's ticket of admission into the governing elite of the city, for which he paid a substantial sum of money. But the marriage had also initiated another process—the integration of ʿAida Khātūn and her family into the local notability. Along with her dowry, ʿAida undoubtedly brought along some of the imperial center's culture, which was to influence local notables for years to come.

At the same time, the families of local governors and their descendants also settled down in the towns of Palestine. Many of the Farrūkhs, Ṭurabāys and Riḍwāns (described in detail in the previous chapter) chose to reside in Damascus, but others remained in Nabulus, Gaza and Jerusalem. Apparently relinquishing their ties to power and politics, they disappeared over time into the big local notable families.

LOCAL NOTABLES AND THE SOCIAL DIVIDE

To the extent that its members were aware of belonging to a separate group, the local notables saw themselves as equal to, or even higher in status than, the governing elite, with the exception of the governor, his deputy and the qadi (who was also usually appointed from Istanbul and formally considered part of the governing group). Evidence in the *sijill* suggests that this was also the view held by the qadi and his court. In long pecking-order lists of participants in special events, local notables figure high on the list. Their names were inscribed in the records immediately after those of the qadi and the governor or his senior representative, preceding all other high-ranking janissary and *sipahi* officers. This is one of many examples:

The paragon of sublime *amīrs*, mainstay of mighty seers, 'Asaf bey, governor of Nābulus and of the noble *ḥajj* arrived in the *majlis* today. It was brought to his knowledge, he announced, that his deputy (*kethüda*), 'Ali *bashsha*,[50] had abused and mistreated the subjects, and took away their money with no legal justification. He therefore summoned all the magnates and *a'yān* of the town—the ulema, the *zu'amā'* (holders of *zeamets*, large *timar* estates), the merchants and the rest of the people (*ghālib al-ra'āya*) in the presence of the qadi, may God show favor to his many qualities. [When they arrived] he made them take an oath, upon God and his Prophet [and asked them:]—"Did you ever inform, or hear, that 'Ali Kethüda had mistreated, hurt or harmed any of God's creatures, or has taken money, or any other object with no legal justification? If something of this kind ever presented itself to you, you are obliged to prove it. And if indeed he did not behave honestly, I shall relieve him of his duties forever, and banish him from my presence for eternity, for I do not seek the abuse of my subjects and will not choose to do so in my reign.

Present in the *majlis* were the pride of teachers, Sheikh Abu Bakr, the *shāfi'i mufti*, the pride of the righteous sheikh Muḥyi al-Dīn ibn Ṣalāḥ al-Dīn the *imām*, the model of the righteous sheikh Kamāl al-Dīn the *imām*, and the paragon of orators Sheikh 'Amīq al-Din. . .and the pride of the high and noble 'Ali ağa ibn Tuqlizade, *müteferrika* at the Sublime Porte,[51] the pride of the noble Mustafa bey, *mīr alāy* Nabulus, pride of the high and noble Muṣṭafa bey ibn Muḥammad ağa, the *za'īm*, pride of the noble 'Ali bey ibn Muḥammad *bölük baṣi* (commander of janissaries) the za'īm, pride of the mighty Ibrāhīm bey the *za'īm*. . .and the pride of merchants 'Ali Tuqqān, and the pride of merchants Khawāja 'Abd al-Raḥhīm al-Ṣabbān (the soap-maker), and the pride of the merchants Zayn al-Din Marwān, and Sheikh Idrīs ibn Sheikh Jarrār, head of most of Nabulus's population (*jull Nābulus*) and a party of Muslims whose names shall be written down at the end [of this record].

They all declared that "We have never heard any of these things about him, and furthermore, we know that he has chosen to walk the straight path. We have not heard of him abusing anyone, or taking anything by deceit."[52]

Taking into account the *sijill*'s bias, favoring those who were part of the ulema establishment, an "old boy" network based on the Ottoman *madrasa* system and shared interests, we still have to consider the very clear hierarchical pattern that emerges from this document and many others like it. The pecking order is offered twice in this document, once in a general form, presenting first the ulema and only later the *timar* holders of all ranks, and the second time by name, following the same pattern. The first to be mentioned are the leading local notables. Members of the military, including very high-ranking officers, are next in line, and closing the list are several prominent merchants and sheikhs. It is precisely this separation between the merchants and the ulema, with officers in between, that emphasizes a formal and structured hierarchy, looked upon as the natural order of things, at least in this context, by all parties involved.

As Robert Darnton has shown, this does not necessarily mean that religious notables were always held in high esteem, or that they occupied the first rungs of the social ladder from everyone's vantage point.[53] But just as urban processions or parades in the early modern period served to express the corporate order of society, to emphasize its essence and quality, to provide "a statement. . .through which the city represented itself to itself—and sometimes to God," so did public gatherings in the city of Jerusalem. Muslim inhabitants of the city used such gatherings in the *majlis*, God's court of law, to recreate and reproduce their own microcosm of social order.[54]

Though it allowed some movement from one elite to the other through marriage, religious learning or the purchase of titles, the borderline separating the two elite groups was relatively well defined. This separation did not generate any special friction between the two groups. Until the late seventeenth century both groups worked together in relative harmony. If the Ottoman Empire could be described as "a military-*sharī'a* alliance," this unwritten contract between two very different groups, which reinforced the cohesion of the empire, was echoed on a much smaller scale in Jerusalem and in neighboring *sanjaqs*. It was only later, towards the end of the century, that this very delicate fabric of relations was disrupted.[55]

In contrast to this degree of permeability between the two elites, the dividing line between notables and the rest of the unpriviledged population was rigid and difficult to cross. The social divide did not distinguish ulema, *ashrāf* and very rich merchants from the rest of the local population. It cut through the ulema and *ashrāf* establishment. There were, of course, many merchants and artisans who did not belong to the elite, but even within the establishments there were many who did not succeed in crossing this very visible border, demarcated by tax exemption and other privileges. Once the border had been crossed, the new status was cemented in marriage agreements and in receptions, as well as in *sijill* lists of summons to court, and in receiving a "green light" from Istanbul, most likely in the form of inclusion in lists of annual grants, or *'ulūfa* (*ulufe*) from the *ṣurra*.

A riot in 1652 highlights the unrelenting struggles for *'ulūfas* in Jerusalem. At the beginning of that year, we are told by the French traveler Jean Doubdan, permission was given to the Franciscan monks to renovate and enlarge their convent on Mount Zion. The Franciscans hired many Muslim masons and workers, who started to dig under the foundations. In the process they discovered ancient caves and cellars. Soon rumors began to circulate in town alleging that the Christians were building a tunnel to connect their monastery to the port of Jaffa, or even to the faraway island of Malta. Through these tunnels new Crusader armies will emerge and conquer the holy city from within.[57]

When Muslim pilgrims came back to Jerusalem from their annual visitation to the tomb of Moses (*qabr nabi mūsa*, on the way to Jericho), several men of religion among them conspired against the Christians. Playing on these persistent rumors, the conspirators instigated the pilgrims gathered in the courtyard of al-Aqṣa to attack the Christians and the "traitors" who helped them. An excited mob tried to attack the chief qadi who was praying nearby, but he somehow managed to escape and hide away. The mob then made its way to the Christian convent's gates, hurling large stones at the windows and doors, and was close to breaking into the grounds. The monks and their terrified guests were saved in the nick of time by a group of armed soldiers from the governor's retinue.[58]

Doubdan tells his story through the eyes of his hosts, the Franciscans, who, though more experienced, had very little knowledge of the motive force behind the riot. A deeper, more complicated set of motives emerges from several accounts of the same incident in the *sijill*:

> On the 19th of Jumāda al-Ūla 1062 (28 April 1652) a group of notables arrived in the *majlis*. Among them were heads of the ulema, the *mutasallim* [the governor's representative], the *sipahi* commander, the commander of the castle, the head of the merchants and a large group of Muslims. They all notified the qadi that sheikh 'Abd al-Karīm al-Ṣāmit, who was present at court, was responsible for the riot among the believers last Friday. When he left for the visitation to Nabi Musa, they said, he conspired with other scoundrels of his sort to start a *fitna* (commotion) upon their return on Friday. They described his evil character and his tendency to instigate riots. Sheikh 'Abd al-Karim was then asked: "Did you not declare that if a sultanic grant (*'ulūfa*) will be paid to you in full, you will not cause this *fitna*, and you will cease to incite the people?" "So I did," admitted the sheikh. And as [by his own admission] he proved the claims made against him by the ulema, the *ashrāf*, and other people present, the judge decreed that he should be punished by *ta'zīr* [whipping,

bastinado], and imprisoned in the citadel. So indeed was he punished and imprisoned, as a deterrence to him and to all who tread the same path.[59]

Sometime later Sheikh ʿAbd al-Karīm's accomplices were arrested and punished. Among them were *sūbāshi al-kilāb* (*sūbāshi* of the dogs) and several artisans.[60]

The riot of 1652 was apparently caused by the local elite's reluctance to include Sheikh ʿAbd al-Karīm al-Ṣāmit among those entitled to be granted an *ʿulūfa* from Istanbul. *ʿUlūfa*s were usually quite small, and could not have made such a difference economically. Their importance lay mainly in being a status symbol of the elite, and one of the ways notables could define themselves and draw the line separating them from the rest of the population, in a society where precedent was of paramount importance.[61]

Another status symbol, one which carried more economic value, was tax exemption. Repeated requests by *ashrāf* villagers in the *sanjaq*s of Nabulus and Jerusalem to stop paying taxes by right of their illustrious ancestry, illustrate the difficulties encountered by the establishment when asked to give a group of peasants, lacking any other traits of the elite, such a blatant symbol of elite power. This strange combination—*ashrāf* working as *fallaḥīn*, presented an almost insurmountable obstacle. Village-based *ashrāf* families had to fight over and over again for their rights to tax exemption by law, precedent and usage. Although some of the reluctance on the part of the local government to grant them their request stemmed from the evident loss of tax income, this sort of consideration never seems to have deterred anyone from allowing tax-paying city dwellers to join the ranks of the *ashrāf*.[62]

Social mobility and attaining inclusion in the ranks of the notables was a slow and painstaking process, as demonstrated by the ʿAsalis. From the beginning of the century this family advanced rapidly, economically as well as socially, but its members were still considered candidates and yet to be approved. Only late in the century, having studied and acquired ulema status and having bought titles and married into the two elites, their status as full-fledged members was finally given formal recognition in the form of various elite symbols of power and affiliation.

THE FOUNDATIONS OF NOTABLE WEALTH

It is widely accepted that local notable families in later centuries built their wealth on *iltizām*, or concessions for tax levies. Auctioned by the government for short terms at the beginning, *iltizāms* rapidly became long-term concessions, and ended up as *malikane*s—lifetime leases, and de facto private property.[63]

In the *sanjaq* of Jerusalem, however, *iltizām* was not the main source of enrichment for notable families. As seen in the short family histories presented above, their wealth and power originated in other economic activities. Its cornerstone was in many cases *waqf* foundations for religious and study purposes, dedicated by notables and ulema from the imperial center, by governors and their households, and by local magnates. In addition to receiving the *waqf*'s yield as charity, ulema, *ashrāf* and Sufis were also appointed managers, supervisors or comptrollers of *waqf* foundations and hence given influence and power in decision-making circles. Old Sufi families, such as the Dajjānis and ʿAlamis, were thus provided with a wide and varied economic basis.

Other governmental sources of income were the imperial *ṣurra*, and *kharāj* (poll tax) payments from locally based minorities. Notables were often allocated well-paying prestigious teaching posts in madrasas, and on rarer occasions appointed qadis or *bashkātibs* (*başkâtıb*, chief secretary in court.) Tax exemption, granted to ulema and *ashrāf*, allowed them to preserve most of their income, including a substantial surplus, usually invested in other transactions.

Another nonnegligible source of wealth was marriage agreements with aspiring merchant families, which led to the infusion of substantial sums of money in doweries, inheritance and joint economic ventures that benefited both sides.

And so, perhaps naturally, many of the notables in later generations found investment in commerce a relatively safe way of preserving and expanding their assets. They dealt in a variety of commodities, ranging from real estate to soap. They rented village taxes from *timar* holders and from *waqf* endowments. They bought land sold by villagers and houses in the city. They rented flour mills, soap factories, workshops, stores, coffee houses, and public baths. They sold the produce and imported goods from near and far.[64]

Towards the end of the century many notable families were economically very well off. They possessed lands and assets in the city and in many villages around it. This economic power generated a considerable deal of political influence both in the city and in surrounding villages. As centralization efforts continued, vested interests of the notables were in danger. They reacted by declaring a revolt at the beginning of the eighteenth century, and enlisted the support of urban dwellers, villagers, and even tribesmen.[65]

ALIENATION AND REVOLT

Local notables in seventeenth-century Jerusalem owe their ascent to the support of governors during the first half of the century. Ties between the two groups were not confined to *waqf* donations and Sufi ceremonies. Many governors saw the notables as important allies, to be promoted and looked after. Al-Muḥibbi's dictionary includes many biographies of governors from old established families—Riḍwān, Farrūkh and Ṭurabāy. He stresses their support for the ulema, and their clear commitment to local religious culture. Governors, led by the senior family—the Riḍwāns—devoted a great deal of attention to religious questions. They appointed *muftis*, granted scholarships, sent promising youths off to Egypt to study, and provided support for the most talented scholars when they came back. Mutual trust, enhanced by Sufi affiliations, was challenged only on very rare occasions. In sum, the era of local dynasties was the golden age for seventeenth-century notables. They had established themselves economically, socially and, to some extent, politically.

But later on in the century, when these local dynasties were broken by the imperial center and replaced by short-term governors, harmonious coexistence gave way to harsh, and at times violent, confrontation. By this time the notables were a powerful group, with considerable economic means at their disposal, strong ties of patronage to village and city populations, and clear vested interests in all realms of economy and politics. The new Istanbul appointed governors were replaced after very short terms in office, and they lacked the kind of intimate knowledge their predecessors had of the district and its problems. Many of them treated the local notability as just another group to be governed and exploited, and failed to understand their importance as a vital link to the population.

As relations between the two groups deteriorated further, notables cooperated with the rest of the population, sending petitions to Istanbul and pleading for action against the new governors. The *mühimme* defters in Istanbul include a growing number of petitions complaining about the brutal behavior of the governors and janissaries, about the unbearable burden of taxes, and about unpaid debts to merchants, artisans and suppliers. In all these petitions names of ulema and *ashrāf* open the list of petitioners. Needless to say, in the centralizing atmosphere prevalent in Koprülü Istanbul, these petitions were commonplace, and were probably shrugged off as the groans of an outdated system being replaced by a new and vigorous one.[66]

In the face of efforts to curb its power, a well-entrenched notability, sure of the support of the population, refused to bow its head as it had in the past. When a new governor, Muḥammad Pasha "Kurd Bayram," harsher and more thorough than his predecessors, arrived in 1701, things came to a head. The pasha demanded more taxes, and cruelly punished those who refused to pay. He apparently ignored the notables and their claims, and joined the qadi, reportedly a vain and corrupt person, in extorting their money. The last straw was the attempt by the governor's retinue to attack and rob a village belonging to the *mufti* of Jerusalem (probably as *waqf* or lease.) The anger of the ulema and the *ashrāf*, pent up for two decades, finally erupted in the violent revolt of Naqīb al-Ashrāf in 1703.[67]

It was precisely this desperate move, however, that set back the development of a strong and influential notability, and dealt a near fatal blow to the rising group of notables. The revolt failed, the *naqīb* and his accomplices escaped from Jerusalem in October of 1705, and were later sentenced to death, and the city was occupied again by Ottoman troops. Thousands of soldiers were stationed within Jerusalem's walls, resulting in a rapid decline in the economy. Some of the old ulema and *ashrāf* families fell from grace, notably the Ḥusaynis, who led the rebels. In the course of the eighteenth century other families emerged, and some of the old ones regained their status and found their way into the Ottoman administration, having given up much of their former independence in the process.[68]

There can be little doubt that the insurrection broke out because of contemporary grievances that had to do with the new governor's cruelty and high-handedness, and with the centralizing tendencies emanating from Istanbul. But it cannot be understood out of context. The rise of a powerful and relatively independent notable group in the seventeenth century was a crucial part of that context.

In the second half of the seventeenth century, the notables became a cohesive social group, resembling in many respects Weber's "patriciate" as defined by Hourani for the Ottoman Empire. Their control of land and commerce gave them control over part of the city and the villages in its vicinity. Their management of *waqf* foundations, along with the patronage of the governing elite, added a significant measure of political power. As centralization increased in the last two decades of the seventeenth century, the power of notables began to decline. It was first felt as they were deliberately distanced from the new centers of government, followed by disregard for their economic privileges. Their achievements up to this point were threatened. At the same time stronger ties were forged between the notables and the rest of the population, bound by shared feelings of neglect and mistreatment. The *reaya* assisted the notables in the revolt, which was a desperate attempt by the notables to regain some of their former political power, and a violent protest against the ongoing effort to rob them of the rest of their achievements.

Can the same conclusions be applied to the contemporary revolts in Istanbul, Cairo and Damascus? There is still not enough material available on these incidents, but it seems that all have a lot in common. In his evaluation of the last years of the seventeenth century, Abdul Karim Rafeq found that as local military forces (*yerliyya*) faltered in Damascus, the ulema became the peoples' sole defenders against autocratic rule. Between 1690 and 1696 several notables who dared protest against the governor's tyranny were banished from Damascus, among them *naqīb al-ashrāf*. In Cairo, the same role of popular leadership was assumed by the janissaries, who became a deeply rooted local notability, and in Istanbul the revolt was carried out under the aegis of the local aristocracy, which had its own axe to grind with the sultan and his vezirs.[69]

All these uprisings had something in common, which set them apart from other, earlier revolts in the empire. Unlike their sixteenth- and seventeenth-century antecedents, the revolts at the beginning of the eighteenth century were not led by autonomous governors who wanted to shake off Ottoman rule and achieve some sort of independence, nor were they led by charismatic religious zealots. Neither were they spontaneous peasant riots typical of the Celali period of unrest in Anatolia. Instead, these revolts were instigated and led by influential local notables—*ashrāf*, ulema or localized military units. They should therefore be seen not only as separate affairs in their local settings, not merely as detached incidents emerging from local grievances, but also as different manifestations of the same historical phenomenon. They were a phase in a wider chain of events, tracing the beginning of the notable spiral: the rise of local notable groups throughout the empire at the beginning of the century, and their attempt to recapture some of the political power appropriated by the centralizing state in the latter part of that century.

Chapter 4

Desert, Village and Town

A UNIFIED SOCIAL STRUCTURE

In the first decades of Ottoman rule, the heyday of the empire's power in Arabic-speaking lands, signs of weakness began to show in the old guard of elite soldiers. Janissaries and *sipahis*, not so long ago the terror of armies across Europe and Asia, became cumbersome fighting units, unwilling to adapt to changing circumstances. Their ranks swelled with people who bought titles and commissions with very little training or fighting experience. They threatened the sultan and his government with ever-growing demands for wages, yet repeatedly failed in the battlefield. Their weakness created a military and political void in the center and the provinces, which was rapidly filled up by other coalitions of power.[1] These subsequent structures of military power, their meaning for society and culture, and the form they assumed in the district of Jerusalem, will be dealt with in this chapter.

A CHANGING OF THE GUARD

Still considered an elite fighting unit at the beginning of the seventeenth century, the janissaries are frequently mentioned in the records of *sharīʿa* courts. In most cases, however, this mention has nothing to do with their military duties or with problems arising from these duties. Throughout the century janissaries were seldom used in combat missions in the province. The collective image that emerges from the sources is one of a social group with very few military obligations, yet formally considered part of the governing elite, well entrenched in the social and commercial life of the district, and enjoying a wide range of economic privileges.

Many of the janissaries mentioned in the records bear Muslim names, and quite a few possess a second or third generation of such names, clearly not of the limited set given to non-Muslims who embraced Islam. Sometimes their fathers were also mentioned as janissaries or local notables. It is evident that they were not a product of the sultanic system of acquisition and training, nor were they brought up in the parallel system based on the purchase of slaves, which was sponsored by the *ümera* in their local courts. Military training was apparently not a prerequisite for joining the ranks.[2]

A record from the year 1636 (1045), one of many dealing with janissaries in the *sijills* of Nabulus and Jerusalem, illustrates clearly the status of some janissaries in Jerusalem in the first half of the century:

> On 9 Dhu al-Qa'da 1045, the *sayyid* Salih and his brother, Sayyid Muḥammad, sons of the artisan (*mu'allim*) Maḥmud ibn Ilyās, arrived in court. These two gentlemen of the janissaries in the citadel of Jerusalem (*min al-sāda al-yinkishāriyya bi-qal'at al-quds*) brought their complaint before the qadi. Up to this day, they said, they or their forefathers were never asked to pay special impositions (*al-takālif al-'urfiyya*)[3] for producing wooden latticework (*sha'āra*), but now the governor's representatives harass them and demand that they pay these impositions.
>
> Upon hearing their complaint, the qadi decided to examine the matter in depth, and consulted with several Muslim notables who were well acquainted with the two brothers and their circumstances. These notables supported the brothers' claim, and affirmed that government taxes were never imposed on them or on their father. They were exempted on two counts, the notables added: their commissions in the janissary corps, and their poverty (*wa-likawnihima bayna yinkishāriyyat qal'at al-Quds al-sharif wa-lifaqrihima*). Following the inquiry the judge ruled in favor of the brothers, and instructed all those persecuting them to stop demanding special impositions, either for production of latticework or for any other reason. The verdict was duly inscribed in the *sijill*.

This portrayal of the janissaries is remote from the image of the institution in its classical period, when janissary units were a symbol of imperial power, recruited and trained in the center. It is also a far cry from the *ümera-mamlūk* form of socialization into the governing elite. The two janissary brothers are referred to as *sayyids*, a title usually reserved for descendants of the prophet, but in this period sometimes used as a general honorific. Their father was a known member of the urban community, a *mu'allim* (an accomplished artisan or artist), and a janissary himself. The two sons, registered as janissaries in the citadel, remained in the old family business of latticework.

Records like this also bear witness to the many tax exemption privileges enjoyed by the janissaries, which made the commission so lucrative. These privileges were not always based on law. In special cases, when the janissaries themselves were manual laborers and were not engaged in trade or financial brokerage, other conditions, like proof of economic necessity, were necessary for tax exemption. Most janissaries did not have a regular fixed income, and being one did not determine economic status. If estates and property registered in cases involving inheritance disputes are any indication, however, poverty was not a widespread problem among janissaries and they were usually well off. Many among them possessed lands and large households.[4]

Some janissaries may have served as bodyguards for governors, members of their entourage, tax collectors, policemen, and even as garrison soldiers in fortresses along main routes. It seems very unlikely, though, that such soldiers could be mobilized and sent off to wars or punitive expeditions. Fighting against well-equipped European armies, or against battle-hardened bedouin tribes in harsh desert conditions, was not the sort of task to be entrusted to artisans and merchants. They could not be depended upon as fighting forces in the battlefield.

*Sipahi*s, the other elite fighting force, were in a similar predicament, though the institution still retained much of its past prestige. Cavalry officers commanded respect, and some still turned up in the provinces now and then, presenting sultanic decrees awarding them *timars*. But by and large the imperial source for professional *sipahi*s seemed to dwindle, and in the second half of the seventeenth century it was no more than a trickle.[5] Instead, fiefs were sometimes allocated to the sons of Ottoman vezirs and other notables in the center. Thus, in 1595, the holder of the large fief (*zeamet*) in the village of Dammun on Mount Carmel was the son of the Ottoman vezir Khalil Pasha. In 1657 the son of Anatolia's chief military qadi (*kazasker*) held the *zeamet* of Bayt Saḥūr near Jerusalem.[6] Slaves brought up as *mamluks* in the houses of provincial *ümera* were another source of manpower for the *sipahi* corps. Upon manumission many of them received a *timār* and a commission in the force. In Damascus, the provincial governor was authorized to allocate small fiefs to *sipahi*s, thus strengthening ties of loyalty and clientage with *ümera* in the province. Larger estates were obtained from Istanbul.[7] Many, perhaps the majority of *sipahi*s in the districts of Jerusalem and Nabulus, were sons or grandsons of local timariots. When called upon to give testimony or answer in court, their lineage presented to the qadi often included the father's name and rank in the *sipahi* corps. frequently the *sipahi*'s family—his sisters, brothers, children or uncles—would also be mentioned.

One incident, in which a *sipahi* was murdered by villagers in the vicinity of Jerusalem, may serve to illustrate the state of the institution:

> On the morning of 5 Jumāda al-Ākhira 1079 (10 November 1668) a group of *sipahi*s arrived in court. Among them were Sheikh Abu Bakr ibn Khalīl and Ḥājj Muḥammad ibn ʿIwad. They notified the qadi that Sayyid Khalīl ibn Sheikh Yūsuf the *sipahi* was found dead in the village of Khirbat al-Lawz, which is part of his *timār*. They claimed that unknown persons from the village killed him and dumped his body in a water cistern.
>
> A team of investigation was sent to the village. The body of the dead *sipahi* was found, bearing marks of violence. The two *sipahi*s who reported the murder turned out to be the victim's uncle, Abu Bakr, and his maternal brother, Ḥājj Muḥammad Bey ibn ʿIwad al-Maʿarri. They told the team investigating the case that the victim, Sayyid Khalīl, spent the night at the house of a certain family in the village. The murderers captured him there, tied him up and killed him. His personal effects, including his money and his sword, were all stolen.[8]

The affair went on for a while, until the assassins were seized and executed. Meanwhile another case was brought to court: a controversy about the possessions of the victim, and his legal heirs. Among those claiming the right to inherit were his mother, ʿAisha *khatun* bint Sheikh ʿAli al-ʿAzma, his sister, Khadīja *khatun* bint Yūsuf, his maternal brother, Ḥājj Muḥammad Bey ibn ʿIwad, and his paternal uncle Bakri (formerly mentioned as Abu Bakr) ibn Khalīl. In due course the relatives agreed on the way to divide the property and possessions.

Another dispute concerned the now vacant *timār*. Ḥājj Muḥammad Bey received his brother's vacated *timār* by imperial decree, but here an unforeseen problem arose. The same *timār* was also allotted to another *sipahi*, ʿAbd al-Karīm Ağa ibn Muṣṭafa, by the provincial governor in Damascus, who apparently assumed that reallocating the *timār* was within his powers. Another prolonged legal debate seemed to be in store for the family, but to everyone's relief and to the reader's surprise, a compromise was reached out of court. ʿAbd al-Karīm Ağa and Ḥājj Muḥammad Bey, the two contestants over the small *timār*, decided that the fief should be divided between them. Each one will receive an equal share, paying 1,100 *ghurūsh* of tribute a year. The unusual arrangement received the qadi's blessing.

This affair tells us a great deal about *sipahi*s and *timār* holders in the period. Sayyid Khalīl, the victim, was neither a product of the *devşirme* system or a parallel imperial institution. Nor was he the *mamlūk* of a local *amīr*. His family hardly fits the classical *sipahi* mould. As in the case of the janissaries, it is difficult to determine whether the victim's title "*sayyid*" implied descent from an *ashrāf* family. This was not a common title for *sipahi*s in earlier times. The father's title of sheikh was also rare among *sipahi*s, certainly in the first generation. Several other family members, like the paternal uncle, Abu Bakr, were also referred to as *sipahi*s. The father married ʿAisha, a local woman who had a son from a previous (or later) marriage. This son was also a *sipahi*, even though his father's name and his *nisba* suggest that he was also of local descent. At least four members of the family, then, carried the title of *sipahi* in the same district. They inherited from each other, and transferred their *timār*s to other family members, with what amounted to an almost automatic approval of the authorities. Other records imply that this approval was obtained in many cases by sending gifts to certain officials in Istanbul.

The affair ended with another highly unconventional arrangement. The *timār* in question was divided into two mini-*timār*s, yielding a very small income. This arrangement, perhaps more than any other part of the story, bears witness to the fact that *timār*s and *sipahi* duties were by that time meaningless from a military point of view. The former sanctity of this institution, upon which an entire Ottoman standing army was based, had become a lucrative source of income, to be rearranged and divided almost arbitrarily.[10]

Transfer of *timār*s to next of kin is relatively frequent in the *sijill*s and in Ottoman sources. In several cases minor sons of *sipahi*s received their father's *timār*, while still under the supervision of a legal guardian. In such cases *fatāwa* and legal opinions enjoin that the minor *sipahi*s should arm and train replacements to take their place on the battlefield. This appears, however, to have been an old legal mechanism which served as a fig-leaf to cover what was in fact an attempt to privatize and bequeath land. In other cases *sipahi*s leased their *timār*s to the highest bidder, and evaded the added task of maintaining law and order in the villages assigned to them.[11]

In the districts of Palestine *timār*-holders were frequently exempted from duty in imperial campaigns. Instead, they were required to perform several security tasks in the area. Pilgrims on their way to visit holy shrines in Jerusalem, Hebron and Nabi Musa were entitled to be accompanied by *sipahi*s to protect them. Evliya Çelebi, who visited Jerusalem in the 1670s recounts that the *sipahi*s in Jerusalem are not required to participate in imperial campaigns, and that their sole duty is to accompany the pilgrims and travelers. But as records in the *sijill* and the Ottoman archives suggest, this was not always the case. From time to time orders were sent to *sipahi*s requiring them to join the Ottoman army on its way to war. They would usually decline, claiming that they were needed back home. More often they were asked to pay a sort of ransom (*bedel, badal* in Arabic) in lieu of participation, which they would grudgingly do.[12] In short, *sipahi*s maintained their titles, their privileges and the pomp of dress and sword brandishing, but lacked experience in war.[13]

Sultans, vezirs and provincial governors soon realized they could no longer rely on the janissaries and *sipahi*s. Instead they began to train and give precedence to other forces, known as *sekban, sarıca* or *levend*, (*sakbān, sārija* or *lawand* in Arabic), based mainly on armed villagers. At first they were recruited on an ad hoc basis for one campaign and then dismissed, but later on they developed into regular army units. *Sekban* (sometimes called *sakmāniyya* in Arabic,) were part of the governor's retinue in Jerusalem. Other units, known as the *yerliyya* (local) forces were modelled after the janissaries and competed with them in the provinces.

In the southern and Western regions of the province of Damascus, the most important military force at the time was undoubtedly the bedouin. In one capacity or another bedouin seem to have participated in almost every skirmish and battle. Their role in the service of Ottoman governors is often played down or ignored altogether.[14] If we are to understand the importance of the bedouin in politics and society, we must now turn to a discussion of the reasons for this neglect.

Desert and Sown—The Paradigm

The enmity between the desert and the sown has been described countless times in literary epics: nomads lead their lives in harsh desert climes, where food and water are scarce and where the heat (or cold, at nights and in winters) is oppressive. On the other side, where water is abundant and the earth fertile, they encounter villagers or townsmen, who guard their possessions jealously and try to push the nomads back into the desert. The envious nomads stare hungrily at the riches of the land, and when an opportunity presents itself, pounce on the sedentary settlements, pillaging and looting.

A wider conceptual framework for the same idea was offered by the famous fourteenth-century Maghribi historian Ibn Khaldūn. Living on the northern rim of the North-African Sahara desert, Ibn Khaldun held clear views on the subject. The war between the desert and the sown, he said, was the center of human history. Both nomads and sedentary societies are ''natural'' societies. Their way of life is dictated by economic necessity. Pasture, the basis of nomad economy, requires enormous tracts of land, thus forcing the nomads to migrate often and lead a spartan life. In time economic conditions improve for some of them, and they are no longer satisfied with their way of life. Finally they settle down, building their own villages and towns. Nomads are therefore the source of all civilization, but as they acquire the habits of civilization they soften and become spoiled, losing their team spirit, the *'asabiyya* which enabled them to survive in the desert. Other nomads do not follow this pattern, however. Although their ability to adapt to desert life is impressive, they seek to improve their lot by attacking sedentary civilizations. Such onslaughts, repeated in an eternal vicious circle, result in the total destruction of civilization.[15]

Thus, in Ibn Khaldūn's masterpiece, and in many other works, a line of demarcation is drawn between the desert and the cultivated areas. An almost tangible border, sometimes moving into the desert, as "civilization" infringes on nomad realms, at other times biting into the perimeter of towns and villages. This reasoning has influenced many modern works on the Middle East, which tend to ignore relationships between nomads and sedentary populations that do not correspond to this mould. When facts crop up to challenge this view, they are often ignored, or explained away as exceptions to the rule. The misconception about the ways nomad and sedentary populations coexist and cooperate leads to distorted views of society and politics in many historical contexts.

Complex relations existed between sedentary and pastoral cultures in Palestine throughout its history. The coastal plain and the mountain ranges in this area form a narrow strip of fertile, arable land, surrounded by deserts: Sinai, the Negev, the Judean desert and the Syrian desert. In times of draught the desert invades areas habitually cultivated, while a long stretch of rainy seasons may widen the settled zone considerably. In many respects the whole area is a desert periphery from ancient history to modern times.

Descriptions of the enmity between bedouin and sedentary populations in this area abound especially in Ottomanist research. One of the most comprehensive research works on the early years of Ottoman rule is Uriel Heyd's *Ottoman Documents on Palestine*, based on a collection of sultanic decrees from the famous Mühimme Defterleri collection in the Ottoman archives in Istanbul.[16] These decrees often discuss bedouin insurrection and insubordination. They appear to have been a constant menace which the government saw as one of its main concerns in the region. From time to time wars erupted between forces stationed in the area and the bedouin.[17] There are frequent reports of bedouin tribes equipped with state-of-the-art firearms, revolting against Ottoman rule. Decrees often encourage governors to fight these rebels, or to impose economic sanctions upon them in the hope of making them submit to authority.[18] Other methods included the taking of hostages, and sometimes even the forced deportation of clans or whole tribes.[19] The Ottoman government, says Heyd, saw the bedouin as a threat and a nuisance, and often inflicted cruel punishment upon them. Here there were no misgivings or remorse of the kind that sometimes accompanied punitive expeditions against troublesome villagers. The war was prolonged and bitter. Being accustomed to desert conditions, sometimes better equipped, and enjoying access to intelligence information about expected raids, the enemy often had an edge over government forces.[20]

In his study on the bedouin in Palestine in the sixteenth and seventeenth centuries, Moshe Sharon endorses Heyd's conclusions. Basing his argument on Arabic chronicles and descriptions provided by European travelers, Sharon adds a flavor of terror: raids on trade caravans and pilgrims, and highwaymen demanding ransom. Here too inhabitants of the desert and the sown are presented as enemies locked in mortal combat. Ottoman governments saw their main duty in the region as protecting the sedentary population from bedouin invasion, and safeguarding the passage of pilgrims to the holy cities of Mecca and Medina. Just like their predecessors, the Mamluks, they failed in this task. the reasons for their failure, maintains Sharon, were their military weakness, a dwindling civilian population too insecure to defend itself, and the growing power of their foes, the bedouin.[21]

The Ottomans tried to cope with the problem, Sharon says, by moving villagers to sparsely populated regions. Some were promised tax deductions in return for resettlement in border areas, others were deported by decree (*sürgün*). These measures, however, were never carried out properly, and the villagers seldom settled in their designated areas. Another method often used was an attempt to buy off bedouin sheikhs and notables by paying them sums of money, and at times by trying to integrate them into the Ottoman governing system. But the central government was weak, and could not impose its will upon potential bedouin allies.

In several cases tribes and clans were integrated into the Ottoman system. One prominent example is the integration of the Ṭurabāy family, a clan of the Bani Ḥāritha tribe, which claimed descent from the famous Tayyi' tribe of the Arabian desert.[22] Such attempts were only partly successful. For a long time Ṭurabāy relations with the Ottomans fluctuated between cooperation and rebellion. In 1677, when their tribe, the Bani Ḥāritha, moved eastward to the area of ʿAjlun and the Jordan valley, they were deposed as governors of Lajjun, and an Ottoman officer was appointed in their place. In the end, he concludes, the Ṭurabāys were just another example of the Ottoman provincial administration caving in to bedouin pressure.[23]

A study by ʿĀdil Mannāʿ supports the conclusions arrived at by Heyd and Sharon. In an essay on the Farrūkh governors of Jerusalem and their relations with the bedouin, Mannāʿ describes the weakness of the central government and its inability to restrain rebellious bedouin: "The relative improvement brought about by the Ottoman government's curtailment of bedouin activity in the first half of the sixteenth century, petered out towards its end. The situation once more resembled the state of affairs which characterized the last years of Mamluk rule in the region."[24] The only ones who were able to check the disastrous bedouin raids were the Farrūkh governors, and they did so only by eventually joining forces with them to raid and plunder villages entrusted to their care.[25]

Mannāʿ has used another source, one that was seldom used before. His was the first research concerning bedouin to have used the *sijill*. The records he uses include firmans from Istanbul, letters from the provincial governor in Damascus, and descriptions of events in and around Jerusalem. These records elucidate the volatile relationship between the Farrūkhs, the bedouin and the fallahin in the district. A relationship which could best be described as a combination of treachery and cruelty, where yesterday's allies are today's victims. Ties between the bedouin and the governors were always at the expense of the settled population. The local provincial elite, claims Mannāʿ (referring mainly to the governor Muḥammad ibn Farrūkh), betrayed their duty of protecting the populace, and allied themselves instead with the ruthless nomads.[26]

The works of Heyd, Sharon and Mannāʿ enhance and reproduce well known stereotypes of the bedouin. Nowadays many scholars tend to accept this view and to incorporate it in their studies as a well-documented historical fact. Thus, Haim Gerber, in his book on the social origins of the modern Middle East, can write that "The problem of nomads in Syria and Palestine under Ottoman rule is well known and needs little elaboration. The vacuum left by the weakening of the government after the sixteenth century (if not before) was a function of the fact that the great bulk of the coastal plain was a roaming ground for bedouin tribes, and was almost totally devoid of permanent villages."[27] In such basic textbooks the facts have already become assumptions that "need little elaboration," and upon which other theories can safely be constructed.

This insistence on the basic stereotype continues even when there are clear contradictions in the sources. These are already evident in Heyd's work. A decree dated 1552 quoted by Heyd claims that the crux of the problem is the close-knit commercial relationship, centered mainly on sheep and wool, between the inhabitants of Jerusalem and the bedouin, as well as the friendly ties between bedouin and *timār* holders, who tip them off about expected punitive raids against them. The firman instructs the Beylerbey in Damascus to punish the rebellious bedouins, to arrest the treacherous timariots, seize their households and families, and send them over to Istanbul.[28]

Another decree of the same year imposes economic sanctions on bedouin tribes, but in discussing the state of affairs prior to the rebellion, the decree conveys a sense of very active commercial ties with the nomads. In the past, it says, such sanctions were the only way to force the bedouin to reach a settlement with the Ottoman authorities. Another firman, dated 1584, describes the hazardous road in the area of Ramle in the district of Gaza, where bedouin highway robbers attack innocent travelers. The solution it suggests, however, is the appointment of a *bedouin* sheikh who holds a *timar* in the vicinity to keep an eye on the road.[29]

Such contradictions are also visible in Sharon's essay. The appointment of bedouin notables like the Ṭurabāys to the high-ranking post of district governor is outstanding in itself. It cannot be seen merely as the result of bedouin pressure brought to bear on the Ottoman government. After all, over a century of Ṭurabāy rule, usually loyal to the government in Istanbul, must have been built on a stronger foundation. But there are other indications as well. Sharon writes of the cooperation between villagers and bedouin against other such groups; payment of fixed salaries (*ṣurra*) to bedouin sheikhs on the *ḥajj* route; and even of an incident where seven thousand soldiers were required to protect a munitions caravan to Jarash and ʿAjlun, but an agreement with the bedouin made it possible to send the caravan through with no military escort whatsoever.[30]

Mannāʿ casts his bedouin in a double role. At the beginning of the century, when Farrūkh Bey was governor of Jerusalem, they threatened the peaceful existence of the district, and organized daring raids against him. But when his son, Muḥammad, became governor in the 1620s, they suddenly turned out to be his closest allies. The bedouin's actions are described as disruptive both when they fight against the provincial government, and when they join forces with it to exploit the *reaya*.

One of the reasons for the persistence of the "desert and sown" paradigm, even when so many contradictions crop up, is the kind of sources used to lay the foundations of modern research on Ottoman Palestine. The centrality of Mühimme Defterleri decrees in Heyd's book is misleading. These are very reliable sources for Ottoman high politics, and reflect to a large extent what bureaucrats in the center thought about affairs in the province. But this is also their greatest single weakness. In the seventeenth century, Istanbul was a distant capital. Local politics in a faraway district seemed petty and meaningless. Communications were at best haphazard. Istanbul bureaucrats lacked insight into the affairs of the district, and in most cases described the situation in vague phrases, seldom seeing more than the one-sided picture presented to them in a letter or a petition. Another distortion is created when all the firmans concerning a small region over a period of seventy years are collected under subject headings. Each of the subjects dealt with in the book was brought to the attention of Istanbul mandarins once or twice a decade at best. Grouping them together creates an artificial sense of importance and urgency.

From Istanbul's vantage point the bedouin were indeed a problem. They threatened trade routes, raided *ḥajj* caravans and too often acted independently, clearly defying Ottoman sovereignty. The sultan and his vezirs were bothered by the growing challenge to their authority, but did not care about other aspects of the relationship with the bedouin. To obtain a better understanding of the situation in the district, one should attempt to read between the lines, and to amplify dim reflections of this distant reality.

The two sources used by Sharon—chronicles and travelers' accounts—present a different bias. Travelers, many of them pilgrims, are sometimes accused of falsifying reports, or copying from predecessors in order to embellish their narrative. In the matter of bedouin, however, another problem looms even larger. Their understanding of local society and culture was at best superficial. In most cases they did not know whether the menacing individual facing them and demanding money was a bedouin thug, a villager, or even a soldier fulfilling his duty. Local chroniclers knew much more, of course, about the local scene, and in most cases present a balanced, well-informed view of affairs. Indeed, most of the contradicting information in Sharon's article was derived from such sources. But the writers of historical chronicles saw their duty as recording great deeds for future generations. While extraordinary bedouin raids and punitive expeditions against them automatically fell into this category, the slow rhythm of everyday life was not deemed worthy of special record in a chronicle.

Sijills, the main source added by Mannā', shed a new light on the matter. Being a quasi-official record of events, trials, business transactions, and government affairs, they reflect another sort of relationship. The governor's special relationship with the bedouin, as it emerges from these records, forms the basis of Mannā''s argument. Yet the paradigm is so powerful that it embraces even these exceptions. Ibn Farrūkh's alliance with the bedouin is described as an aberration, a deviation from the expected code of conduct. A reexamination of these and other records reveals another side of the picture, and suggests a new way of looking at the role of the bedouin in the politics, culture and economy of the district. Rather than a dichotomy between the desert and the sown, we can now propose a more complex representation, in which bedouin were as much a part of society in the districts of Palestine as villagers or town-dwellers.

BEDOUIN DEFENDING THE REALM

Bedouin participated as soldiers and commanders in the armed forces of all local governors in the seventeenth century. This was the rule rather than the exception. They were incorporated into the military establishment in various ways. Sometimes they were soldiers in army units or in governors' entourages. In other cases a contract was signed between local officials and a certain tribe to employ all, or part of its members, as an allied defense force. Some of these contracts were fairly stable and long-term, while others were signed only when special needs arose. In yet another variety, bedouin clans were entrusted with the defense of a road or a strategic point in their own vicinity.

The beginnings of this system can be traced back to the early days of Ottoman rule, when the territory known as Lajjun (later to become a formal *sanjaq*) was entrusted to the Ṭurabāy family. As Heyd shows in his book, this was not an unprecedented or isolated incident in the region. In the year 1584, for instance, the fief given to the bedouin sheikh Abu al-ʿUways, was enlarged from a *timar* yielding 17,000 *akçe,* to a *zeamet* of 20,000 *akçe,* in return for which he was to guard the stretch of coastal road leading northward to Ra's al-ʿAyn (Rosh Ha-ʿAyin). In a later firman, dated 1585, the district governor was ordered to entrust the defense of another stretch of road, this time to the north of Ra's al-ʿAyn, to a clan of the Bani Jayyūs tribe. Other districts in the province of Damascus were assigned to bedouin sheikhs, like the Ibn Furaykhs, who controlled the northern regions of Trans-Jordan for several decades. The Ottomans were quite content to entrust defense tasks, *timars*, and even whole districts, to bedouin sheikhs.[31]

This system was improved and articulated during the seventeenth century. In 1693 a certain *amīr al-ḥajj,* ʿAssāf Pasha (not to be confused with ʿAssāf Pasha ibn Farrūkh), presented a petition to the sultan. Ever since the offices of sheikh (*şeyhlik*) of Gaza and Damascus were taken away from Sheikh Kulayb and sheikh Walīd and given to others, he claimed, troubles never ceased. The new people were incapable of defending the road properly, and as a result the pilgrims and travelers were constantly harassed. He pleaded with the government in Istanbul to restore the two sheikhs to their old appointments. A decree addressed to the vezir Mustafa Pasha, the governor of the province, instructed him to look into the matter. If, as ʿAssāf Pasha said, the two sheikhs were more adept in keeping the bedouins at bay, under discipline and control, and if they were capable of protecting the *ḥajj* pilgrims better than others, they should be reappointed to their former positions. If, however, the *ümera* are expected to do a better job, then they should be the ones to be appointed. Mustafa Pasha was ordered to report back his conclusions and the course of action he had chosen.[32]

As this firman demonstrates, in the course of the seventeenth century the provincial government had already created formal titles, and probably formal salaries for sheikhs appointed to guard the *ḥajj* route. The Ottoman attitude, as emerges from this and other documents, was entirely pragmatic. The only criterion to be taken into consideration is the ability to perform the task. Another method of securing the cooperation and loyalty of bedouin sheikhs was payment of money from the *ṣurra*. Such yearly tributes, begun in the sixteenth century, became part of the administration's budgeted expenses a century later. When, in 1689, the payment was late, several bedouin tribes attacked the *ḥajj* caravan. An imperial decree sent to the governor of Damascus instructs him to pay the money promptly, and in future to avoid reneging on such agreements.[33]

Bedouin were not employed exclusively as stationary defense forces in a delimited area. They were frequently used as mercenary forces in the governor's personal guard or in his provincial cavalry. They were used to collect taxes and levies from the villages, and to protect caravans and officials against assault. A record in the Jerusalem *sijill* demonstrates the role of bedouin troops in such circumstances:

> In the month of Shawwāl 1024 (1615) a representative of the provincial governor of Damascus, named Ḥusayn ağa, arrived in court. He brought with him a white leather pouch containing 1,000 *ghurūsh* and bearing the seal of the *vali*, Muḥammad Pasha. The money was intended for the district governor of Jerusalem, and was accompanied by a letter which Ḥusayn Ağa read aloud in court: "We have sent you a thousand *ghurūsh* for the purchase of cement, mortar and other building materials," wrote the *vali*. "You are to take these materials and set out to repair the castles of Dhāt Ḥajj, Qalʿat Ḥaydar and Qalʿat Tabūk on the *ḥajj* route."
>
> The governor of Jerusalem, Muḥammad Bey, was summoned and asked to take possession of the leather pouch and the letter, but refused to execute the orders. He claimed that a short time prior to

this date he received two imperial decrees instructing him to repair the city walls, and it would be impossible for him to embark on another task of this magnitude.

To support his claim the governor invited many of the city's notables. Among them were the Shāfi'i *mufti* Sheikh Ishaq, *naqīb al-ashrāf* Sayyid 'Abd al-Qādir al-Wafā'i al-Ḥusayni, the *imām* of the Ṣakhra (the Dome of the Rock) Sheikh 'Ali Nur al-Din and his colleague the *imām* Sheikh Abu al-Fatḥ, as well as a group of *zu'amā'* (holders of *zeamets*) *sipahis* and *mustaḥfıẓān* (local garrison forces) stationed in Jerusalem. In response to the governor's question they all answered that such a request was never made before. The inhabitants of Jerusalem, they claimed, were exempt from special impositions ever since the Ottoman conquest, and were living in conditions of extreme poverty. There were no camels strong enough to carry the building materials over such a long, sparsely populated distance, and anyway, all the camels in the district were weak and ailing as a result of the long draught years.

Furthermore, they declared, even had we been able to organize such a caravan and send the materials, we would have failed in our mission, *because the bedouin ('urbān) of the district of Jerusalem cannot go into these regions. For there is enmity between them and the bedouin who reside there. (Wa-'inna 'urbān liwā' al-Quds al-sharīf la yastaṭi'ūn al-dukhūl ila tilka al-arāḍi lima baynahum wa-bayna 'urbāniha min al-'adāwa.)*

In light of these arguments the district governor, Muḥammad Bey, refused to accept the sealed money pouch, and the messenger, Husayn ağa, refused to return it to Damascus. It was therefore decided to deposit it in the city's citadel, until the *vali* in Damascus decided what was to be done. The commander of the citadel (*dızdār*) Muḥammad ağa "Bosna" was then brought to court, and the pouch was entrusted to his safekeeping.[34]

This record provides a glimpse of the extent to which the governors of Jerusalem relied on their contacts with the bedouin, and the importance of the latters' services. It can be safely assumed that the district governor and the notables made up a series of excuses to explain why they could not execute the order: the governor was instructed by a higher authority to repair the city walls; the inhabitants were always exempt from such impositions (clearly the sum was not sufficient to pay for the whole project); the camels were too feeble after years of draught. . . Still, these had to be reasonable excuses, of the kind that might convince the governor in Damascus and his emissary in Jerusalem to look for another scapegoat.

The provincial governor probably knew the extent of the draught and the state of the camels, just as he was well aware of the use of bedouin as soldiers and camel drivers, and of their internal disputes. It appears, therefore, that the claim that such a trip would be impossible because of the animosity between "our" bedouin and the inhabitants of these regions was a plausible and convincing reason. The fact that it was brought up in the presence of cavalry and infantry officers only emphasizes their incompetence in such situations. The tensions, feuds and alliances between bedouin tribes have thus become an integral part of the province's politics.

The reliance on bedouin armies is made plain in the series of battles against Fakhr al-Dīn in the early 1620s. The Lebanese chronicler Ahmad al-Khalidi describes a battle between the forces of Fakhr al-Din on the one hand, and the joint forces of the Ṭurabāys, Farrūkhs and Riḍwāns on the other, waged on the banks of the ʿAwja (Yarkon) river. Defeated in the first round, Fakhr al-Dīn's forces were now retreating northward along the sea shore. At some point they were attacked at dawn by some 2,000 men. The horsemen of Ṭurabāy (bedouins themselves) and Farrūkh were joined by their bedouin allies of ʿArab al-ʿĀʾid, ʿArab Ghazza (a general reference to several tribes in the vicinity of Gaza) and others. All along that day bedouin forces dogged the *amīr*'s army, and he suffered many casualties and was forced to flee.[35]

The use of bedouin forces was not limited to the first half of the century, or to the rule of the dynasties. They appear in several other events along the century. In 1689, for instance, they accompanied the governor on a mission to the port town of Jaffa. This is how the incident was described by a member of the small community of French traders who resided in Ramle and conducted trade through the port of Jaffa:

> On Tuesday three pirate ships entered Jaffa harbor. Upon arrival they fired some 200 shells at the harbor and the warehouses. The terrified inhabitants pleaded with the governor to come to their rescue, and *he arrived with about 2,000 bedouin*, accompanied by some inhabitants of Ramle. When the force was deployed at the top of a hill, the pirates fired once again and killed four soldiers. The governor's troops returned fire but were unable to force the pirates to retreat. At that stage the pasha decided to summon the French merchants and the priests in Ramle, and to send them as a delegation to the pirates, demanding that they cease fire. Meanwhile the pirates decided to retreat, and when the French delegation arrived they were already some ten miles offshore. When the incident was over, the enraged

inhabitants of Jaffa wanted to take revenge upon the merchants, but the governor and his troops defended them.[36]

Unlike other Western travelers and pilgrims, weathered French traders who had been doing business for years with local authorities knew how to tell a bedouin from an Ottoman soldier. They did not express surprise or astonishment at the sight of such a large bedouin contingent escorting the governor, and regarded it as the natural course of affairs. Thus, throughout the seventeenth century bedouin operated as a military force in the service of district governors in Jerusalem and in neighboring districts. They were employed both as stationary forces charged with guarding roads and borders, and as a highly mobile and efficient cavalry, equipped with firearms, fighting battles and escorting caravans. In the course of the century they may have acquired an official, or semi-official standing in the Ottoman administration.

AN INTEGRATED ECONOMY

The economy of the district in the early Ottoman period was based mainly on agriculture, and on the manufacture of several industrial products. Cash crops in one form or another constituted a major part of the agriculture. Most of the produce was intended for internal consumption, although a slowly growing share was exported to Europe by French, Venetian, Dutch and English merchants.[37] Communities of European traders were established in the coastal towns. More ships frequented the harbors of Acre and Jaffa, especially in the second half of the century. Side by side with the cash-crop economy, many villagers carried on subsistence-level agriculture, sometimes based on barter. Imports were mostly luxury items: coffee, tobacco, spices, paper, special cloth, firearms and foreign currency.[38]

Local produce included mainly wheat and barley; cotton in a variety of forms—unprocessed, carded, combed, spun, and woven in several ways; olive trees which provided a range of products from olives and olive oil to soap and finished olive wood craftwork; cattle and sheep raised for milk, meat, hides and wool; the many fruit trees cultivated in the mountainous regions of Safad, Nabulus and Jerusalem.

The role of bedouin in the local economy is known mainly in its consumer aspects. Bedouin needed the markets of towns and villages in order to buy agricultural products, firearms, leatherware, ironware and clothes. Many imperial decrees deal with the attempt to break the spirit of rebellious tribes by imposing sanctions. The 1552 decree presented by Heyd describes the success of such sanctions in breaking a revolt of the Ṭurabāy and the Thawba clans. The villagers were warned not to sell arrows, bows, horseshoes, nails, food or clothing to members of these tribes. Their compliance with the decree forced the rebels to cease their revolt and seek accommodation with the authorities. In many other cases, however, the sanctions were not so successful, and trade with the bedouin went on. In his book on the Jewish community in Jerusalem, Amnon Cohen recounts that Jewish merchants of the city used to trade with the bedouin. In several cases in the sixteenth century such merchants were caught and put on trial, but, as Cohen adds, the incidents we know about may be seen as indications of spheres of commerce and economic relations too widespread for the authorities to control effectively.[39]

In the course of the century such issues continue to preoccupy the Ottoman central government from time to time. In a decree sent to Damascus in 1692 the governor is warned against the sale of weapons, lead (for bullets) and clothes to bedouin in a state of rebellion (*ısyan üzere olan urban-ı eşkiya*.) It was also forbidden to buy things plundered by tribesmen from pilgrims on their way to Mecca. In 1706 a decree sent to the governor of Jerusalem, Ibrahim Pasha, informing him that villagers on the road from Jerusalem to Nabi Mūsa and to Wādi Zarqā' are selling arms and ammunition to rebellious bedouins (*itaatten huruc eden eşkiya*.) The governor was instructed to fight against them and prevent the continued supply of arms. These decrees and many others clearly separate between "obedient" tribes and rebellious ones, who decided to shake off Ottoman rule.[40] (This separation, as we shall see later, was crucial for understanding the socio-ecological system that united bedouin and sedentary populations).

Bedouin contribution to the economy, however, involved much more than buying arms and munitions. For one thing, bedouin were the main source of supply of cattle, sheep and their produce. They also provided camels and horses for transportation. livestock was raised in pasture land in the desert, and in draught periods, or as summer approached, increasingly close to villages on the desert's edge, where villagers also raised their cattle and sheep. The need to share pasture was the source of much friction between the bedouin and the villagers, but it also created a special sort of relationship between shepherds on both sides. Village shepherds needed the goodwill and protection of the bedouin, who in turn needed the markets of villages and towns to sell their produce and buy munitions. The shepherd community, sometimes referred to as *al-baqqāra*, used to mediate and help defuse crisis situations.[41]

One domain in which the bedouin were considered unparalleled experts was the breeding and training of racehorses. Arabian mares of noble stock were a rare and expensive commodity. Many members of the governing elite and the local notable elite, including *sipahi*s, janissaries, ulema and merchants, bought horses and mares from the bedouin, and frequently left them to be trained and cared for by the breeder. A special relationship evolved between the owners and the trainers, sometimes reflected in records of trials involving a breach of agreement. One record in the *sijill*, dated 1615, refers to several aspects of such a relationship:

> On 23 Shawwāl 1024 a suit was filed by Khudāwardi (Hudaverdi) ibn Yaʿqūb, the *turjumān* (translator, negotiator) of the Armenian community in Jerusalem, against Samariyya ibn ʿAmr, of the tribe of ʿArab al-Jāʾila, who [according to the suit] laid his hand upon a bright-colored thoroughbred filly, in which the plaintiff had a share. The plaintiff declared that another share, a quarter of the said filly, was owned by Ḥajj Dāʾūd ibn Muḥammad ibn ʿAbd Rabbihi, and the remaining quarter by Khalīl ibn Aḥmad, a Janissary in the city's citadel. In his suit the plaintiff demanded his share, allegedly unlawfully appropriated by the defendant.
>
> The bedouin defendant replied that the share in question was given to him by Ḥajj Daʾūd as payment for the care, training and fodder of the filly, as is customary among horse breeders (*arbāb al-khayl*). In response the plaintiff brought several witnesses who supported his claim of ownership. In light of the evidence, the qadi ruled in favor of the plaintiff, and instructed the defendant, Samariyya ibn ʿAmr, to transfer his share, half of the ownership, to the plaintiff.[42]

The strange partnership between a Christian with a Turkish name, a local notable, a janissary, and a bedouin, does not concern us here, although it poses some interesting questions. Neither do questions pertaining to the use of the filly and the way it was being shared. The thing that is most striking, perhaps, is the ongoing relationship between a group of city dignitaries and members of a bedouin tribe. The fact that the young mare was left at the bedouin encampment outside the city walls required the conclusion of complex and costly agreements, and necessitated a great deal of stability and mutual trust. It appears from the document that such deals were common and provided solutions for expected problems "as is customary among horse breeders." In addition to the economic aspects of such transactions, they must have involved an unusual social dimension. Since Bedouin trainers kept the horses, members of the elite had to leave the city and visit the horse at the trainer's encampment.

Camels were also raised by tribesmen. In an arid land they provided the best, and sometimes the only effective means of transportation. The persistent involvement of Ottoman authorities in matters concerning the supply of camels for the *ḥajj* caravan, and the squabbles between province officials over the right to ride one during the long trip to Mecca, emphasize their importance. Correspondence between the center and the provinces alludes to the constant tribulations in Istanbul and Damascus between the wish to rent many camels in order to allow the officers and officials a comfortable ride, and the high cost of these vehicles. In a decree sent to the governor of Damascus in 1637, the problems are clearly defined:

> A petition was sent to my palace [lit., "my threshold of felicity"] by the guards stationed at the citadel in Damascus. Ever since the Ottoman conquest [the petitioners wrote] each year a task force is appointed to defend and maintain the forts on the Ḥajj route: twenty-six soldiers, two *cebeci*s (arms and armor experts,) six *ʿarabacı*s (carriage drivers) and a carpenter. Apart from their expenses and the camels they are allocated in accordance with the *defter*s, they were also accustomed to be given five additional camels for the people of the armory (*cebehane*). In the last few years some of the distinguished officials, including the *kâtip* (secretary) of the janissaries, the *mukabeleci* (administrative clerk), the *baş çavuş* (janissary commander) and the *serdar* (commander), were not allocated camels for the Ḥajj. As a result [these officials took possession of the camels intended for the armory and] the armory people are forced to walk on foot or ride in the carriages. This state of affairs causes much disorder and difficulty. The decree instructs the governor to allocate a camel to each member of the convoy, including five to the armory, and to refrain from obstructing them in their duties.[43]

The problem was not limited to the military and government spheres alone. Pilgrims on their way to the *ḥajj* were just as anxious to rent camels to transport them and their munitions. As the *ḥajj* period approached, and the pilgrims assembled, bedouin camel drivers also appeared at the gates of Damascus, Jerusalem and other cities. Soon they were all concluding deals, renting camels and presenting their drivers. Many women, fearing they would be unable to withstand the rigors of the road to Mecca on foot, rented a camel and a driver, or sometimes shared one with other pilgrims. In most cases the camels were supposed to carry water and munitions on the long and arduous way to the holy shrines. Prices ran high. In the middle of the seventeenth century a sum of 85 *ghurūsh* was paid for "half a camel" to be shared by two pilgrims.[44] The high sums that pilgrims were willing to pay were an enticement for fraud, and an Ottoman decree of 1690 criticizes the practice and its outcome:

> When pilgrims gather in Damascus, camel-renters arrive and promise them a regal trip to Mecca, for which they demand payment in advance. When the deal is concluded they bring old, weak and sick camels. The pilgrims are obliged to carry large quantities of expensive

> food and water not just for themselves, but also for the camel and its driver. They are often forced to seek loans from the city's merchants. Along the road they throw away part of the munitions in order to lighten the camel's load, and as their journey comes to its end they are left miserable and bitter.[45]

Yet, despite the central importance of camels and horses as vehicles and status symbols, the main role of the bedouin in the local economy lay elsewhere. Bedouin tribes had a central role in one of the most widespread and lucrative industries in Palestine—the production of soap.

Soap, and the alkaline ashes needed to produce it, were a substantial part of local exports since the beginning of the century. The quantities exported rose considerably in the course of the century. According to records in Marseilles' Chamber of Commerce, the quantity of soap and ashes exported from Jaffa rose sevenfold between 1615 and 1636. The same was true in the other ports of Palestine. "In Gaza," wrote a merchant who visited the country in 1655, "the greatest tread is in sope and lining cloth." Another traveler, who visited Jaffa in 1669, claims that ashes for the production of soap, along with cotton, are its major exports. In the course of the 1670s a battle for the rights to acquire and export soap was waged between the French traders in Acre and those in the Lebanese port of Sayda (Sidon). Ashes continued to be a major item of export well into the eighteenth century.[46]

In the production of soap cooperation between townsmen, villagers and nomads was crucial. Soap was manufactured from a mixture of olive oil, limewater and alkaline ashes (from the Arabic word *al-qali*) obtained by burning desert wormwood bushes. Villagers supplied olive oil, and bedouin supplied the ashes. In the sixteenth century merchants used to venture into the desert to obtain ashes, but in the following century supply routes were maintained, and the tribesmen themselves delivered loads of alkaline ashes to the manufacturers. Large camel caravans frequently visited the city of Jerusalem unloading sacks of ash, and probably stocking up on other commodities. In his book about the history of Nabulus and the Balqā' area, Ihsan al-Nimr mentions caravans of up to a thousand camels carrying qali from the desert to the cities of Nabulus and Jerusalem.[47]

These essential components were brought by the villagers and the bedouin to special workshops in the city, where all the ingredients were compounded and soap was manufactured by a long process of cooking, pouring into moulds, cutting and drying. Such workshops were owned and operated for the most part by notables and members of the governing elite. Periods of strife between the tribes and the city were liable to cause considerable financial damage to these owners, who enjoyed most of the added value of the finished product. Notables in the city therefore had a vested interest in maintaining good relations with the bedouin.[48] Soap manufacturing also entailed financial gains for bedouin and villagers. It appears to have propelled power struggles in which villagers and bedouin tribes cooperated against other similar groups. A series of records in the Jerusalem *sijill* from the beginning of the century describes such an incident and its aftermath:

> On 11 Dhu al-Ḥijja 1032 (1623) the *kethüda* (deputy) of Jerusalem's governor arrived in court. He reported to the qadi the events of a violent incident which took place on the way from Jerusalem to the Jordan valley: Members of the obedient Balāqina tribe (*'Arab al-Balāqina al-ṭā'i'īn*) who bring *samnah* (clarified butter), sheep and ashes to the city of Jerusalem, brought a large shipment of ashes and sold it in town. On their way back east they were attacked by villagers and other tribesmen near the village of al-'Azariyya.
>
> In the battle that ensued two of the [Balāqina] tribesmen were killed, as well as a large number of camels. The *kethüda* requested that the court conduct an inquiry into the incident. With the qadi's consent an officer of the court was appointed and dispatched to the scene along with the *kethüda* and his team. Inside the village the team found the bodies of two people, and thirteen dead camels. They conducted an investigation and found out that the Balaqina had been attacked by the tribes of 'Arab al-Ka'ābina, 'Arab al-Ramtaḥāt(?) 'Arab Zubaydallah, and 'Arab Haytham al-Baghāritha, along with villagers from Tūr, al-'Isāwiyya, 'Ayn Silwān, Dayr al-sadd, Bayt Sāḥūr, Ṣūr Bāhir, Dayr Abu Thawr, Abu Dīs, Dayr Bani Sa'īd and Bayt Laḥm (Bethlehem), as well as the group of shepherds (*tā'ifat al-baqqāra*). The Balāqina retreated in the direction of the main road leading to the Jordan valley. Sixteen of the camels, pushed to the edge of the road, tumbled each other into the creek below. Thirteen died and the other three are kept, injured, at the village. Among the dead camels the villagers found the bodies of two Balāqina tribesmen. Two of the assailants were also killed.[49]

In the style and custom of *sijill* investigations, there is no attempt to clarify the motives and explain the causes which brought about this lethal incident. Motivation and cause were apparently irrelevant to the description and adjudication of criminal cases. These were always dealt with on the basis of events alone. On the other hand, the reasons were probably so obvious to the qadi and his people that no further discussion was needed. It may have been sparked by jealousy and resentment of the Balāqinas' good relations with the city, or of their monopoly of the trade in ashes. But there may have been other reasons. 1623 was a drought year, and the shortage of water caused tensions inside and outside the city. In any case it should be noted that the culprits who attacked the Balāqina caravan included both bedouin and villagers, who cooperated in what seems like a carefully planned and concerted ambush. The court saw the Balāqinas and their alignment as its allies, and the rest, including the villagers, as the offenders who should be punished and forced to compensate the victims.[50]

From the background given in the record we learn that tribesmen used to bring quantities of alkaline ashes, as well as sheep and milk products to the city. These products were carried by large camel convoys, attested to by the number of camels killed in the incident, and by the very long list of villages and tribes who took part in the attack. The convoys were allowed to enter the city and sell their produce to prospective buyers. The document bears witness to the economic importance of the bedouin in the district, and to the complexity of social ties between the sedentary population and the nomadic tribes.

ONE SOCIAL SYSTEM?

Borders delineating geographic zones are sometimes imaginary. Even when the border separates two political entities, and its definition serves a clear purpose—blocking the enemy, collecting taxes, recruiting soldiers—it is not always clearly defined. In many cases the border is a vast middle area where a unique culture is created. All the more so when the border is said to define a society, a culture, or a climatic zone.

In his classic work on the Mediterranean in the era of Philip II, Fernand Braudel sets out to classify the shores of the Mediterranean according to their landscape and their climate, assuming that each landscape and climate leads to the development of a different culture. The sea itself, its coasts, the plains, the hills, and the mountains around it, all gave rise to different kinds of societies in premodern history. Great civilizations usually evolved between the coastal plains and the mountains, where the climate was moderate and transportation simple. In these areas it was easier to create structures of discipline and hierarchy. In the mountains, on the other hand, where inhabitants tended to protect their independence jealously, the hold of "civilization" was always precarious. Sea shores and plains were prone to be flooded or swamped, but when their inhabitants managed to control and direct the water flow, they soon became rich agricultural societies. The sea itself, and the islands in it, also generated a particular culture of fishermen and sailors.[51]

Braudel also discusses the nomadic cultures typical of considerable parts of the Mediterranean basin. Nomads, he says, are a mountain culture by nature, moving in yearly cycles between the mountains and the sea. Their mobility and the effortless manner in which they cross climatic borders should not blur the distinct features of the nomads as a separate society different from the others. Braudel agrees with Ibn Khaldun that nomadic culture, and especially that of the desert nomads, the bedouin, is opposed to that of other sedentary cultures. It is "the clash between two economies, civilizations, societies and arts of living."[52]

Though sometimes general and inaccurate, Braudel's definitions may help us pinpoint the main differences between mediterranean societies. Yet they might also obfuscate distinctions and divert our attention from other forms of Mediterranean social culture. These are perhaps more prominent along the southern and eastern shores of the sea, where lines of demarcation between landscapes are not so clear. In Palestine, for instance, the mountains are relatively small in size and height. In the south the desert merges with the coast. What sort of cultures would develop here? Do Braudelian categories apply, or should other categories be determined? In short, are we to describe nomads and sedentary populations as two different societies, or as part of one social structure?

Dale Eickelman, focusing on relations between nomads and sedentary populations from an anthropological point of view, refers mainly to the proximity and mutual reliance of nomad and settled societies on the periphery of the desert. He stresses the importance of this reliance to the actual existence of the nomads. According to Eickelman, in no historical period can nomads be regarded as an autonomous society:

> Both in recent decades and in earlier historical periods, the political and social relations of pastoral groups with the peasant settlements, towns and states that are on the periphery of zones of intense pastoral activity have been as important for their livelihood as pastoralism itself. . . . Pastoral agriculture and trade activities are part of a single economic system articulated by various forms of social and political domination.[53]

From the source material presented above, however, we can draw the further conclusion that at certain points in time the dependence of towns and villages on the nomads was no less crucial to their own existence and well-being. The two groups, or, should we say, three—nomads, villagers and townsmen—needed each other, and their interdependence is a key element in understanding their economy, their politics, and even their culture. These communities were not divided by a boundary. The border surrounded climatic and geographic divides, transforming them into the focal point of a unique social experiment.

Early functionalistic theories would describe society as a body within which members cooperate to form a functioning entity. A later version would regard the attainment of complete integration as an almost impossible task, which societies might strive toward, but seldom reach. If we accept these premises, then the district of Jerusalem in the Ottoman period may certainly be defined as one society in the way it adapted to its ecological and economic surroundings, and in its ability to attain its political goals.[54]

For other schools of thought the only valid definitions of a society are economic: "We take the defining characteristic of a social system," says Immanuel Wallerstein, "to be the existence within it of a division of labor, such that the various sectors or areas within are dependent upon economic exchange with others for the smooth and continuous provisioning of the needs of the area. Such economic exchange can clearly exist without a common political structure and even more obviously without sharing the same culture."[55]

Such a definition would regard the district of Jerusalem as an almost perfect social system. Admittedly, the district paid a tribute to the imperial center (or, in other words, the division of labor stretched beyond its borders) and was not an entirely self-sufficient economy. But in practical terms most of the economic surplus flowed back into the local economy, in what may be termed "short taxation cycles" (see Chapter 6). It may be claimed therefore that an almost full division of labor—and hence an entire social system integrating bedouin, villagers and townsmen—existed within the district's borders.

But was this society merely a well-rounded economic structure? Was it just a politically effective group of people? In functionalist terminology we may ask to what extent can it be considered one society in terms of its *integration*—the willingness of its members to cooperate with each other—and in terms of its *latency*—the internal "programming" of individuals to willingly join and fulfill roles in society? Adherents of yet another approach would put the question differently: Was there any form of coherent *discourse* between subgroups? Did they use the same set of signs and symbols? Did they intermarry? Did they refer to the same set of social norms?[56]

Source material pertaining to these questions is scarce. In most cases we do not possess what Clifford Geertz would call a "thick description" of this society. There are no reports of discussions between individuals, and relatively few descriptions of its levels of contact. It is almost impossible, for instance, to assess the attitude of the bedouin towards sedentary groups, and even the way bedouin were regarded by townsmen and villagers is hard to gauge. We can only point out a few facts which are relevant to this quest.[57]

Through descriptions of bedouin activity in the military and economic spheres, we can draw some conclusions about their attachment to local society. Army service brought them closer to the governing elite. Control of fiefs, ranging from the smallest *timar*s to entire *sanjaq*s, was considered by some bedouin sheikhs a recognition of their status as part of the elite. From descriptions of the Ṭurabāy court in Lajjun, it appears that they embraced some traditional Ottoman status symbols—scribes, secretaries, eunuchs, music bands and perhaps even Ottoman dress. They bound themselves to other governing families through marriage, and probably saw themselves as part of a ruling elite with shared interests which overshadowed their identity as bedouins.[58]

Other townsmen, belonging to the local notable elite, met and associated with bedouin under different circumstances: active and widespread commercial relations, transportation needs, and a shared interest in horses and equestrian sports. In the lower echelons of society it is even more difficult to trace the evidence of a common sociocultural system. In the *sijill* there are few records of marriage between bedouin and others, but this in itself does not mean that no such marriages took place. Most of the marriage contracts outside the city walls were not registered in the *sijill*. Another significant indication of bedouin cultural impact on town dwellers may be the popular custom of parading the bride and her dowry on decorated camels prior to the wedding banquet.[59]

Other points of contact were religious and legal institutions. From time to time bedouin arrived in town to obtain a *fatwa* or a ruling in matters that concerned them. Muḥibbi claims that the good relations between bedouin tribes and the governors of Gaza in the seventeenth century stemmed in part from their respect and admiration for the *mufti* Khayr al-Din al-Ramli. In other cases tribesmen were summoned to court, or came there of their own free will to file a complaint. The *sijill* records several instances in which bedouin were summoned as defendants, or asked to give testimony. Some of those summoned actually arrived and presented their case. This would suggest the existence of constant channels of communication between the court and the tribes around the city. It also implies a willingness on the part of the bedouin to accept the court's authority and to see it as an arbitrator and peace-maker.[60]

The fact that bedouin were often summoned by name, or sued as private people, suggests that they were seen by local authorities as individuals. When crimes were committed, there was an attempt to apprehend the culprits themselves. At least in some cases only the perpetrators of a crime were punished, and not the whole tribe. The image of the nomad in the mind of city dwellers was apparently not monolithic and stereotypic. It reflected a recognition that the nomadic world was more complex and varied.

On the other side of the equation, bedouin and villagers cooperated in resisting authority, and in raids on caravans, other villages, or other bedouin tribes. Such raids were seldom perpetrated by bands of thieves or marauders joined on an individual basis. In most cases a village joined forces with a bedouin clan or tribe. At times the gang was headed by a charismatic leader, leading it from raid to raid. At other times forces were joined for a single raid upon enemies, like the raid on the Balāqina. Some of these alliances of villages and tribes may have originated in the Qaysi-Yamani dispute, which split the Palestinian and Lebanese countryside in later centuries, but there is no mention of such a motivation in the *sijill* and little in other contemporary sources.[61]

The district of Jerusalem and its surroundings at the time may be described as being comprised of several zones or tiers. There was an inner zone of permanent towns and villages along the watershed line and westward to the coastal plain. Another unstable sedentary zone traced the periphery of the desert, which fluctuated in times of drought between pastoral and agricultural activities;[62] A third zone, included "obedient" tribes; and a fourth, made up of other tribes, some of them rebellious. Clearly this last division, between obedient and rebellious tribes, originated in the Ottoman center, and was much more volatile and uncertain than the others. Obedient tribes rebelled from time to time, while tribes in a state of insurrection were appeased and incorporated.

Social interaction existed between all four zones. A particularly strong bond tied together the second and third tiers—villages on the desert's edge and bedouin tribes residing in proximity—based on their common livelihood, and perhaps on a myth of common ancestry. There may have been some genuine family relations and past migrations from village to tribe and vice versa, although we have no evidence to support such assumptions. Military service and economic activities connected towns in the first zone to tribes in the third and fourth zones.

The social system drawing nomads and settled populations together was therefore deep and multilayered. Social relations ranged from the local Ottoman governing elite, even at the level of district governors, to the lowest echelons of society in remote villages and tribes. Aside from the crucial importance of bedouin to the economy, and from their role in political affairs, a meaningful sociocultural relationship bound together bedouin, villagers and townsmen in the district of Jerusalem. This relationship found expression both on the establishment side of the political system, and in its resistant opposition. All contributed to the creation of a single discursive structure.

It is harder to say whether this was a constant state of affairs, or whether, on the contrary, the seventeenth century was a unique period in history that does not resemble other periods. There is hardly any doubt that parts of this unified social system existed in earlier and later centuries. Other elements are distinctive of this time and place. It may be worthwhile to point out the historical context, the unique features of the seventeenth century that reinforced such a social system.

At the beginning of the sixteenth century, the Ottoman conquest introduced the massive use of firearms, almost unknown before. Until that time bedouin tribes, like their Mamluk overlords, relied heavily on lances, swords, bows and arrows. Due to their use of firearms, Ottoman forces defeated their Mamluk rivals with ease, and managed to instill fear and discipline among the bedouins. In the following years, however, bedouin tribesmen mastered the use of guns. Soon guns became commonplace and the bedouin excelled at the new type of warfare. Victory, so easily attained by the Ottomans at the beginning of the century, became a bitter continuous struggle a few decades later, in which bedouin frequently had the upper hand. Ottoman governments, realizing the dangers inherent in the situation, tried in vain to block channels of arms supply. The situation was exacerbated by the growing incompetence of *sipahi*s and the janissaries, and by the gradual withdrawal of the Ottoman government from provincial affairs.

Local governors had to choose between two options: a costly, perhaps futile war against the beoduin, and finding a *modus vivendi* with them to maintain the peace. They chose a third: Some bedouin tribes were incorporated into the system, while others were branded rebels. Thus the governors sometimes took over existing feuds between warring tribes, and found themselves involved, not always willingly, in internal bedouin affairs. In general, however, this policy allowed the local government considerable room for action, and provided the district of Jerusalem and adjacent districts with a measure of security.

Several generations of local rulers, most of them scions or *mamlūk*s of former governors in the region created a stable relationship with the bedouin, based on payments of money, alliances and marriage. For the governing elite ties with the neighbors in the desert also meant considerable profits accruing from trade, and from lower spending on security. As long as they stayed in power, they did not prohibit ties between bedouin and other social groups. On the contrary, allying themselves with the nomads, they enhanced social and cultural norms already in existence in society. The process of integration was accelerated by a decentralized system of government at the beginning of the seventeenth century. Local governors soon filled the void left by the central government, and were free to pursue their policy of rapprochement with some of the bedouin.

This tendency was reversed towards the end of the century, when the government in Istanbul decided to enforce central rule upon the provinces. A first step on the way to resume control of the empire was the destruction of local dynasties and their replacement by appointed governors. At this stage ties may have been severed, or at least damaged, between the new governors and tribal sheikhs. The Ṭurabāys and other bedouin dynasties were eliminated, and there was no one to bridge the widening gaps.

Economic and social relations were somewhat more stable, but they too were endangered by political realities. At the turn of the century ties between sedentary and nomad populations were weak and unstable. Still, the relatively short period of central dictate did not cut all ties, and another cycle of decentralized rule brought the two components of local society closer together once again. The rise to power of bedouin leaders like Ẓahir al-ʿUmar, who ruled most of Palestine several decades later, can thus be seen in a different light. It was not another incident demonstrating the extent of bedouin encroachment on the sedentary regions of Palestine previously held by the Ottomans, but rather a continuation of a long-term phenomenon in the political and social life of the region: the bedouin were part of society, and played a pivotal role in all spheres of life. With the rise of Ẓahir al-ʿUmar, foundations were laid for a new cycle of integration.[63]

Chapter 5

Layers of Ownership

LAND AND AGRARIAN RELATIONS

Wherever land and agriculture play an important part in local produce, and comprise a large share of people's income, understanding the systems of land tenure provides an insight into the social structure. Agrarian relations indicate tensions between social groups, and even provide a glimpse of changes before they occur. In the context of the Ottoman Empire, several questions have dominated research in recent years. These questions are relevant both in the "macro" overview—understanding Ottoman economy and society in the early modern period—and in smaller historical environments—the lives of small groups, families and individuals.[1]

One such issue is the change of emphasis in the empire from an agrarian system based on *timārs* to one based on tax farming, known as *iltizām*. In Marxian terms both systems could be described as techniques of surplus appropriation and redistribution, or, in other words, as ways of collecting taxes and reallocating them. Both existed in the Ottoman Empire from its early days, but until the sixteenth century the *timār*—allocation of income from fiefs to those favored by the sultan and his government, in return for the collection of taxes and for the provision of a small contingent of cavalry—was the dominant system. Only later, in the so called "period of decline," did *iltizām*—leasing the right to collect future taxes from a district or province in return for a sum of money paid to the treasury in advance—become a primary tool of surplus appropriation. The change of emphasis from land-based *timār* to money-based *iltizām* was a result of several simultaneous developments: the need to pay salaries to new mercenary troops, the abundance of silver coins, and the monetarization of the economy.[2] It has been assumed that the shift from one system to the other was always a simple, one-phase transformation which gained the upper hand when the outdated *timār* mechanism failed to meet the requirements of the state, and the Ottoman bureaucracy and war machine were desperately short of money. A closer look at local sources may suggest that at least in some areas the shift was gradual, involving many small incremental changes in local economy and land tenure.[3]

The same question is examined from a different point of view in neo-Marxist economic theories, where Ottoman history from the sixteenth century onward is viewed mainly as the process of the empire's transformation into a peripheral zone of the European and Atlantic world economy. In this context the shift from *timār* to *iltizām* is seen as part of the region's peripheralization. The new agrarian system gave rise to a stratum of local notables and to the commercialization of agriculture. Notable groups, which gained political and economic ascendancy through their control of tax farms, relinquished the old economic system, depleted land resources, and brought the entire region under the hegemony of Western Europe. An accurate description of agrarian relations may therfore indicate whether such a process took place in the seventeenth century, and the state of subsequent integration into the world economy.[4]

Tensions between the state and the elite are also reflected in systems of land tenure. In many authoritarian states a permanent conflict exists between two concepts of surplus appropriation. Some states collect taxes directly from cultivators through a bureaucracy of tax collectors. Others evolve a more decentralized system, in which cultivators pay a *rent* (as money or other services) to a quasi-feudal landowner. When the state entrusts a land-based elite with the collection of taxes, the natural tendency of the elite is to privatize the land and to bequeath it to descendants, or, in other words, to convert the tax into rent. This is a sure sign of the state's weakness.[5] For hundreds of years the Ottoman Empire resisted the provincial elite's attempts to privatize lands allocated as *timārs*. In view of the fact that most *timār* holders did not emerge as a landholding group in later centuries, we may ask ourselves whether they succeeded at any time in converting tax into rent, and, on the other hand, what were the means and the mechanisms by which the state managed to maintain its ultimate control over land tenure even in remote provinces. Another aspect of the tax-rent tension is its implications for the cultivators themselves. In tax-collecting states the actual distance between the state and the cultivator frequently results in a lack of interest in crops and in techniques of production. In contrast, in a feudal system landowners are in direct contact with cultivators, allowing for rapid development on the one hand, and increasing social tension on the other.

By describing agrarian relations in the district of Jerusalem throughout the seventeenth century, we may begin to answer some of these questions, and to analyze their meaning for the district and for the empire as a whole. Let us first turn to an overview of the most common Ottoman systems of agrarian relations in the period, and to the form they assumed in the region.

SYSTEMS OF LAND TENURE—AN OVERVIEW

The *timār* was a well-established economic and military system long before the Ottomans adopted it. Some trace its origins to the Byzantine *pronoia,* while others emphasize its Islamic origins in the Seljuq and Abbasid periods. In its adapted Ottoman version, it was intended to provide an income for one officer, in most cases a *sipahi,* and for his crew of trained horsemen. A regular *timār* was a small fief, comprising one or several smaller villages, and yielding up to 20,000 *akçe* per year. Larger fiefs called *zeamet* (or *za'āma* in Arabic) yielding between 20,000 and 100,000 *akçe* a year, were given to higher-ranking officers or officials. An even bigger estate, called *has* (*khāṣ* in Arabic) yielding more than 100,000 *akçe,* was earmarked for district and province governors, or for senior officials in the provincial administration. Timariots were required to help collect the taxes imposed on the inhabitants of their fiefs, to act as a local garrison when needed, and to report to duty with their contingent when the imperial army went to war. Some of the *timār* holders were originally the sultan's slaves (*kapı kulları*), while others were part of a native military elite incorporated into the Ottoman army. In the fifteenth and sixteenth centuries most *sipahi*s were stationed in areas remote from their native lands. This policy may have been intended to prevent the consolidation of rebellious local forces based on ethnic or regional solidarity.[6]

*Sipahi*s, and other dignitaries who received a *timār* or a *zeamet,* were not the owners of the land. Most of the empire's territory was considered state land, officially the property of the sultan himself. It was entrusted to his servants for a limited duration, ranging from several years to a lifetime. As a rule all *berat*s (deeds conferring an estate or any other privilege) were invalidated with the death of a sultan and had to be renewed by his successor. The sultan could divide fiefs as he saw fit, pass them on from one person to the next, or change their designation. In most cases *berat* holders were not allowed to sell their fiefs or to divide them. They needed special permission to bequeath them to their sons. The *berat* enabled them to collect taxes defined by law, either in money or in kind, and to keep a certain share for themselves.[7]

Timārs were typically rurally based. In towns and cities, however, a similar system was implemented, based on urban crafts and commerce. *Timārs* were part of this system known as *iqṭā'*—the allocation of a tax yielding segment of the economy to a person or institution. In Ottoman usage *timars* were just one form of *iqṭā'*. Many Ottoman officials received nonagricultural *muqāṭa'as* in the provinces. Such a *muqāṭa'a* might have consisted of the taxes and customs levied from ships entering a port, or from the *hisba* taxes in a town's market. In addition to being a prevalent system of tax collection and wage payment, the *iqṭā'* soon became a status symbol and a cultural building-block of the governing elite in the provinces. Those who aspired for a place at the top regarded the acquisition of an *iqṭā'* as a symbol of their entry into the elite. Control of an *iqṭā'* placed them on a higher rung on the social ladder, not only above the *reaya*, but also above junior officers and officials.

Alongside the *timār*, *waqf* institutions were a common mechanism for controlling and overseeing rural land and urban assets, and for the redistribution of economic surplus. *Waqfs* could be consecrated by any owner of property (including, of course, the sultan himself and members of his household.) The endowment of property as a *waqf* was based upon the Islamic principle of separation between the actual ownership of the property (*raqaba*) and the usufruct (*taṣarruf*)—profits accruing from its use. A man dedicating a *waqf* (*muqīf*) could name any person or group as beneficiaries: himself, his family, the poor of the city, a school, a mosque or a Sufi brotherhood. These beneficiaries were entitled to part of the usufruct. They did not own the property, and could not dispose of it or exchange it by sale or other means, except by authorization of the *waqf*'s supervisor (*mutawalli*, or *mütevelli* in Turkish).[8]

In this respect *waqf* and *timār* were very much alike. In both systems the ultimate ownership and the usufruct were clearly separated. The differences between the two lay in the purpose of the endowment, and in the social groups entitled to the profit. While those who benefitted from the *timār* were exclusively members of the governing elite, *waqf* institutions frequently designated the poor, the Sufis or students in a *madrasa* as beneficiaries. And while a list of the *waqf*'s beneficiaries could only be changed in court, in keeping with the original endowment deed (*waqfiyya*), timariots were replaced by the sultan's decision, or in some cases by the provincial governor.[9] In Palestine vast tracts of land, including many villages, were designated as *waqf*, the profits of which went to institutions of charity, piety or learning in Jerusalem and in other towns.

In the late sixteenth century, a time of dire economic straits, high inflation, and a decrease in the pace of conquest, the Ottoman Empire gradually neglected the *timār* system and replaced it with *iltizām*. The main reason for the change was the economic inadequacy of the old *timār* system, the impact of European warfare techniques, and the rapid evolution of the battlefield, which turned the *timār*-based cavalry into an obsolete fighting force. The new Ottoman army, based to a great extent on paramilitary armed units, had no need for old-fashioned knights, and could not rely on the very slow recruitment mechanism of *sipahis* in the provinces. Furthermore, the impoverished empire could not afford to pay its growing new standing army, while allocating most of its land resources to *sipahis*. Although no formal decision is known to have been made in the matter, Ottoman governments refrained as a rule from allocating new *timārs* to officers, and instead tried to convert as much land as possible into tax farms.

In the new system, the guiding principles were entirely different. The tax-farmer (*multazim, mültezim*) used to pay a sum of money in advance, in return for the right of collect taxes for a short duration (in the 1600s usually one to three years). Having received authorization, again in the form of a *berat*, he would proceed to the region, or send a representative, to collect his due. As a result, it is claimed, the quality and produce of agricultural land declined rapidly. Unlike his predecessor the *sipahi*, who intended to keep using the territory for several years, the *multazim* leased the right to collect taxes for a short period, and was only interested in maximizing profits.[10]

In parts of the province of Damascus *iltizām* was already a widespread agrarian system in the sixteenth century, and according to Abu Husayn, the economy of the entire province was based on tax farming.[11] It appears, however, that in the district of Jerusalem and in neighboring districts *iltizām* was limited to very small areas until the end of the seventeenth century, and represented just a small fraction of taxes collected. Most of the region was divided into *timars*. A direct testimony is brought by Evliya Çelebi, who visited Jerusalem in the early 1670s:

> The district of Jerusalem is allocated as an *arpalık* [literally, "barley fee"—an estate granted to provide temporary income to a member of the elite with no appointment]. It is a *has* estimated at 257,485 *akçe*. The district includes 9 *zeamets* and 106 *timārs*. . . . This is a prosperous region, but the timariots residing in it do not have to serve in the battlefield, and their only duty is to accompany the pilgrims to their destinations.[12]

Evliya's testimony cannot be taken at face value. It is often inaccurate and embellished. But in this case it is corroborated by the *sijill*, by the *mühimme defterleri* and by *fatāwa* books throughout the period.[13] A reference to the number of *timars* in the neighboring district of Nabulus can be found in a *sijill* record from the mid-seventeenth century:

> On 16 Jumāda al-Ūla 1066 (13 March 1656) the *alaybey* of Nabulus (a commander of *sipahis*) Muḥammad Ağa arrived in the *majlis*, accompanied by several of the timariots and holders of *zeamet* in the district. Among them were Mustafa Bey ibn ʿUmar Ağa Arnaut (the Albanian), ʿAli Bey ibn Muḥammad, Sayfūsh Bey ibn ʿAbdallah, and others. They all filed a complaint against one of their peers. The timariots claimed that they possess a sultanic decree exempting them from paying the *bedeliye* tax (a tax imposed on *sipahis* who did not participate in an imperial campaigns). The reason for this exemption is their official duty of protecting the pilgrims and travelers on their way to Jerusalem and Hebron. They also presented letters from the governor of Damascus to that effect.
>
> In spite of these assurances, they said, this time they were all demanded to pay a fine of 1,800 *ghurūsh*, because they failed to join the army on a recent campaign. Dividing the fine between them they decided that every thousand [each income unit of 1,000 *akçe* in a *timār*] should pay 4.5 *ghurūsh*. They claimed that the defendant promised to pay his share, and since the income from his *zeamet* is 31,000 *akçe*, he has to pay 140 *ghurūsh*. The defendant denied the charge, but the testimony of two janissaries from Damascus convinced the qadi of his guilt, and he was instructed to pay his share of the fine.[14]

A perfunctory glance at this record would reveal that timariots and *zeamet* holders were still very prominent in Nabulus late in the seventeenth century, while simple arithmetic would show us that the official estimate of income from *timars* and *zeamets* in the district at the time was 400,000 *akçe* {(1800:4.5) × 1000 = 400,000)}. This represented a substantial part of the small district's surplus, and does not leave much room for tax farming.

The abundance of documents dealing with *timār* in the *sijills* of Jerusalem and Nabulus, in the *Mühimme* and in *fatāwa* books, as opposed to the trickle of documents concerning *iltizām*, support this conclusion. A sample check of twenty-five villages in seventeenth-century *sijills*, compared to their status in the previous century according to *tapu-tahrir* (tax assessment and census) registers of Jerusalem, reveals that most villages did not change their status, and none were referred to as part of an *iltizām*. Wherever minute changes did occur, they did not transfer the village from one designation to another. Thus the village of Bayt Imrin, which the *tahrirs* listed as a *timār*, was referred to as a *zeamet* a century later. In other cases the *tahrir* describes a village as divided between two or three authorities, while the *sijill* mentions only one. The village of Bayt Safafa, for instance, is mentioned in the *sijill* as part of a *timar*, while the *tahrir* register describes it as part *timār* and part *waqf*. But even in such cases it may be assumed that there was no change, and that scribes in the qadi's *majlis*, writing in the *sijill*, referred only to the part of the village that was of interest at that particular moment for the case pending in court.[15]

Inalcık suggests a possibility of change into another agrarian mode as an interim stage. In his essay on centralization and decentralization in the empire, Inalcık states that in the wake of the dissolution of the *timār* system in the seventeenth and eighteenth centuries, many districts in Anatolia were allocated as *arpalık*s to holders of senior positions in Istanbul, or to commanders of forts on the borders. A government official or a commander who was entrusted with such a *sanjaq* did not reside in the district in person, but appointed a deputy to run it in his absence. These deputies were frequently local notables, who, as representatives of a distant governor, were able to consolidate their political status. Thus, little by little, control of the provinces passed into the hands of the notables.[16]

There are clear indications that the use of *arpalık* was widespread in the region, and especially in the district of Jerusalem. From the beginning of the seventeenth century large estates, like the governor's *has* in Jerusalem, Gaza, Safad or Karak-Shawbak, were entrusted from time to time to Ottoman officials or to senior provincial governors waiting for an appointment. In Ottoman documents these temporary arrangements were referred to as *arpalık*, or "barley-fee," suggesting that they were intended to cover the expenses of maintaining a small cavalry. The rank of those receiving the *arpalık* was often higher than that of the district's regular governor. Many held the title of Pasha, and had already governed a province. In several cases this separation between the function of the district as a unit of administration, and its role as a source of income for grandees, caused tensions and misunderstandings between the center and the province. It is not clear whether the bone of contention was control of the district, or whether it was related to sources of income. But it appears that the Ottoman government itself failed to clearly define the duties of an *arpalık* holder, and did not specify whether he had to assume all the responsibilities of the governor.[17]

Such disputes are recorded in the *sijill* from the early seventeenth century. Occasionally the qadi was asked to arbitrate between a governor, and a distant *arpalık* holder who saw the district as his fief. Sometimes the two held valid letters of appointment and argued over the income of the province. In one case the *arpalık* holder claimed he had received the district for his entire lifetime (*ʿala al-taʿbīd*), but was soon forced to relinquish control of the district. Frequent changes in district governorships indicate that *ümera* from local families and *arpalık* holders appointed by the central government vied for control of the district. In a register of provincial appointments from the mid-seventeenth century, governors are replaced in rapid succession. In 1041 (1631) Muhammad Pasha was appointed governor. in 1046 (1636) the district was given as an *arpalık* to ʿAli Pasha, the deputy (*kethüda*) of the grand vezir. Two years later, in 1048 (1638) it was allocated to Muḥammad, brother of the *silahdar* pasha. A year later it passed hands again, this time as an *arpalık*, to Muḥyi Pasha. Throughout this period members of local dynasties in Palestine, the Farrūkhs and the Riḍwāns, also aspired to govern the district, and frequently took control, forcing the government's hand.[18]

Allocating the district's *has* as an *arpalık* caused severe problems and may have been the cause of further disruption of the traditional system. In the past, the district governor was also the commander of the local *sipahi* battalion. The distant politics promoted by the *arpalık* system left the *sipahi*s with no clear chain of command, and contributed to the destruction of the *timār* system. It may have also aided the rise of local notables to power by further decentralizing the system in the district. But the *arpalık* did not constitute a major change in land tenure and the economic structure of the district. Whether appointed as an *arpalık* holder or a "regular" *sanjaq bey*, the governor had direct economic control only over his own estate, the local *has*. The great bulk of the territory was still administered by timariots and *waqf* institutions. In the context of Jerusalem and its neighboring districts, *arpalık* did not replace the *timār* system. Both institutions existed side by side for a long time, with no apparent change in the patterns of agrarian relations.

We may sum up, therefore, and conclude that in the seventeenth-century district of Jerusalem state-generated *iltizām* concessions did not constitute a major threat to the old *timār* system, nor did the introduction of *arpalık* grants change the basic pattern of land tenure. Side by side with the *waqf*, it was the old *iqṭāʿ* system that served as a principal means to control land and its produce. *Waqf*, *iqṭāʿ*, or *timār*, however, were merely names for institutions the structure and contents of which changed dramatically in the period under consideration, to resemble a local variety of *iltizām*. In order to observe and understand these changes, we must now turn away from the formal Ottoman sources and look at these questions in their local context.

SYSTEMS OF LAND TENURE—AN UNDERVIEW

Since the beginning of the seventeenth century, *timār* holders attempted to discard the burden of overseeing quarrelsome, recalcitrant villagers, and to maximize their returns by leasing parts of their *timār*, and sometimes the entire fief. The lessees were in most cases other timariots, members of the governing elite from other districts, or local notables. The *timār* was usually leased for a year, sometimes for two or three years, and the lease payment for each year was made in advance. The lessee was entitled to collect legally sanctioned taxes as specified in the lease document. The leasing of *timār*s had its roots in the fifteenth and sixteenth centuries, but as their main function was blurred by other considerations, such practices became more widespread and, later on, institutionalized. One document which bears evidence to the practice and to some of its inherent difficulties is a record of a trial in 1656:

> At the end of Muḥarram 1067 (mid-November 1656) a suit was filed in the *sharīʿa* court of Nabulus, by the pride of his peers (*fakhr aqrānihi*) Aḥmad Bey ibn Sulaymān ibn Marʿi, against the pride of his peers Muḥammad Bey ibn Shaʿbān. In the trial, held in the presence of both, the plaintiff claimed that he had leased his *timār*, in the villages of Tima and ʿArfit, to the defendant. The *timār* is registered at a value of 3,300 *ʿuthmani* [a local name for *akçe*]. It was leased for a period of six years, and the defendant agreed to pay a rent of 34 and ⅓ *ghurūsh* per year. Three years passed from the day the lease was signed, and now the plaintiff reached the conclusion that it was not profitable, and that he had lost money as a result of the deal. He demanded the cancellation of the lease. When the defendant was questioned he confirmed the plaintiff's description of the deal, but refused to "remove his hand" from the *timār* until the end of the lease period, in three years' time.
>
> In his conclusion, however, the qadi presiding over the case notified the defendant Muḥammad Bey that this lease is null and void from its inception (*inna hādhihi al-ijāra bāṭila min aṣliha*), and instructed him to return the *timār* to the plaintiff. Then, having resolved their monetary differences the plaintiff paid the defendant twenty *ghurūsh*, and the lease was cancelled.[19]

This condensed record, which leaves many questions unanswered, describes a practice which in later years became a common feature of agrarian relations. The two timariots[20] had concluded a private deal for leasing the *timār*. It appears that the plaintiff failed to calculate his expected income. Perhaps he did not take inflation into account, or did not expect the defendant to be so efficient in collecting taxes. In any case, he regreted having made the deal, and asked the defendant to revoke it. When the defendant refused, the plaintiff took the case to court, where the two were notified by the qadi that the leasing of *timār*s is intrinsically illegal (according to the *kanun*), and that therefore the deal has to be cancelled immediately.

Since it was common knowledge, certainly among timariots, that it is illegal to rent *timars*, the appeal to the *majlis* must have been calculated on the part of the plaintiff, who hoped to have the contract revoked. Yet, as many other records in the *sijill* reveal, such contracts were not considered illegal *a priori*, and many of them were formally recorded in the *sijill*. Qadis had no compunctions about recording such deals, and even provided the parties with the legal jargon and flowery language suitable for concluding major contracts. Here is a somewhat shortened version of such a record:

> ʿAli Ağa, the *muhẓir bashi*[21] rents from Muṣṭafa Ağa ibn Maḥmūd Jāwīsh,[22] holder of a *zeamet* in Jerusalem, half of all summer and winter crop taxes, olive taxes, [and taxes for] *rijāliyya*,[23] *khamīsiyya*,[24] marriage[25] and *subashiyya*,[26] and half of the *bad-ı hava*,[27] which he would be able to collect (*ma ʿasāhu an yataḥaṣṣal*) from the village of Mikhmās near Jerusalem. The lease period is one year, and the rent is 50 *ghurūsh*, to be deducted from the sum owed ʿAli Ağa (the lessee) by Muṣṭafa Ağa (the lessor) for a horse which he bought from him.[28]

Towards the end of the century such records became very widespread, perhaps ignored by the state, but in many cases encouraged by the participation of senior officials from the provincial capital. Often several *sipahis* took part together in a deal offering a greater tract of land to a potential lessee, not infrequently a high-ranking officer or governor in Damascus or Istanbul:

> On 8 Rajab 1091 (4 August 1680) a lease agreement (*muqāṭaʿa*) was signed between Maḥmūd Bey ibn ʿUthmān, the representative of ʿAbd al-Karīm Pasha, the *çorbacı* in Damascus, and several *sipahis* in Jerusalem, in the presence of two witnesses—ʿAbd al-Bāqi the *bölükbaşı*[30] in Jerusalem, and Ibrahim ibn Sharaf. The lessors are Ahmad ibn Darwish, legal guardian for the minor Ḥasan Bey ibn ʿAli al-Asbaki (the Uzbek), Sulaymān Bey al-Ṣāri, and ʿIwaḍ Bey, all *sipahis* in the city of Jerusalem.
>
> The above-mentioned *sipahis* transferred into the hands of the pasha's representative a *muqāṭaʿa* comprising the yield of summer and winter crops, sheep tax, honey tax, *bad-ı hava* and all other taxes he is able to collect from the villages of Bayt Ṣāḥūr and Bayt Ṣafāfa in the *timār* held by the above-mentioned minor, and from a specific part of the village of ʿAjjūl, held jointly by the *sipahis* ʿIwaḍ Bey and Sulaymān Bey. The lease is given for a period of three years, from the beginning of 1091 until the end of 1093. The rent is 150 *ghurūsh*, of which 50 *ghurūsh* will be paid into the hands of the minor *sipahi*'s guardian, and the rest, 100 *ghurūsh*, will be paid to the two other *sipahis*.[31]

This last record is a further example of how the arrangement became a recognized fiscal practice in the late seventeenth century. Lease agreements were referred to as *muqāṭaʿa*, implying that they are a continuation of the government policy allocating fiefs to members of the governing elite. It is recorded in the *sijill* as a legal transaction. The boundaries of the territory, the exact rental period, the amount of money specified and the kinds of taxes to be collected are explicitly referred to. Nowhere is there any clue to the fact that the contract and all its contents, from the demarcation of the area's boundaries, to most of the taxes mentioned, is completely illegal.

Leasing villages or their potential yield was not limited to *timārs*. In fact, timariots may have followed the practice of an older establishment—the *waqf*. Both institutions, as was mentioned earlier, were based on the Islamic separation between *raqaba* and *taṣarruf*, but unlike *timārs*, *waqf* institutions were allowed to lease their possessions under certain conditions, and often did so. This was an established practice meant to provide income for the *waqf*, especially in times of economic hardship. *Waqf* supervisors leased houses, shops and workshops in town, and villages or farms in rural areas. The rent was used to acquire nonagricultural products, especially if the *waqf* included a soup-kitchen or a madrasa, to pay debts, and even to provide for the day-to-day administration of the *waqf*. The leasing of villages by *waqf* institutions was also recorded in the *sijill*, although sometimes *waqf* administrators did not adhere to rules of honest business:

> At the beginning of 1033 (1623–24), Nasir *Bashsha* (*beççe*)[32] ibn Muḥammad arrived in court, representing Sulayman Ağa, a servant of the Sublime Porte. He leased from Muḥammad Ağa, supervisor of the *waqf* of *Khāsiki Sultān*,[33] the whole village of Qāqūn which belongs to the *waqf*. A contract was then signed, leasing the village for three years, for a sum of 500 *ghurūsh* a year. But on 17 Ṣafar 1033 (10 December 1623), shortly after the signing of the agreement, Sulayman Ağa's son, Muṣṭafa *çavus* came to court, accompanied by the said supervisor of the *waqf*. Having been identified as the law requires, Muṣṭafa told the qadi that he had received from his father the income from the village (*intifāʿ*), but to his astonishment he found out that the village was deserted by its inhabitants. It appears they were terrorized by the former governor of Nabulus and had all run away. In light of this new evidence it was decided by mutual consent to revoke the lease contract, and the money was returned to the lessee.[34]

Waqf supervisors leasing a village did not hesitate to sign contracts with anyone who could come up with the money or a suitable substitute. Villages were frequently leased to ulema, rich merchants, or former *waqf* officials, to *sipahis*, and even to the villagers themselves, in return for supplies and services:

> Muḥammad Ağa ibn ʻAbdallah, *çavus* of the sublime porte and the current supervisor of *waqf* al-ʻImāra al-ʻĀmira (Khāsiki Sultān waqf), has leased the village of Jīb al-Fukhkhār, in the vicinity of Jerusalem, to Muṣliḥ ibn Ṣāliḥ, ʻUmar ibn ʻUmayra, Ibrāhīm ibn Ismāʻīl and Barakāt ibn ʻĪsa, all of them sheikhs (*mashāyikh*) of the said village. They have leased it for themselves, and as representatives of the rest of the people in the village. Part of [the taxes of] this village belong to the above mentioned *waqf*, while another part belongs to the *waqf* of al-Malik al-Mu'ayyad, but the said supervisor has presented a permit to lease both parts. The lease includes winter and summer crops, olive and vineyard tax and other taxes accruing to the two *waqfs*, all together estimated at 10,000 *qiṭʻa miṣriyya*.[35] This sum was subtracted by Muḥammad Ağa from the value of [work done by the villagers] cutting timber and carrying it to the *waqf* daily, summer and winter. All together this is estimated at six hundred Jerusalem *qintārs* from the beginning of Muḥarram 1009, to the end of that year. The price of this service is 9,000 *qiṭʻa Miṣriyya*, on the basis of 15 *qiṭʻa* per *qintār*. The sheikhs all gave mutual guarantees for this.... The lessees paid [the rest of the money] as required, and the lease was lawfully signed. Then the said supervisor came to an agreement with the lessees that if during the year the villagers would bring more than the amount of timber agreed upon, he would recompensate them for it.[36]

The central government in Istanbul frowned upon some of these lease contracts. Not infrequently such agreements involved embezzlement of funds intended for the *waqf*. In a series of documents from 1642, the governor of Damascus was instructed to punish the supervisor of a *waqf* in Hebron for leasing parts of the *waqf* and putting the money in his own pocket.

> A decree to the governor of Damascus, the vezir Ahmad Pasha, to the qadi of Damascus, to the governor of Jerusalem as an *arpalık*, and to the qadi of Jerusalem.
>
> The governor of Damascus, the above-mentioned vezir, sent a letter to my palace. After my former decree was sent, [the letter recounts] the *waqf* was seized, and its action suspended. The super-

> vizor and his clerks were arrested; an investigation was carried out; and it was forbidden for those who took over the *waqf*'s villages through lease contracts to go on exploiting them. When the supervisor's accounts were checked, it was discovered that he owed a sum of 3,600 *ghurūsh* for the period of one year and two months. He was therefore incarcerated in the citadel of Damascus, and his son, Ja'far, pledged to pay the money.
>
> The vezir informed us that he had sent a new supervisor to Jerusalem, and put a stop to the further exploitation of villages by those who laid their hands on them by lease (*icare ile*). He further requested that when the money is received [from the former supervisor's son] it shall be expended for the *waqf*'s vital necessities. My sublime decree was therefore written.
>
> I command that when my decree arrives you shall act accordingly. When the *waqf*'s money in the possession of the former supervisor is received, it should be lawfully given to the *waqf*, and expended for the *waqf*'s vital necessities.[37]

Other documents in the same series refer to the illegal leasing of villages, the profits of which were stolen by the supervisor, and to the steps taken to make sure the incident does not repeat itself. But on the whole, the government accepted the necessity of leasing *waqf* property, and was either oblivious to, or turned a blind eye towards the leasing of *timar*s. We may conclude therefore that this special form of "sublease" of villages and other rural areas was a dominant feature of agrarian relations throughout the seventeenth century. It preceded the *iltizām*, and in many respects prefigures tax-farming. Pressures of inflation and a stagnated economy enticed timariots to lease their fiefs.

It may have come about as an interim stage of the shift from a tax system based on payment in kind, to one based on money. Selling tons of wheat, cotton, or olive oil for the right price was a demanding task. In an unstable economy it required a special expertise which many timariots simply did not possess. The task was further complicated by the rapidly growing burden of state taxes. Tax collection became a continuous contest between producers and fief-holders, and the latters preferred to reside in urban centers, leasing their *timar*s in exchange for a lump sum of money. Let someone else take care of recalcitrant peasants, of collecting the harvest and of converting it into money. Probably some *sipahi*s, janissaries or even local notables, as may have been the case, specialized in overseeing the villages and collecting taxes, while others leased their estates and elected to invest the returns in commerce or in the acquisition of immovable property.

This type of sublease, a local form of *iltizām*, was not directed by the central government. Unlike state-controlled *iltizām*, it was characterized mainly by leases of small holdings, usually one or several villages. Another difference lay in the shorter time-spans of such leases. In many cases a village was leased for a few years, and then returned to its former status as part of a *waqf* or *timar* land. Only in rare cases was the rental period extended beyond a few years, to resemble the ubiquitous tax-farming of later centuries. Still, this change in structures of land tenure brought forth many of the ills later attributed to the *iltizām*: mistreatment of cultivators, oppressive taxation, and abuse of land resources. This is made evident by the many petitions sent by fallahin to the Sublime Porte towards the end of the century, complaining of abuse by the governing elite.[38]

In its local version described above, the leasing of state land did not create conditions for a massive takeover of the surplus by a localized elite. In other words, notables, merchants, or other aspiring elite groups, could not become large-scale tax farmers. Perhaps in the minds of local notables state land and tax collection were still by and large the domain of the governing elite. In any case, the formal connection between *sipahi*s or *waqf* officials and the villagers remained largely intact. Notables, it seems, hesitated to invest in tax-farming. With few exeptions they did not tend to lease large estates. They preferred to purchase land, and to invest in urban crafts.

The emerging pattern—sublease of small *timār*s or parts of them—also postponed the emergence of large farms, and market-oriented farming. On the contrary, it split the former *timār* system into smaller parcels of land, and added other varieties of land tenure and administration systems. The absence of a clear system of agrarian relations and the lack of a well-defined group of land holders that could direct production and meet demands halted the movement towards peripheralization and European control of the economy.

We may assume that some of the *timār* holders improved their economic status and filled their coffers, but on the whole their effort to privatize *iqtā*ʿ land and bequeath it to their sons failed. Until the end of the century, and well into the following century, timariots and *zeamet* holders still needed the authorization of the central government to pass their fief onto their next of kin. *Sijill* records dealing with such authorization suggest that it could be bought for a sum of money lavished on officials in the capital:

> At the end of Rajab 1091 (1680) a suit was filed by Dhīb ibn Iṣḥāq, guardian of the minor Muḥammd, son of Muḥammad Ağa, the former *sipahi* commander in Jerusalem, against Ismāʿil ibn Rajab,

> representative of the minor Ḥasan, son of the deceased *sipahi* ʿAli Bey al-Asbaki (the Uzbek). The plaintiff claimed that Muḥammad Ağa, his protegé's father, brought from Istanbul a *berat* authorizing the minor represented by the defendant to take over his deceased father's *timār*. In order to obtain the authorization he had to spend a sum of 120 *ghurūsh* in Istanbul.
>
> Before his death Muḥammad Ağa gave the *berat* to the defendant, telling him that it cost 120 *ghurūsh*, and subtracting 40 *ghurūsh* as a present. They agreed that the defendant should pay the rest of the sum—80 *ghurūsh*—in three years' time. Meanwhile Muḥammad Ağa died, and now the plaintiff claims the money on behalf of Muḥammad's son (who is also named Muḥammad).[39]

Paying for a *berat* was apparently a well-established norm, and inheriting the fief did not require any special qualification or distinction. The potential heir to the estate did not have to prove his valor or administrative skills. Still, the quasi-formal act of going to Istanbul or Damascus, spending money and buying presents for high officials, was enough to make it clear to all concerned that the Ottoman government still had ultimate control of the land, and could allocate it at its whim.[40] In this capacity *timār* holders were always the state's servants, and did not develop as an autonomous feudal institution. In order to insure a safe future for their families they had to direct their efforts to other avenues of land tenure, to which we shall now turn.

THE BATTLE FOR LAND OWNERSHIP

We have seen that although state-sponsored *iltizām* did not make much headway in the seventeenth century, the former dominant system, that of the *timār* and the *waqf*, changed considerably. *Timār* and *waqf* possessions were farmed out on a local basis. On the other hand, this did not constitute a shift towards privatization. Tax did not become rent. The battle for privatization was not fought in the realm of the *taṣarruf*, the usufruct. Instead it was the gray area between the *taṣarruf* and the *raqaba*, the ownership itself, that provided the best chance for privatizing land.

Sometimes the emphasis in Ottomanist research on *timār* and *iltizām* overshadows another point of interest in Ottoman systems of land tenure. Most of the land, as Ömer Lutfi Barkan and Gabriel Baer have shown, formally belonged to the state, or more specifically to the sultan himself. The sultan could grant it, or confiscate it at will. From time to time the sultan decided to change its designation, from *timār* to *waqf*, for instance. Rarely he (or his servants) would replace the cultivators, sending them off to colonize a newly acquired province. But other than that, the sultan's ownership remained in the realm of political or philosophical thought, having no direct bearing on the ground.[41]

Sultanic land granted as *timars* or *waqfs* was left in the hands of its cultivators. Officially they were allowed to till it in return for part of the crop, but in effect they had a hold over their land. This hold was by no means unequivocal. It was affected by many factors. First there was the type of land and its produce. Since growing trees, for instance, was a long-term project, requiring several years until they bore fruit, the state, in accordance with *sharīʿa* law, considered them private property. By recognizing private ownership of trees, Ottoman law recognized the cultivators' de facto ownership of the land where orchards, groves and vineyards were concerned. Owners of orchards were allowed to bequeath them, sell them or even to assign them as *waqf*. Fields or vegetable gardens could not officially be considered the property of cultivators, but these too were passed on by fathers to their sons and daughters, and sold inside the village community. In some places where vegetables were grown among the trees, for example, the definition was more problematic. Such definitions were crucial in mountainous areas like Jerusalem, Safad, Hebron or Nabulus where large fields or plantations were few, and orchards constituted the lion's share of cultivated land.[42]

Ottoman lawmakers deliberated definitions of ownership concerning fields and orchards, and questions of taxation emanating from these definitions. Their deliberations are reflected in the *kanunnames*, or legal codes, prepared separately for each of the empire's provinces. A subsection of the *kanunname* prepared for Damascus in 1548, indicates one of several potential problems:

> For certain places where vineyards or orchards existed in state lands in the said province, a *kharāj* tax was specified according to a certain index. Later the vines in the vineyard, or the trees in the orchard whithered and died, and their land was sown. If [their cultivators] now wish to pay taxes according to the old rate by claiming "it is our property" (*mülkümüzdür*), they should not be allowed to do so, since by prevailing custom the taxes to be collected from the villages should be determined by a fixed ratio, according to the regulations.[43]

Thus, when the vines died, and the vineyard became a field, or when the farmer failed to cultivate the land for several years, the land could no longer be considered "private" property, and a higher amount of tax had to be paid. The notion of private property, therefore, was much more supple and changeable than in later years. It was defined by the uses of the land, and the definition changed with the change in usage. This allowed cultivators to "increase" the level of ownership in the land by changing its designation, and by planting trees.[44]

Other reflections of the Ottoman difficulty in defining private property can be found in *fatāwa* books of the sixteenth and seventeenth centuries. The famous sixteenth-century *mufti*, Şeyhülislam Ebüssuud Efendi, the leading *ʿālim* of his day and a companion of Sultan Süleyman, was asked to define the categories of *mülk* (Arabic *milk*—private property) and *miri* (state land). Although the question itself indicates that definitions were problematic, his response, it seems, is unequivocal:

> Lands inside cities (*şehirler içinde olan yerler*) are *mülk*. Their owners can sell them, give them away as presents, or dedicate them as *waqfs*. When they die, the whole area passes into the hands of their heirs. *Miri* lands are those cultivated areas in villages, which each cultivator is allocated for his own use. They cannot be sold, given away or dedicated as *waqf*. When [the cultivator] dies, if he has sons they continue using the land. If not, the land is reassigned to the *sipahi*'s *tapu*.[45]

But even Ebüssuud's own *fatāwa* seem to question his simple definition of *mülk* as referring to areas inside cities. "Qadis in the province of Rumeli," he was asked, "grant documents of ownership (*hüccet*), and record in the *sijill* authorizations for sale and purchase, pawning and mortgaging, exchange and preemption, concerning lands which are now in the hands of the general populace (*reaya*). Is this fact in line with the *sharīʿa*?"

> It is contrary to the *sharīʿa*, [he replied]. These are now considered lands which have been registered in the *sipahis*' *tapu*. Recording their sale and purchase in the qadis' books is an error. It should be recorded in the following manner: "Zeyd delegated the use of the land which was his usufruct to ʿAmr, and took a certain sum for vacating it [the term used is *ferağat*, which also means *selling*]. Bekr, the *sipahi*, also took a certain tax, and gave [the fields] to ʿAmr.[46]

In this and other *fatāwa*, Ebüssuud suggested a fictitious legal mechanism which would allow people to own land for almost all practical purposes, while formally maintaining that no sale occured. The fields are transferred from Zeyd's possession to ʿAmr's, and the *timār* holder, Bekr, also receives a sum of money. (The names Zeyd, ʿAmr and Bekr are common names used to give theoretical examples in legal sources.) Since these questions of de facto ownership did not matter to the timariot and, moreover, he had something to gain from such transactions, it may be assumed that the sale and transfer of land was even encouraged. In later times, as the sway of fief-holders over the population diminished, this kind of transaction was already a well-established norm, and the villagers did not even request their permission.

In a series of questions posed to the famous *mufti* Khayr al-Dīn al-Ramli, who lived in Gaza and Ramle in the first half of the seventeenth century, questions of ownership appear to be a constant problem. It seems that such questions were still not resolved, and that a certain tension existed between cultivators and the state's agents:

> Fallahin who possessed a tract of sultanic land which they have inherited for several generations, have come into some difficulties and mortgaged their land with their fellow villagers in return for a known sum of money, on condition that they will get their land back when they return the money. Years later they returned the sum owed, and the land [should have been] returned to their possession. Now the villagers claim that the land belongs to them, and deny it has ever been mortgaged. If the above is proven, is it possible to drive them off the land?
>
> Yes, [answers al-Ramli], they should be driven off the land because the inheritors still have a right to it, on condition that they paid their debt in its entirety.[47]

In this case al-Ramli justifies the cultivators' claim to possession of the land by a sort of preemption. In other cases his ruling is more in line with formal views of land tenure. He is opposed, for instance, to the selling or leasing of *timār* and *waqf* land by their cultivators, on the grounds that they themselves are considered lessees, and are not allowed to sublet the property.[48] But as usual in *fatāwa* works, the questions are more indicative of prevailing customs and moods than the answers. From the numerous questions dealing with such issues addressed to al-Ramli, we may conclude that the definition of ownership was complex and multifaceted. Any attempt to define it by *shar'i* and kanuni definitions of *milk, raqaba, taṣarruf, waqf, mīri* or *sultāni* is doomed to fail. Very often cultivators sold sultāni land to others, leased or mortgaged it, even though according to *shar'i* definitions they did not own any of it. Many such transactions were officially recorded by the state in the *shar'i* court. Other deals were made by the parties themselves, with no state intervention, and were brought to the *majlis* only when one party to the transaction brought charges against the other party.

A glance at the *sijills* would indicate that selling orchards and vineyards was a daily occurence. In Nabulus, where most of the area was covered by olive trees, the majority of transactions involved olive groves. Records of sale always indicated that this was "the seller's property, whose usufruct he possessed until this sale" (*ma huwa lahu wa-taḥt taṣarrufihi ila ḥīn ṣudūr hādha al-bay'*). Unlike the procedure in Anatolia during the same period, in Jerusalem or Nabulus sales deeds never mentioned the *timār* holder or the *waqf* institution (*sahib-i arz*), and did not include a special payment for the grant-holder.[49] One suit filed to the qadi's court in Nabulus in 1066 (1656), sums up many characteristics of such sales deeds:

> The woman Ṣāliḥa bint Muḥammad of the village of Nāqūra, identified for the court by her husband, Fāzi' ibn Qarqūr, sues Aḥmad ibn Salāma of the village of Bayt Līd. The defendant, also present in court, represents the pride of his peers Bakr Bashsha ibn Zakarīyya.
>
> The plaintiff claimed that the defandant and his representative both took possession of one half—12 *qirāṭ*—of the whole, 24 *qirāṭ*[50]—of an olive grove, the roots of which are planted in the land of Ḥallat Marj, within the boundaries of Bayt Līd; an area undeniably recognized by both parties, and well known in its region, which makes its boundary definition here unnecessary. The plaintiff submits that this is her own property, and demands that the defendant and his representative vacate the said share of the grove.
>
> Asked whether it was his property, the defendant claimed that he had bought this half of the olive grove from Fāzi' ibn Qarqūr, the plaintiff's husband, and paid him 30 *ghurūsh* for it. At this stage the said Fāzi' retorted, "This sale I made is cancelled (*mawqūf*) because the share I sold to Aḥmad ibn Salāma, the representative, is part of my wife's property (*milk min amlāk zawjati*), and she did not sell it. The other part of the grove which is in my possession (*al-Jāri fi milki*) is mortgaged to Nāṣir ibn Zuhayr." In saying this he denied the actual sale, but the said Ahmad, the defendant, did not accept his words, and said he has *shar'i* proof that Fāzi' sold him his own share, and it is in fact the other half, which belongs to his wife, that was mortgaged. He asked the qadi's permission to leave in order to obtain that proof.
>
> Having obtained permission he left and came back at a later date with two witnesses. They both testified, in front of the woman, the said Ṣāliḥa, and in front of Salāma, son of the said Fāzi', that Fāzi' himself said to them during the transaction: "Bear testimony that I sold my share, comprising half of the olive trees, to Aḥmad ibn Salāma." Thus they provided ample *shar'i* proof. In consequence the qadi forbade the woman Ṣāliḥa and the said Salāma ibn fāzi' from objecting with no legal cause to the ownership of Aḥmad the said representative, and notified them that the olive grove is now part of the aforementioned Bakr Bashsha's possessions. All this was

proven according to the *sharīʿa*, and registered in mid Dhu al-Qaʿda 1066.[51]

In Jerusalem orchards and groves were of a more varied nature. The vague description of their contents in many sales records may imply that some of these were not strictly arboreal plantations. Some of the properties sold may have included vegetable gardens or fields, where trees were scattered. It is interesting to note that in al-Ramli's *fatāwa*, cotton is referred to as "cotton trees" (*shajar quṭn*), perhaps an indication of the different way the term 'trees' was used at the time. By describing the land sold as an orchard, it would have been easier to claim that it was private property, and to register the sale. Such cases were usually recorded in the *sijill* in the formal and elaborate language of business transactions, reproduced here with some ommissions:

> Ṣāliḥ ibn Ṣalāḥ al-Dīn, Manṣūr ibn Nāṣir and ʿAwda ibn Shaḥāda, all inhabitants of the village of Lifta in the vicinity of Jerusalem, buy with their own money, for themselves, in equal parts between them, from Badrān, son of the deceased Ḥajj Ḥasan al-Ṭanbugha, who is a legal representative of the sisters Ṣafiyya and Alfiyya, daughters of the deceased Ḥajj Amḥad al-Ṣaydāwi. . .that which belongs to his authorizers (the sisters) in equal parts between them, and constitutes part of their property, which they have received as part of their inheritance from their father, and has remained in their possession until the execution of this sale. [The property in question includes] all of the orchard which consists of vines, figs, olives, apricots and more, the roots of which are planted in the vineyard known as Karm al-Ṣaydāwi in the land of Al-Ṣarāra, including half of the structure (*qaṣr*) and the water cistern in the said vineyard, owned in partnership with Mūsa al-Ashram. The boundaries of the said vineyard are: on the south side, the main road; to the east, the part owned by the said Musa al-Ashram and beyond it a vineyard owned by the heirs of the deceased Sheikh ʿAbd al-Jawwād al-ʿAsali; to the north, the vineyard of Abi al-Khayr which is in the hands of the buyers; and to the west the main road and beyond it the said vineyard. [The sale includes] all the rights to the property. . . . The price is 40 *ghurūsh*, paid in full to the said representative by the said buyers.[52]

Other records in the *sijill* indicate that some sort of private land ownership was considered even by the Ottoman authorities as the natural state of affairs:

> On 19 Rajab 1078 (2 January 1668) Sheikh ʿUbayd ibn Muḥammad from the village of Jaljūlya in [the subdistrict of] Jabal Nabulus arrived

> in court, and presented to the qadi an imperial decree dated Rabīʿ awwal 1077 (September 1666). According to the decree, the said Sheikh ʿUbayd, and his friend, Sheikh Muḥammad, complained to the authorities that although they possess no land or taxable property in the village, its inhabitants harass them, demanding that they pay their share of special taxes (*ʿawāriḍ wa-takālīf*). The decree orders the qadi to look at the matter, and if indeed the petitioners possess no land or property in the village, they should not be forced to pay taxes. If any of the inhabitants of the village goes on annoying them, his name should be passed on to the palace. Sheikh ʿUbayd requested that this decree be recorded in the *sijill*. The qadi consented, and instructed the inhabitants of the sheikh's village to refrain from harassing him and his friend.[53]

There are several conclusions to be drawn from these documents. Primarily, ownership of land, whether de facto or de jure, was very widespread. It was not confined to towns, and was practically ubiquitous. This fact can also be gleaned from descriptions of the boundaries of sold land. In almost every case the plots of land adjacent to the one sold were also registered as owned by individuals—a notable from the city, a fallah from another village or the daughter of a local inhabitant. People would sell their land, bequeath it, mortgage it or pawn it, with the possible exception of consecrating it as a *waqf* (as this would be a long-term commitment unacceptable to the authorities).

Another interesting conclusion refers to the acquisition of land by local notables and members of the governing elite. Governors, officers, *ümera* and their decendants, ulema, rich merchants and *ashrāf*, all bought landed property in great quantities. Bequests of governors or ulema registered in the *sijill* frequently include large tracts of private land, indicating the process whereby a group of notables consolidated economic power in the seventeenth century. It also traces the process of enrichment and localization of the ethnically foreign governing elite, and its assimilation into local society. This process was not based on the *iltizām*, or on the privatization of *timars*. It was based, instead, on the acquisition of *sultāni* land turned private. Even when their political power was destroyed at the beginning of the eighteenth century, these families still retained most of their landed assets, providing a basis for future development.

AGRARIAN RELATIONS AND THE RISE OF A LOCAL NOTABLITY

In her book on towns in Anatolia, following in the footsteps of Ömer Lutfi Barkan, Suraya Faroqhi claims that in the course of the seventeenth century the importance of private ownership rose considerably in Anatolia, and that *miri* lands were more and more frequently treated as private property:

> The expression *bey* (sale), which should not have been used at all with respect to *miri* lands, began to find its way into the documents. As the kadis were trained in the *şeriat* and therefore mainly accustomed to dealing with the legal problems presented by freehold property, fields that could be sold might in the long run have come to be regarded as *mülk*.[54]

However, according to Faroqhi, the meaning of *mülk* (*milk*) was uniting the *raqaba* or actual ownership, with the *taṣarruf*. In the district of Jerusalem and in neighboring districts, however, the definition of a property as *milk* simply meant that the words *raqaba* and *taṣarruf* themselves came to acquire a different meaning. Even though the inhabitants of the district knew well that the land was still *sultāni*, or even *waqf*, they considered it private, in the sense that parts of the *raqaba*, and parts of the *taṣarruf*, were theirs to dispose of as they wished. Yet they went on paying taxes and impositions to the *sipahi* or the supervisor of the *waqf*, they still kept a very small part of the income, and were dispossessed from time to time. In this respect private ownership mattered very little. Only in the highest echelons of society, where most people paid no taxes, did *raqaba* and *taṣarruf* really unite.

Agrarian relations in the district of Jerusalem during the same period were, thus, more complex than a century earlier. Land ownership, which Cuno rightly sees as a "shared control," or "shared ownership," was constructed of several layers of Muslim law, "secular" Ottoman law, pre-Ottoman custom and an elusive local ingredient that found its way into the legal documents, even though it did establish itself in legal codes.

In principle the sultan owned most of the land. At his behest he could have transferred cultivators from their plots of land, settled others in them, and allocated the *taṣarruf* to whomever he wished. Another limited layer of ownership belonged to the holders of *timār*s and other *iqṭā*'s, and to *waqf* institutions—those who appropriated most of the economic surplus, and had a say in sale transactions and ownership disputes. Their mandate did not include any direct rights of ownership of the land, but they could have purchased land, and did so extensively. Finally, the cultivators, the fallahin themselves, had a share of the ownership, stretching from officially recognized freehold, to a temporary hold on the land, subject to its cultivation.

In the seventeenth century the whole region could be described as a battlefield between all these layers of ownership. The state sought to maintain its ultimate ownership, and the right to appropriate surplus and reallocate it at will. Its main goal was to prevent its slipping into the hands of the localized provincial governing elite. This was done by frequent transfers of officials from one district to another; by confiscation of property from rebellious *timār* holders; by a close supervision of *waqf*s; by fighting against unlimited subletting of *timār*s and *waqf*s; and, later on, by replacing the *timār* system with the state's own version of sublease—the *iltizām*.

Members of the Ottoman-local governing elite tried to retain and even increase their portion of the surplus and their control of land. They strove to bequeath estates to their offspring, and to collect more taxes. Another track, which proved more efficacious, was the purchase of large quantities of landed assets. Exempt from most taxes, and unhampered by their own bullying of the *reaya*, they enjoyed all the benefits and suffered few of the shortcomings of this system. Many would sublet their own *timār*s and use the money to amass land and city-based property.[55] This process was detrimental to the rest of the unprivileged populace. It may be assumed that in lands bought by members of the elite fallahin worked as hired hands and lost the small measure of control they once held over their land. On the other hand, the gradual decline in tax-paying area, resulting from the acquisition of land by the elite, increased the already heavy load of taxes on the *reaya*, whose own dwindling income made the purchase of more land almost impossible.

Members of the local notable elite also bought land, with money earned from other economic activities and from state-sponsored wages. Like their rival peers in the governing elite, they sought to increase their control over the land, and to pry away from the state, the sultan, and the cultivators their respective parts of the ownership. Being senior ulema and *ashrāf*, or having purchased military commissions, many local notables had the advantage of tax exemption.

A classic example of this process is Khayr al-Dīn al-Ramli himself. During his lifetime the famous *mufti* acquired enormous quantities of land. His biography, written by one of his disciples, mentions that he had also planted more than a hundred thousand trees on these lands(!). By the mid-seventeenth century he was the biggest landowner in Ramla, his native town, and his income was estimated at more than one hundred *ghurūsh* a day.[56] Several years after his death, a case was brought to the *majlis* in Jerusalem: The supervisor of the Khasikiyya *waqf* told the qadi that Khayr al-Dīn's son, Najm al-Dīn, had inherited land, houses, flour mills and soap factories from his father. Much of this property was located in the village of Ludd (Lod), which forms part of the domains of the *waqf*. The supervisor complained that Najm al-Dın does not pay special taxes which were imposed on the *waqf*. Following a long debate about the nature of these assets, the qadi decided that Najm al-Dīn should not pay taxes since this was the custom in his father's time, and precedents should be respected.[57] Thus Khayr al-Dīn and his heirs, like many other notables, enjoyed both the right to purchase land, and at least some tax exemption on the acquired property.

The last group, the cultivators themselves, fought to preserve what ownership rights they still had. This is evident from their insistence on recording transactions in the *sijill*, from their frequent requests for *fatwa*s on questions of land and ownership, and even from complaints to the Sublime Porte in Istanbul. In the course of the century they managed to retain their share of the ownership, but on the whole the portion of landed assets owned by villagers gradually decreased. Heavy taxation and cruel treatment often forced the fallahin off their own land, and compelled them to relinquish their claim to land and property.

In its silent struggle against the provincial elite, the government managed to prevent the conversion of *iqṭāʿ* from tax to rent, from state ownership to total private ownership. In this struggle to prevent privatization, the central government found a staunch ally in the local cultivators. Both parties—the sultan and the fallahin—strove to keep their part of the ownership, and their joint actions, uncoordinated though they were, prevented the locally based governing elite from gaining the upper hand. We have no way of knowing whether the central government anticipated this sort of cooperation from its humble subjects, but the vezirs in Istanbul may have understood the advantages in turning a blind eye to land transactions as a means of curtailing the power of local governors. The unstated yet very real principle of shared ownership stood fast against attempts to destroy it by the governing elite. Even when parts of *timar*s were bought by *berat* holders or other officials, the land did not lose its official status as state land. A timariot could buy a layer of ownership in a tract of land, but was prevented from uniting his rights as an estate holder with his rights as a landowner to produce full ownership.

Still, the same principle allowed members of that group to gradually acquire landed property on a smaller scale, and expand their economic base. This process went on mainly in the first half of the seventeenth century, reaching its apex in the 1650s and 1660s. A few years later, however, when the local dynasties were decapitated, entire chains of patronage and clientship collapsed. Remnants of this local elite, for the most part replaced by new Istanbul appointments, lost most of their landed assets, which reverted to the state.

For a while, the real winners were local notables. Unlike the governing elite, they were not considered dangerous opponents by the state, and no battle was waged against them. Other groups—the governing elite, and even the cultivators themselves—failed to recognize the threat inherent in the local notables, and in fact saw them as allies. In the course of the period they amassed property and power with no apparent opposition, and emerged at the end of the century as a dominant local political force to be reckoned with. When their vested interests were jeopardized at the turn of the century by a new, foreign governor attempting to impose a new order of taxation, the result was revolt, led by the ulema and notables of Jerusalem. This revolt was an agrarian setback for the notables from which they did not recover until later in the eighteenth century.

Chapter 6

An Economy in Transition

COMMERCE, CRAFTS AND TAXATION

The very detailed taxation surveys made by order of the sultan during the fifteenth and sixteenth centuries supply an abundance of data on Ottoman provinces. In spite of their many shortcomings and inconsistencies, these *tahrirs* supply historians of Ottoman economy with information of a kind known only in modern bureaucratic states and having almost no parallel in the premodern Islamic world. Balanced by information in *sijill* registers of local courts and in other sources, depictions of the economy in Palestine, as in many other regions, can be lucid and sharp.[1]

In the second century of Ottoman rule in Palestine, however, this meticulous system of control changed considerably. The survey routine declined before the end of the sixteenth century, and in the ensuing period was all but forgotten. The reasons had to do with changes in the structure of government, with the internal balance of the governing elite, with different systems of agriculture and agrarian relations, and even with the continuous decline in the empire's population. We therefore have no source comparable to the *tahrir* surveys for the seventeenth century, and have no way of gathering accurate statistical data. To compensate for this shortage, we must turn to other sources. Our main venue for this period is still the *sharīʿa* court. Part of the court's duties was control of the fiscal system, registration of tax payments, sale and purchase of land and movables, internal trade of all kind, and prices of basic foodstuffs. Another important source is the archives of European states, ports and trading companies. Prominent among them during the seventeenth century was the chamber of commerce at Marseilles, which conducted the main volume of French trade with the eastern Mediterranean. Another source, of lesser importance for this region, is the English Levant company. Ottoman archives supply information mainly about agrarian relations and the initial demands of taxation. None of these sources can provide a clear quantitative answer to the main problems of Ottoman economic history at the time, namely the questions of decline, decentralization, and the process known as peripheralization in the rapidly expanding world economy. But all these sources taken together, each in its own domain, may shed some light on the issues discussed in this chapter.

For the Ottoman economic mind, the basic unit of taxation at the time of the conquest was a household, usually headed by an adult male. The types of social structure implied by the term ranged from the nuclear (sometimes polygamous) family to an extended one with a single recognized head. *Tahrir* surveys assessed the amount of taxes to be collected from each unit's revenues accrued in agriculture, industry and commerce. For cultivated lands, taxation assessment was based on the *çiftlik* system. *Çiftlik* (literally, "pair"), a Turkish word of Persian origin, referred to the amount of land that could be cultivated using one pair of oxen. It was assumed that each village household had at least one such pair at its disposal, and therefore was capable of tilling a *çiftlik*. In towns and cities other yardsticks were used to measure the household's productive capabilities.

There were many differences between provinces in regard to the fertility of the land, climate, average annual rainfall, traditions of agriculture and industry, and even pre-Ottoman taxation systems. All these considerations had an influence on Ottoman taxation policies, and were integrated into regional *kanunnames*—official collections of sultanic edicts. In many cases *kanunnames* which contained taxation laws concerning a certain province were to be found in the preamble to *tahrir* surveys of that province. Appraisals in the surveys were used by tax collectors to determine the estimated yield of each taxation unit, and to allocate the tax thus assessed according to the needs of the treasury. At the same time these appraisals were used to determine the size and value of *timārs*, the main source of income for the *sipahi* cavalry and other high-ranking officials in the provinces. Such estimates served as a basis for allocation of *timars* to deserving officers and officials.[2]

Until the 1590s the Ottoman government managed to retain its hold over the economy in the district of Jerusalem. It avoided complete privatization of *timārs* and *waqf* endowments, maintained its legal ownership of lands cultivated by villagers, and stressed its right to define taxes, and to receive and allocate the economic surplus. The economy was centralized. Important economic matters were decided in Istanbul and later communicated to the provinces. Within this rigid system there was always some leeway as a result of structural constraints—distance, faltering communications, or local forces vying for a part of the action. Still, *tahrir* surveys supplied a powerful and reliable means of economic control. Although they provided only approximations of produce, the surveys enabled treasury officials in the imperial center to assess with reasonable accuracy the income expected from a province, to check whether a governor was filling his pockets with too much of the government's money, and to investigate the petitions of villagers overburdened by the local government's greed.

At the end of the sixteenth century the surveys were neglected. One reason was the rapid decline of the *sipahi*s. The provincial cavalry, reluctant to adapt to the use of firearms and modern military tactics, was now useless as a military force. It was soon replaced on the battlefield by other forces, better adapted to modern warfare. Unlike their predecessors, these new military units did not receive *timār*s. Their income was based on salaries and bonuses, sometimes on a temporary basis. Since the determination and allocation of *timār*s was an important reason for conducting the surveys, the decline of the *timār* system subtracted from the overall importance of the survey. Coupled with rapid changes in agrarian relations, and probably with a visible decline in the population which led to smaller tax yields, there was little incentive to conduct new surveys.[3]

When the *tahrir* system was abandoned, the Ottoman government lost a tool of immeasurable value. The gap between the old survey data and changing conditions on the ground expanded rapidly. The ability of the sultan and his servants to control and assess taxation diminished, and central control over the provinces decreased in direct proportion. *Timar*s and *waqf*s, still the main agrarian systems, became more decentralized. *Sipahi*s and local officials often leased lands and property in their trust to others. Decentralization found even more acute expression in matters concerning the monetary system, taxation regulations, and internal and foreign trade.[4]

Officially the *akçe*, sometimes called *osmani* (*'uthmāni*), and known in the West as *asper,* was still legal tender in the seventeenth century, but it has long ago ceased to be in circulation. Its only use was as "money of account," symbolic units of money to be added and subtracted by treasury clerks.[5] The majority of business transactions in Jerusalem and Nabulus were conducted using foreign currency. The most common coin was the Dutch *löwen rikstaler,* a gold coin depicting a lion's head, referred to as *arslanlı kuruş* in Turkish, or as *ghurūsh asadi* in Arabic. Use of this coin was so widespread that in *sijill* documents it was simply called *ghurūsh,* and no other adjective was needed. It was often used as a basic currency unit that other coins were measured against. Slightly less popular was the Spanish real, *ghurūsh riāl* in Arabic. The real, slightly more expensive than the *rikstaler,* was one of the major import items from Spain into the Ottoman Empire. These coins also served to determine the value of Ottoman currency. The main Ottoman coin used in Palestine at the time was the Egyptian *qiṭʿa,* a version of the Ottoman *para* minted in Cairo. The Damascene *para—qiṭʿa shāmiyya—*was also used frequently. Its value was slightly lower than that of its Egyptian counterpart. At mid-century one *ghurūsh asadi* (Dutch *rikstaler*) was worth 40 *qiṭʿa shāmiyya* or 30 *qiṭʿa miṣriyya*.[6]

Currency values were determined by the content of precious metal (gold or silver). The use of so many kinds of currency, frequently with no clear indication about their actual value, made trade and taxation difficult. From time to time, mainly in the first years of the century, new exchange rates were announced for different coins. A typical record of the court summons the commander of the citadel to receive his soldiers' pay, and to formally declare that he received "two hundred *ghurūsh,* worth 60 *qiṭʿa shāmiyya* each, and 25 *sulṭāni,* worth 108 *qiṭʿa shāmiyya* each."[7] In other court records the local community requested the qadi's intervention in order to determine exchange rates:

> Several people were summoned by our noble qadi. [They included] Ḥusām al-Dīn *efendi:* Sheikh ʿInāyat Allah al-Ghazzi, the preacher (*khaṭīb*) Sheikh ʿAbd al-Ḥaqq ibn Jamāʿa, Sheikh Yaḥyā ibn Qaḍī al-Ṣalṭ, the teacher (*mudarris*) Sheikh Raḍiy al-Dīn ibn Abi al-Luṭf, and the Sufi master Sheikh Shāfiʿi al-Ghazzi. And of the merchants the *khawājā*[8] Muḥammad al-ʿAṣali, head of the merchants (*raʾīs al-tujjār*), *khawāja* Muḥammad ibn Mūsa al-Duhayna, *khawāja* Aḥmad ibn ʿAbd al-Qudūs, the *muʿallim*[9] Aḥmad, the *muḥtasib*[10] in Jerusalem, the *muʿallim* Yūsuf, head of the market (*bazār bashi*), Sheikh ʿAbd al-Qādir, the deputy inspector of the *waqf,* and others from the market.
>
> When they all gathered the qadi asked them about the exchange rate in Jerusalem, and the reasons for its confusion. Those present consulted on the matter and came to the conclusion that the value of one golden *dinār,* whether *sharīfi, Ibrāhīmi* or *Venetian,* should be 48 Egyptian *qiṭʿa,* and [the exchange rate of] a true *ghurūsh* should be 30 *qiṭʿa,* and [the exchange rate of] other types of *ghurūsh* coins should be 30 *qiṭʿa,* so that the value of the *dinār* is 1.5 times the value of the *ghurūsh.*

In later years fluctuations in the value of coins were less extreme, and the impressive forum convened by the qadi did not have much reason to assemble again. The ratio between the foreign *ghurūsh* and the local

Egyptian *qiṭ'a* remained stable throughout the century, and so did other exchange rates. The galloping rate of inflation characteristic of the late sixteenth century seems to have slowed down considerably, and to have reached a lower steady state.[12]

Towards the end of the century, the Ottomans minted their own *kuruş* coin, with a smaller content of gold than its European counterparts. The introduction of this new coin did not reduce the use of European currency in circulation. It was used by all social groups, from the governor and his retinue, through the *sipahis* and janissaries, to the ulema, the merchants, the villagers and the bedouin. It was used in commercial transactions, loaned, and paid as bride-price. It was even collected as taxes, although the official taxation currency was still the *akçe*. In the last decades of the century, the use of Egyptian and Damascene *para* coins diminished, and foreign currency became even more popular.

Western European currency was popular for several reasons. The sixteenth century balance of trade with Europe was based on the import of (originally American and African) gold and silver into the Ottoman Empire, in return for raw materials and finished products. Most of the metal came in the form of coins minted in Europe. These rapidly became popular as a dependable kind of currency with a stable ratio of pure gold or silver to base metal. Later on, when the central government's ability to influence exchange rates and money markets diminished, Europe became the only reliable source for currency. The imperial *divan* succumbed to the pressures of the market, and allowed the use of foreign currency inside its own fiscal and monetary systems for payments, taxes and wages. In addition to losing an important symbol of sovereignty, this capitulation signifies a conscious decision on the part of the Ottoman government to give up trying to control the money market and the economy. Such loss of control was also manifest in other domains of the economy.[3]

DECENTRALIZATION OF TAXATION

In its Syrian-Palestinian version, Ottoman taxation combined a Mamluk heritage, which reached its final form at the time of Sultan Qayitbāy,[14] with several Ottoman modifications and ideas from other provinces. In 1517, the Ottomans left the Mamluk system almost intact, and introduced only a few changes, intended primarily to improve tax collection and to help integrate the new provinces into the Ottoman network. In the course of the first century of Ottoman rule, however, this relatively simple system became complex and cumbersome. The central government itself added a patchwork of new taxes, inconsistent with the old ones, until the principles guiding it were forgotten and the basic pattern was completely lost.

The principle at the base of the initial taxation system was the collection of a proportional tax from all tax-paying populations. The dividing line between those who paid taxes and those who did not was almost identical to that which separated the *reaya* from the *askeri*. The estimated income of taxpayers was recorded in *tapu-tahrir* registers, and each family was supposed to pay its taxes in accordance with the estimate. The system was not progressive. It did not take into account the relative poverty, the different income or the inherited property of each family, or its ability to pay the required tax. But the average standard of living in the area and the potential yield of the land were taken into consideration. *Tahrir* registers set a lower tax rate for less fertile land, or where problems of irrigation did not permit intensive farming. Different rates were set for different kinds of olive trees, for wheat and barley, and for cattle, in accordance with their various market values.[15]

Rates were also fixed for industry and trade activities, in accordance with estimated gains. Some of these taxes were collected by the *muḥtasib* and his adjutants directly from merchants and craftsmen in the market. In villages the person responsible for coordinating tax collection was the village headman, in the sixteenth century most often referred to as *ra'īs al-fallāḥīn*. In later centuries the title used in court records was *mutakallim* (speaker, representative), usually in the plural, *mutakallimīn*, perhaps suggesting some devaluation in the status of village headmen. The way taxes were divided inside the village was of no consequence to the authorities. Village headmen were required to collect the tax in money or in kind, and deliver it to the city. In some areas of Palestine this encouraged the system known as *mushā'*, which entailed a revolving responsibility for cultivation of the village's plots of land. This system was not very widespread in the district of Jerusalem at the time, and is very rarely referred to in *sijill* records. Much of the land in the district quietly slipped into quasi-private ownership, with or without official approval.[16]

As the revenues of the central government dwindled at the end of the sixteenth century, a new excise was levied. The *avarız* (or *'awāriḍ* in Arabic) was first described as a special tax levied only when Ottoman subjects were required to lend a hand in anticipation of a new campaign against the infidels. But since the empire was very often in the midst of a war against one or more of its many enemies, this special levy soon became a regular tax, paid every year. The *avarız* system, as McGowan has shown, competed for some time with the *iltizām* as the taxation system intended to replace the *timār*, and even gained precedence over it for a while. This tendency is reflected in imperial rescripts and *sijill* records which, from the middle of the seventeenth century, increasingly mention *avarız* taxes side by side with the old taxation systems.[17]

Ignoring the inherent logic of the established taxation system, the government now decided that new *avarız* taxes are to be levied from the district as a whole, and not from each household separately. Inside the district the governors and their henchmen allotted the burden, somewhat arbitrarily, to villagers and to other revenue-producing sectors. The records show that *avarız* were levied on the majority of the district's population, including villages that formerly paid their taxes to *waqf* institutions exclusively. As current government policy dictated, the new taxes collected in the districts of Palestine were often transferred directly to the Yerliyya janissaries of Damascus.[18] Several imperial rescripts sent from Istanbul to Jerusalem quote petitions sent by Yerliyya commanders complaining that the *avarız* levied in Jerusalem did not find their way to the Damascus garrison. Instead, it appears, the money was appropriated by the imperial treasury to finance campaigns elsewhere. But whether it went to Istanbul or Damascus made little difference to the dwindling population of the region, forced to shoulder yet another tax.

New excises were also imposed on the *sipahi*s themselves. By the early seventeenth century the central government considered the *sipahi*s more a nuisance than an advantage, although it was unable to rid itself of the *timār* system altogether. Instead, it attempted to minimize the *sipahis*' revenue from *timār* estates by imposing substantial *bedel* fines (*badal* in Arabic), to be collected whenever the *sipahi*s failed to join the ranks of the imperial army in one of its many campaigns. Other taxes, referred to by the general term *tekalif* (Arabic *takālīf*, literally, "expenses, impositions") were added soon, and the military personnel stationed in the area were also required to pay them from time to time. The *sipahi*s, for their part, did not hesitate to lift the added burden off their shoulders and transfer it to those of the *reaya*. Sometimes they even used the new taxes as an excuse to extract a bit on the side for themselves. Firmans sent from the capital to the provinces attest to the government's dismay at such injustice:

> Edict to our lord Muṣṭafa, qadi of noble Jerusalem, may his virtues be plentiful. A letter was sent to my palace, [according to which] the ulema, sheikhs and Sufis (*fuqarā'*) of Jerusalem came to the *sharī'a* court [and testified that] the *timār*s and *zeamet*s belonging to timariots in the district of Jerusalem are of stony ground and poor of yield. Apart from the fact that the [*sipahi*s] themselves are poor, their lands are surrounded by bedouin, and they are charged with the duty of guiding the pilgrims safely and securely to visit [the gravesites of] the honorable Ibrāhīm Khalīl al-Raḥmān (Hebron) and the honorable Musa Kalīm Allah (Nabī Mūsā) may the best prayers and the most perfect peace be upon them and upon our prophet.

> In return for their efforts they were given permission to pay *bedel* and *tekalif* as a substitute for their absence from battlefields this year, as were all other *sipahi*s in the province of Damascus. But in view of their aforementioned predicament, the *timār* and *zeamet* holders in the district of Jerusalem requested total exemption from the war toll (*sefer teklifi*).
>
> Therefore I have written my noble firman to instruct you, the qadi, to look into the matter and to confirm that bread is indeed in short supply in the *timār*s and *zeamet*s of Jerusalem. If that is the case, see that the [timariots] are exempted from payment as of this year, 1103 (1695), on condition that the holders of *zeamet*s and *timar*s continue to lead the Muslim pilgrims safely to their destinations.[19]

It seems improbable that the local leaders of Jerusalem's religious and lay communities, who petitioned the sultan to exempt *timār* holders from payment of the special taxes, did so just out of pity for their poor colleagues in the governing elite. A more plausible explanation would suggest that they knew, as did everyone else, that the fief-holders would pass the yoke of payment on to the seemingly bottomless pit that absorbed all previous demands for heavier taxation—the tax-paying *reaya*. The double gain of the timariots thus became the double loss of the rest of the population. The *sipahi*s were not required to join the increasingly dangerous military adventures of the Ottoman Empire, nor did they pay a fine for this evasion. The *reaya*, on the other hand, had no refuge from their landlords even in times of war, and on top of this were forced to pay the indemnity as well. The insistence on checking whether the district is as poor as the petition claims it to be, and if so, authorize exemption, seems to imply that the decision taken by the authorities in Istanbul stemmed from awareness of this problem.

This, then, may have been the course of events that led to a disintegration of the coherent structure at the base of the sixteenth-century Ottoman taxation system. Alongside the traditional taxes assessed according to output capacity, other payments were imposed by the central government, including *bedel* and *avarız*. At the same time the old system of economic control, based on *tahrir* surveys, ceased to supply basic data for decision-makers. Taxation was decentralized, and central control over tax collection systems weakened. New taxes, incompatible with the old ones, were imposed by local governors and *timār* holders. The people of the region failed to perceive the logic in the new system, lost their faith in it, and began to see it for what it was—an arbitrary pattern of taxation, devoid of any social logic, striving mercilessly to exploit them.

Exploitation was not unknown in the previous century, but what was then treated as an exception, now became an established norm. Local traditions of hospitality, expressed in lavish banquets and expensive gifts for honored guests now became a tax, to be paid on a regular basis. Often called *selamlık*[20] or *muṣahara*,[21] these taxes infuriated the *reaya*, helpless in the face of such exploitation. At the beginning of the century feeble attempts were made to hold this tendency in check, as a firman of 1606 recounts:

> An edict to the governor and qadi of Damascus, to the governors of districts in the province of Damascus, and to qadis in these districts.
>
> The inhabitants of the province have sent a petition to my royal council. In the past, [they claim,] the province governor, the district governors and the qadis have accepted their allocated revenue from crops, taxes and *bad-ı hava*,[22] and treated their subjects in a just and honest manner. Now, for the first time, they are not content with the revenue from taxes, crops and other sources sanctioned by the *ṣeriat*, the *kanun* and the *defter*.[23] Several hundred officers (*subaşıs*) raided poor subjects, seized their food, and imposed new (*bid'at*) taxes named *selamlık* and *piyade*.
>
> Let it be known that I am not content with any sort of exploitation and harassment of my blameless *reaya*. I have therefore published my noble edict instructing you to remove all these new blasphemous inventions. I have ordered that when the firman arrives it is to be legally copied [into the *sijill*] and you, the governors of the province and the district, are to cease at once sending horse-riding officers and to stop collecting the *selamlık* and *piyade* from my subjects.[24]

Efforts to curb the rapidly growing tendency to invent new taxes failed altogether. The central government kept trying to compel local governors to get back in line and stop collecting what came to be known as "governing elite impositions" (*takālıf ahl al-'urf*). In contrast to formal government taxes, these new local ones were imposed on populations formerly exempted from payment, among them villagers of *ashrāf* and *sādāt* families. In the second half of the century increased taxation pressures kindled feelings of anger and hostility among the *reaya*.

An edict of 1657 records a complaint sent by the inhabitants of a village in the district of Jerusalem. Even though they had always paid their dues on time as requested, the villagers complained, the governors of the province and the district, and others of the governing elite (*mirmiran ve mirliva ve sair ehl-i örf taifesi*) have imposed new taxes on them, unsanctioned by royal edict. Among the many taxes mentioned in the complaint were *mufill* (uncultivated land), *mecani* (harvested fruit?), *yemek* (food), *kabūl* (reception?), *kozu* (sheep), *bal* (honey), *bağ* (orchards), *arpa* (barley), *cemali* (or *deve,* camels), *at* (horses), *sud* (profit?), *odun* (firewood) and *tavuk* (poultry). Other taxes were *nefl-i paha* (payment by "voluntary" work), *kaftan paha* (payment for robe), *küçük* (children), *zor* (need or compulsion, or perhaps *zevr,* visit), *selāmiye* (selamlık), *hak tarik* (road toll) and *ziyafet akçesi* (forged coins, or entertainment, banquet).[25]

The edict ends with an order to stop this reprehensible conduct of officers and governors, but even the clerk who composed the firman knew, it seems, that these were "words in the wind" as the local Arab saying goes. Governors and their henchmen ignored such edicts, and went on inventing new taxes. The central government finally gave in and allowed these decentralizing tendencies to take root in the provinces. This attitude can also be discerned in the increasing tendency to allocate official taxes collected in the district in a "closed circuit," to sectors in the province itself, sometimes within the district's borders. As with other such arrangements, this was not an entirely new idea. Ever since the conquest of the Fertile Crescent, much of the money collected in the region was allocated to specific goals in the region itself. In the sixteenth-century district of Jerusalem this was indeed the rule, not the exception. The greater part of the revenue was allocated for use inside the district: to royal *waqf* institutions, to *timār* and *zeamet* holders, and to other official bodies.

This financial arrangement—a direct link between payer and receiver within the confines of the province—became ubiquitous in the following century, spreading in ever widening circles. One such example, the payment of *avarız* collected in Palestine to *yerliyya* battalions in Damascus, was discussed above. Other examples are the *iḥtisab* taxes, collected in Jerusalem's markets, which were allocated to the soldiers stationed in the district's citadels and fortresses; the custom duties levied at Jaffa's harbor, dedicated to preparation of the pilgrimage caravan to Mecca; and the poll tax (*jizya* and *kharāj*) collected from Jews and Christians, given as payment to ulema in the mosques of al-Aqṣa and the Dome of the Rock.[26]

Sometimes the link between payer and receiver was direct and immediate, as in the case of timariots and *waqf* inspectors who were accustomed to collecting taxes on their own behalf. In other cases the taxes were collected by state officials. The *muḥtasib,* an appointed functionary charged with overseeing the market and checking weights and measures, collected taxes from merchants and craftsmen in the city. Another official, usually an officer, was charged with collection of the poll tax from non-Muslim communities. The use of appointed tax collectors enabled the state to control its revenue to some extent, but weak and withdrawn as it was at the beginning of the seventeenth century, the Ottoman government could not have had much influence on the scope and intensity of tax collection. Such matters were left to the end-receivers to worry about. These latter did not hesitate to put pressure on officials and to encourage them to collect more money from taxpayers, and to deliver it faster. A series of records in the Jerusalem *sijill* describes such a chain of events:

> On 3 Muḥarram 1080 (3 June 1669) several people came to the *sharī'a* court in Jerusalem. Among them were Muṣṭafa Ağa, the commander of the city's citadel, and Sayyid 'Abd al-Salām, his deputy (*kethüda*). They informed our lord the qadi that the local *muḥtasib*, Ḥasan the *bölükbaşı* (janissary company commander), left for Damascus, and has appointed in his place a certain Muḥammad Abu Sunayna to collect the city's market taxes, which are then to be distributed among the soldiers stationed in the citadel. The two men explained that the money is distributed as salary, and requested that the above-mentioned Muḥammad be summoned to court, and forewarned that he must collect the year's market taxes from merchants and craftsmen, and that he has to commit them to the safekeeping of a reliable person. Later they suggested that the money be kept by Muṣṭafa Ağa, the citadel commander, after having collected the sum and duly inscribing it in the *sijill*.
>
> In view of their request the qadi summoned the *muḥtasib*'s representative and cautioned him that he is expected to collect the money accruing from this year's market taxes and to commit the revenue for safekeeping with the said Muṣṭafa Ağa.[27]

Later records in the same register disclose that other soldiers, this time stationed in a small new fortress near the village of Arṭās near Bethlehem, received their salaries from the same source.[28] When they found out that their colleagues in Jerusalem demanded and received the money, they too appealed to the qadi, and demanded their share. The case of market tax revenues and their allocation went on for several sessions of the *sharī'a* court until all claims were settled.

An intricate socioeconomic relationship can thus be discerned through the matter-of-fact description in the *sijill*s. The closed circuit of tax payment, and the proximity between those who paid taxes and those who received the money, created a direct and permanent link between segments of local society. Just as the soldiers in the citadel made sure that the taxes accruing to them are properly collected and distributed, so did other tax-receiving groups. Representatives of Yerliyya battalions sent to Jerusalem checked to see whether "their" *avarız* were collected on time, and ulema in the mosques closely monitored the numbers of Christians and Jews in the city to make sure they were not cheated out of their rightful share of the *jizya*. Local society did not question the moral basis of the clear cut division into rulers and ruled—those who paid taxes and those who received them—as long as this division remained a remote and vague issue, but allocating taxes within the confines of a small district juxtaposed well-defined social groups and created tensions between them. Those who demanded swift and full payment were in direct contact with those who tried to minimize it. The natural outcome of such a system was continued fragmentation of the social system, and even hostility between segments of society which, were it unbridled by this continuous confrontation, could have been avoided.

In an article called "Agenda for Ottoman History," Huri Islamoğlu and Çağlar Keider examine the relationship between the Ottoman Empire's economic structure and its social and political fabric. One of the main reasons for the empire's social stability and for the persistent nature of the "Asiatic mode of production" in its domains, they suggest, is the consistent separation between producers, mainly farmers, and members of the ruling class that received all economic surplus. Peasants in the Ottoman Empire worked as independents, not as serfs, and their only contact with the upper class was through tax collectors. Class tensions were thus alleviated and social integration maintained, to the detriment of more advanced modes of production.[29]

The situation in seventeenth-century Jerusalem, however, points to one of the main weaknesses of this assumption. In the district of Jerusalem direct links developed between taxpayers and tax-receivers in the governing and notable elites. Peasants, merchants, craftsmen or members of religious minorities had to pay tribute directly to janissaries, *sipahi*s or ulema. Negotiations between payers and receivers, pressures for more thorough tax collection, and demands for prompt payment were very much a part of the local reality, and probably led to strife and conflict between segments of society. If the set of production relations typified as the "Asiatic mode of production" did exist in the Ottoman Empire for long, the reasons must be found elsewhere. Exploitation in the Ottoman provinces almost always had a name and a face attached to it.

One way to opt out of the taxpaying cycle was to join a privileged group that did not have to pay taxes, or preferably one that was located at the receiving end. *Ashrāf* were exempt from payment but did not have a stake in the state's treasury. Governors and their retinues, *sipahi*s, janissaries, other military men and ulema were all tax receivers. As the system lost its guiding principles, differences were more apparent within the various componenets of the elite itself. The military used their power to collect taxes even from other elite members. Ulema and other notables petitioned the court and the sultan to grant them tax bonuses, usually on grounds of ancient precedent. Most desperate were the *ashrāf*, who had to fight for tax exemption. This was discernible in villages where families of *ashrāf* descent claimed recognition:

> A group of venerable *ashrāf* from the village of Farkha[30] in the *nāḥiya* (subdistrict) of Jabal Nabulus came to court and notified the qadi that while all *ashrāf* in the region are exempt from local taxes, the governor [of Nabulus] ʿAssāf Bey, leader of the *ḥajj* caravan (*amīr al-ḥajj*), and his officers, harass them and demand all kinds of payments and taxes. These demands are contrary to the *sharīʿa* and to local custom. They requested the qadi to put an end to this harassment and to unreasonable demands for payment made by the governors, their officers, their slaves and their servants. This should be done in accordance with ancient custom, and in honor of their illustrious forefather the messenger [the prophet Muḥammad]. In view of this the qadi sent a message to his highness ʿAssāf Bey *amīr al-ḥajj*, demanding that he and his men stop harassing the villagers of Farkha, and stop demanding payments and taxes. Today a messenger came to court, and brought a letter from the governor. In his letter the honorable ʿAssāf Bey announces that he has received the qadi's message and that in honor of the prophet and the qadi he will instruct his slaves, servants and officers to refrain henceforth from harassing the *ashrāf* inhabitants of Farkha. The qadi then issued a notice prohibiting governors and their representatives from harassing the inhabitants of Farkha in matters of tax collection. Written on 20 Jumāda al-Ūla 1066 (15 March 1656).[31]

Several months later the villagers of Farkha raised a similar claim. In this instance the governor, ʿAssāf Bey, demanded that they pitch in, like all other villages, to pay the expenses of the *ḥajj* caravan. The inhabitants of the village refused and complained to the qadi. This time the governor was more adamant. He brought representatives from the adjacent villages of Jamāʿīn, ʿAqrabā, Balītā, Ḥawārā, Būrīn and al-Kafr. They all testified that from the day they were born it has been common knowledge that the inhabitants of Farkha pay all impositions where the *ḥajj* caravan is concerned. ʿAssāf Bey then told the qadi that some time ago the villagers turned to the qadi in Jerusalem, and asked him to defend them against this demand. In response to a query he wrote to the qadi in Jerusalem and explained that even though they are not entitled to exemption, and there is no such precedent, he decided to honor the qadi's request and refrain from collecting this imposition from the *ashrāf* of Farkha this year.[32]

Similar claims were raised by other villages, some of which sent petitions to the sultan and received firmans exempting them from payment of taxes and impositions. Such attempts were not always successful, however, and in some cases the petitioners' hopes to establish precedents were dashed. It appears that decision-makers in Istanbul required a higher status set (*ashrāf* who were also town dwellers and owners of property, or ulema of certain rank) in order to grant full exemption. Another facet of this struggle for tax exemption is the tension between those who opted out of the taxpaying community, and their neighbors who had to keep paying, and shoulder the burden of those who left. The people of Jamāʿīn, ʿAqrabā, and the other villages mentioned above, were undoubtedly hostile to their Farkhāwi peers who left them to carry the tax burden alone. They were probably happy to oblige the governor and testify in court.[33]

Decentralization of the tax system thus brought forth increased exploitation. As tensions mounted, vertically as well as horizontally, between members of the same social strata, the prospect of internal political crisis loomed ever nearer. In the last decades of the seventeenth century, new, centrally appointed governors joined hands with army officers already serving in the region, to expand the circle of exploitable taxpayers. The ulema, a group that more than any other provided social cement, was a prime target. Soon they too had to pay, either directly or through cruel exploitation of villages they had rented. Profits and property amassed through decades now started to dwindle rapidly, and soon the ulema joined the widening ranks of the oppressed.

INTERNAL TRADE, MERCHANTS AND CRAFTSMEN

While the older Mamluk tax system was taken for granted by the Ottoman authorities, they had much more to say about the organization of urban trades and crafts. In this realm local conditions and precedents were not as crucial, and the Ottoman legislator felt that the system developed in the empire was superior in many respects to anything the Mamluks had to offer. As in other regions of the empire, internal trade in the district of Jerusalem was founded on town-based unions of merchants and craftsmen. Such unions were locally called *ḥirfa* or *ṣinf*, and the *sijill* often uses the term *ṭā'ifā* (pl. *ṭawā'if*—group, sect).[34] These unions resembled medieval European guilds in many respects, but differed from them in other significant ways. In order to avoid the automatic assumption that these institutions were identical, we should make use of local terminology.

Local sources very seldom refer directly to the internal structure and the hierarchy of the *ṭā'ifa*. Details must be inferred and restructured from travel literature and sijill records. These latter also provide a lot of information on the way these institutions operated, and on their important role in social and economic life. It appears that during the century merchant and artisan *ṭawā'if* did not go through major structural changes. They remained dominant economic and cultural institutions.

Ṭawā'if were structured hierarchically. They were headed by a sheikh, sometimes called *ra'īs,* and when representing his peers usually referred to as *mutakallim* (spokesman, representative). Licensed merchants or craftsmen were termed *usta* or *mu'allim*. There seems to have been no differentiation between these two ranks. Apprentices were called *çırak* or *ilf* (companion). The special relationship between master and apprentice was based on personal loyalty, as this short description of a case tried in the Nabulus *sharī'a* court in 1656 demonstrates:

> Muḥammad, of the village of Isdūd in the district of Gaza, sues master barber Yūsuf ibn 'Abdallah.[35] In his complaint the plaintiff claimed that the master Yūsuf has employed his son, Ḥasan, without due authorization from the child's father. He demands that the master return the son to his parents' custody. Master barber Yūsuf, questioned on the matter, said that the boy joined his employ of his own free will, and wishes to stay with his master and learn the trade. The boy was therefore summoned and questioned, and he too replied that he wished to stay with his master in order to learn the barber's profession.
>
> In view of these declarations the qadi informed the plaintiff that he is not to get custody of his son, unless the son himself so wishes, since the boy is now a mature companion (*ilf 'āqil*). He warned the plaintiff against trying to harm the defendant or harass him.[36]

The *ṭā'ifa* sheikh was formally appointed by the qadi in a ceremony which took place inside the *sharī'a* court.[37] In most cases, however, the qadi did not intervene in choosing the person to head the organization. Neither did he have any say in appointing the master craftsmen or merchants in the *ṭā'ifā*. Deciding these matters was left to the members themselves. In all *sijill* cases where the qadi appoints a head of a *ṭā'ifa*, it is done, at least ostensibly, by request of the masters of that *ṭā'ifa*, and the person chosen is the one recommended by the members. On the other hand, the qadi was authorized to remove a sheikh who was found guilty of crimes or wrongdoing:

> On 13 Rabī' al-Awwal 1033 (4 January 1624) Muḥammad ibn Nuḥaysi sued the Christian Arslān, the sheikh of the jewelers' *ṭā'ifa* (*al-ṣuyyāgh*) in Jerusalem. In his claim the plaintiff declared that he had paid the sheikh 11 *ghurūsh riyāl* (Spanish reals) and 8 Egyptian *qiṭ'a*, worth together 12 *ghurūsh asadi* (Dutch *löwen rikstalers*). In return the sheikh was to buy one hundred *dirham* of silver, and cast a sheath

> for the plaintiff's sword. The plaintiff claimed that the defendant bought impure silver, and stamped it with the stamp of pure silver, to deceive the client. The defendant claimed that, on the contrary, he bought more silver than he was asked to buy—122 *dirham*—and therefore the plaintiff owes him 2.5 *ghurūsh* more.[38]
>
> In order to check both claims, the qadi ordered that the sheath in question be melted down, and the silver content examined. Another jeweller, a certain Constantine, was summoned to melt down the sheath in the presence of the qadi, but while this examination was taking place, the defendant was caught throwing 15 *dirham* of silver into the melting pot. When the examination was over, the pot was found to contain only 105 *dirham* [and not 115 *dirham*, as would have been the case had the 15 *dirham* thrown in by the defendant been added to 100 *dirham* in the bowl].
>
> In view of this result the qadi ruled that the defendant is a liar and a forger, and is not worthy of the title of *sheikh ṭā'ifa*. He is to be chastised and removed from his office.[39]

Several days later a new sheikh was appointed for the jewelers' *ṭā'ifa*. This time it was Yūsuf ibn Muṣṭafa, a Muslim, appointed, the record declared, because his predecessor was found out to be a liar. The new sheikh was apparently elected by the members of the *ṭā'ifa* and the qadi was required to give his consent to the choice. The government's involvement in the way the *ṭawā'if* were conducted was thus limited mainly to cases where the person in charge failed in his duty, or breached the authorities' trust. Yet the qadi had no qualms about removing the sheikh, and the heads of the *ṭā'ifa* accepted his jurisdiction in the matter.

The *ṭā'ifa*'s code of conduct required that its members coordinate the rules of their trade, the prices and the division of revenue among themselves. In the former century the qadi, assisted by the *muḥtasib*, would publish a detailed and compulsory price list from time to time. These lists reflected the state of demand and supply of most basic foodstuffs, and at the same time influenced the market and prevented artificially induced high prices. Later on such lists became more infrequent, and at the beginning of the seventeenth century the price lists disappeared altogether. So yet another important tool of economic supervision was forsaken. From this time on merchants and craftsmen were authorized to determine their own prices for commodities and the quality of products offered in the market. A dispute in the greengrocers' *ṭā'ifa* in 1702, is a typical example:

> In mid-Rabī' al-thāni 1114 (August–September 1702) several members of the greengrocers *ṭā'ifa* (*al-khuḍariyya*) in Jerusalem arrived in court, among them ḥājj Qāsim, ḥājj Ḥijāzi, Ḥājj Ismā'īl, Ḥajj

> Muṭāwi', Dawūd and Badr. They claimed that their colleague from Ramla, Ḥijāzı, buys and sells vegetables in the market as he pleases, and does not share with them his gains and losses, as he should according to the old custom that requires all those who buy and sell vegetables in the market to be on a par with their colleagues.[40]
>
> At this stage Ḥijāzı declared that from now on he does not intend to stand in opposition to his comrades' sale and purchase of vegetables. He mentioned that according to his reckoning his friends owe him four *ghurūsh*, but he will waive this debt as a sign of good will on his part.[41]

The qadi, then, did not determine the level of prices and the allocation of profits. He was approached in this matter as a neutral arbitrator who had no say of his own in determining prices. He indicated that both sides should adhere to the rules prevailing in the union, and refrained from commenting about these rules. The qadi accepted the greengrocers' claim that they are free to set their own prices as a cartel, and to prevent free competition between merchants. This attitude, which defined the *ṭā'ifa* as the center of economic decision-making, is also apparent in another case, tried in court some thirty years earlier:

> On 11 Jumāda al-Ākhira 1081 (26 October 1670) several people came to the *sharī'a* court in Jerusalem, among them Ḥājj Maḥmūd al-Dawūd, Ḥājj 'abd al-Ḥaqq ibn Muḥammad, the sheikh of the *ṭā'ifa* of the oil-press workers (*ma'ṣariyyā*) in the city, and Ḥājj Badr al-Dīn, the former *muḥtasib* of Jerusalem, all members of the oil-press *ṭā'ifa*. They claimed that the porters of sesame seed [for the production of oil] have started delivering dirty loads of merchandise, full of shells and dust, and heap it up on their thresholds in the street. Until the present time they were used to getting their sesame free of dirt, and the new practice is harmful to their trade and property. They requested that the qadi order the sesame seed porters to cease this new practice, and threatened that if this state of affairs continues, they may have to consider going out of business.

The qadi, unimpressed by the threat, made it clear to the members of the *ṭā'ifa* that sale and purchase are only possible when both sides come to an agreement (*'ala tarāḍ min al-bā'i' wa-l-mushtarı*) and that no one can oppose anyone else wishing to undertake a certain line of work or to abandon it. The members of the *ṭā'ifa* have a right to receive their sesame seed in better condition, as they have in the past, but this is something they must agree upon with their colleagues, the porters of sesame seed.[42]

A similar spirit of laissez-faire prevailed in most areas of trade and commerce. Local government, taking its cues from Istanbul, reduced its involvement in the daily management of the province's economy to a minimum. But this relative freedom was restricted to the *ṭā'ifa* level. Its members were allowed to set prices according to the state of supply and demand, or to make internal arrangements for the allocation of profits. In order to protect the *ṭā'ifa*, the Ottoman authorities, represented by the qadi, would defend its members in their struggles against individuals or groups who threatened to take away the *ṭā'ifa*'s monopolist control over a certain domain. Such was the case when members of the dyers' *ṭā'ifa* in Jerusalem found out that a group of merchants from Hebron was conspiring to take over their line of business:

> On 25 Shaʿbān 1081 (7 January 1671) Yūsuf *bashsha*[43] ibn Mahmud came to court. He notified the qadi that he was representing the dyers (*al-ṣabbāghīn*) *ṭā'ifa* in Jerusalem, and claimed that several people have arrived in the city from Hebron, among them a certain Shaʿbān and his brother. Having purchased clothes and indigo dye (*nīl*) in Hebron, these people sell their products directly to the inhabitants of Jerusalem, thus threatening the livelihood and standing of *ṭā'ifa* members. Yūsuf *bashsha* requested that the qadi prohibit this practice. After checking the details of the complaint, the qadi did so.[44]

The qadi was prepared to go a long way to protect *ṭā'ifa* members against the assaults of individuals, but even he drew the line at attempts by certain groups of merchants to cooperate in illegally storing foodstuffs or other necessary commodities in order to create an artificial shortage in the city and then raise prices. Local authorities were also afraid that real shortages might be created by this kind of unethical commercial activity. In such cases the qadi would summon the members of the *ṭā'ifa* suspected of breaching the regulations, and warn them that they will bear the consequences:

> On 4 Rajab 1080 (28 November 1669) the *muʿallim* Sharaf ibn Muṣṭafa *al-Raṣṣāṣ*,[45] the *kayyāl bāshi*[46] complained to the qadi that several of the merchants in the market, including Muḥammad ibn Muṣṭafa al-Raṣṣāṣ (a relative of the *kayyāl bāshi*?) as well as Aḥmad ibn Abi ʿAlā' and others, are buying great quantities of wheat and storing it in their depots near the market, in order to sell them later at exorbitant prices. These practices, he claimed, are detrimental to the interests of the people. He requested that the culprits be summoned to court.
>
> Having verified the details the qadi summoned the suspected merchants and warned them against creating artificial shortages in town.[47]

Motivated by the belief that constant supply of basic foodstuffs to the city at reasonable prices was the first duty of any government, Ottoman officials saw such practices as a serious offence, and did their best to prevent real or artificial shortages in the market.[48] Any attempt to make financial gains out of such shortages was severely punished. On the other hand, however, the qadi and his officers provided no protection for merchants and craftsmen against exploitation by the governing elite.

Up until the 1670s and 1680s a relatively stable system of give and take was established between local ruling dynasties and the *ṭawā'if*. In the last three decades of the century, however, as the central bureaucracy, headed by vezirs of the Köprülü family, managed to reassert its control over the provinces and to destroy most local dynasties, the internal balance in the districts of Palestine was shaken. Unlike previous governors, the new ones sent by Istanbul did not feel any attachment to their new dominions, and usually saw them as a brief stopover on the way to greater glory. In many cases their treatment of the local populace was unusually harsh and cruel.

The plight of merchants, many of whom were obliged to supply the governor and his retinue with food and luxuries free of charge, finds expression in petitions and letters sent to Istanbul to protest against such humiliating practices. These petitions were often aimed at the *"ahl al-'urf,"* the local-Ottoman governing elite which included army forces stationed in the area, *sipahis*, bureaucrats, the governor's retinue, and retainers of his servants and henchmen. Some letters were sent directly to the sultan in Istanbul, while others reached the governor's palace in Damascus. All testify to the qadi's inability to assist the petitioners:

> In the middle of Jumādā al-Ūla 1114 (October 1702) Ḥājj Kassāb al-Fakhri, the sheikh of the potters *ṭā'ifa* (*al-fawākhiriyya*, or *bardakcılar* in Turkish) came to the *sharī'a* court in Jerusalem, and presented a sultanic edict dated mid-Rajab 1113 (December 1701). The firman (summarized briefly in the *sijill*) recounts that the potters' *ṭā'ifa* had sent a petition to the sultan and claimed that *ahl al-'urf* in Jerusalem often seize pottery and earthenware objects from them by force, and do not pay for them. The edict instructs the governors[49] to stop this kind of mistreatment, and to instruct their entourages to cease this habit of forcibly taking merchandise from the potters.[50]

Local notables, mainly *'ulamā*, sympathized with the struggle of these merchants and craftsmen, many of whom were related to them through marriage and business partnerships. Here and there a group of local notables joined together to help them, as the following record in the *Mühimme Defterleri* demonstrates:

> Mid-Rabīʿ al-Thāni 1112 (end of September 1700). An order to the qadi of Jerusalem.
>
> You, the above-mentioned qadi, have sent a letter to my palace, and the rest of the ulema, the *sādāt* and the notables of Jerusalem have sent a petition [claiming that] the governors of the district and their appointed deputies (*mütesellim*) do not pay the prices of goods they take. Moreover, they abuse people and mistreat them. The petitioners requested a royal edict in the matter.
>
> Therefore you, the qadi, should see to it that governors, deputies and others of the governing elite pay the full price of goods to those entitled to such payment, and that they do so every month. Do not allow any postponement or evasion, and prevent harm or suffering.[51]

Small wonder, then, that when rebellion broke out at the end of 1702, the merchants and craftsmen hurried to collect their debts from the few officials still trapped inside the city:

> ʿAli Ağa, pride of the *aʿyān*, former deputy of the former governor of Jerusalem, Muḥammad Pasha, came to court today and reminded the qadi that when Muḥammad Pasha left the city at the beginning of Ṣafar (June 1702) he was appointed deputy. During the three months from the beginning of Rabīʿ al-Ākhir to mid-Rajab (September to November) this year, he had expenses totalling 230 *ghurūsh asadī*. His expenses included payment for bread, meat, coffee, *dibs* (grape syrup), olive oil, barley for camels, onion, the wages of the water carrier and the gatekeeper, and expenses for the lodging and food of *sekbān* soldiers sent there from Nabulus by the pasha. He asked the qadi to summon the heads of merchant unions (*aṣnāf*) in town and to inspect his statement with them.
>
> Consequently, several merchants including ʿĀmir the butcher, Shaʿbān the *bazār bāshi*, and Ḥājj Mūsa the baker came to court and confirmed that they have received payment in full from ʿAlī Ağa for meat, bread, oil, *samn* (clarified butter) and other merchandise for the said period, and that ʿAli Ağa does not owe them any money. ʿAli Ağa also confirmed these words, and by doing so was declared free of his debt towards them for all the above-mentioned commodities. Established in accordance with the *sharīʿa* at our lord the qadi's court, on 12 Rabīʿ al-Thāni 1114 (5 September 1702).[52]

Could it be the rage of Jerusalem's merchants, exploited for so many years by the governing elite, that hides beneath the surface of this record? Public announcements of merchants and craftsmen at court that they received payment from the governor and his household for goods supplied was a regular feature of economic life. Such announcements were recorded in the *sijill* from time to time. Yet here the governor's deputy, the *mutasallim* himself, humbly appears in court as a public servant accounting for his actions, and specifies his expenses, including items never before discussed in public. The debtors do not wait for him in court in awed silence. They show up only when summoned by the qadi, and graciously accept the money. But the merchants' satisfaction, if that is what it was, did not last long. Soon the revolt was put down, and the new governors, backed by a bigger and hungrier army, were no better than the old ones.

All in all, Jerusalem's commercial world was based on the same basic concepts and assumptions as the one laid out by taxation systems. The central government's ability to oversee traders and craftsmen and to regulate their unions had waned considerably in the sixteenth century. A relative measure of law and order gave way to a loose agglomeration of incoherent rules. The representatives of Ottoman rule adhered to a few basic principles, such as preserving the monopoly of each *ṭā'ifa* in its realm, constant supply of basic foodstuffs, and prohibition of arbitrary pricing. Yet they allowed trade and commerce to take their course, abandoning old practices of price regulation and production quotas.

Under different conditions this could have sufficed to give commerce a much needed boost and allow it to take off again, but such a market economy had a darker side. The local government did not provide protection for the merchants and craftsmen against its own representatives, members of the governing elite, who did their best to skim most of the economic surplus, took away much needed capital, and thus allowed very limited scope for expansion and development.

FOREIGN TRADE AND CONTACT WITH EUROPE

During the Mamluk period Palestine's trade via the Mediterranean littoral was very limited. In the wake of the Crusades all coastal towns were deserted and most harbors were destroyed. These conditions provided no safe haven for ships, and none of the necessary services. The main bulk of trade with Europe and North Africa was directed by the Mamluk rulers to the ports of Lebanon, Northern Syria and Egypt. Right after the conquest the Ottomans prohibited export of commodities such as wheat and cotton. This prohibition, meant to prevent the draining of vital commodities by a rich and thirsty European market, slowed down the process of restoration. But in the course of the seventeenth century, the coastal towns of Palestine were gradually revived.[53]

During the century foreign trade went through two significant shifts. First, the ban on exports to Europe was either lifted or eroded by repeated infringements. Throughout the period, in documents from both the center and the province, there is no mention of such a ban, or of the need to fight exports to Europe. The central government (unlike local one) even tried to encourage foreign trade, with France in particular, and to alleviate the tax burden on foreign and local traders. The second shift had to do with the type of commodities and the trade balance. In the former century the most important items of trade, exported to Europe in spite of the ban, were wheat and other cereals. In the seventeenth century, however, cereals diminished in importance, and were replaced by other items, mainly cotton, soap, and alkaline ashes for the production of soap. Wheat was of secondary importance, and bought by foreign traders only in years of bad harvests in Europe.[54]

Muslim sources tend to remain silent on the matter of foreign trade with Europe during the century. This is perhaps an indication that some of the old prohibitions on export were still enforced, but even more than that, it indicates that the volume of trade with Europe was relatively small. Had it been of more consequence, its problems would have found their way into *sijills*, *fatāwā* collections, or other written documents. In the course of the century this volume of trade may have developed somewhat, but not enough to leave a serious impression in local legal or historical records. Another indication is the fact that income from port customs was usually not a serious bone of contention between officers, officials and local magnates.

Most of the source material concerning this trade is to be found in European archives, mainly in France. French merchants were among the first to establish a *nation*, a small trading community, in Acre and in Ramla (for the port of Jaffa). These merchants, as well as men of commerce and diplomats from other European states, passed on valuable economic information to their countrymen and authorities. They sent in reports about encounters, terms of trade, weather conditions and potential values. In the ports of Europe, particularly in the port of Marseilles, these reports coincided with an attempt to regulate the flow of commodities in and out of the country, and local harbors started recording ship movements and merchandise to and from the Levant. Important information, of a more impressionistic nature, can be obtained from the descriptions of travelers and pilgrims.

On the Palestinian coast, Acre was the most important port, vying with its northern neighbor, Sayda, for primacy as the major port of the region. Jaffa, the coastal town closest to Jerusalem, was much smaller in comparison, and at the beginning of the century only a trickle of trade passed through it. From the beginning of the period it was described by pilgrims as a half-deserted village, with no harbor to speak of. This is how it was described by the Russian monk Sukhanov in 1649:

> Ancient is the town of Jaffa. Once very big, now only traces remain: a few Arab tents beside the sea, and a little food market near the ships' docking place. A small new fortress was erected on a mountain by the sea. It is guarded night and day.[55]

And a similar description by an Englishman twenty years later:

> We arrived at Joppa, which hath no harbor to defend ships from storms, but very good ground to anchor in, about ten fathom water. It is a poor town and hath one castle to defend those ships that come in close to the shoar. The chief trade thereof is pot-ashes for soap, cottons and cotton yarn, which the Franks bring from thence.[56]

Jaffa had no harbor. Its moorings, exposed to the wind and the waves, were sometimes dangerous. The only advantage was its proximity to Jerusalem and to the fertile plains of Ramla, the main source for cotton in the area. Yet this was not enough to create a need for further development until well into the eighteenth century. Another factor which slowed down development was frequent attacks by pirates on ships at anchor. Such attacks were carried out by Christian and Muslim pirates alike. Christian pirates, many of them French, were particularly detrimental to European trade, because they sometimes hoisted European flags on approaching the coast, and surprised the unsuspecting Muslim ships docked there and the inhabitants of the small community itself. The damage caused by such raids made the authorities suspicious of European merchants, and they were often accused of trying to assist the pirates. Similar raids by Muslim pirates on French ships were seen as retaliation for Christian atrocities, and sometimes even encouraged by the local garrison, as we learn from a letter sent by local French merchants to Marseille:

> While soap was being loaded on a [French] ship in Jaffa, a small vessel from Salé (in Algeria) entered the docking area. The vessel, manned by a crew of forty corsairs, attacked the ship. The captain and four of his people were taken prisoner and reduced to slavery, and their ship was burned. When the raid was over, the captain of the pirate vessel, *ra'īs* Ibrāhīm, went ashore, brought presents to the customs master, and both sat down to have coffee together.
>
> Since the pasha had gone away on the pilgrimage to Mecca, the [French] merchants complained to his deputy, but it is clear that this one, who is not as honest as his master, will not do anything.[57]

Whether Christian or Muslim, these corsair attacks hampered the development of Jaffa and its vicinity, and delayed the development of trade with Europe. Such incidents became more frequent in the 1680s and 1690s, until, under pressure from Western ambassadors in the sultan's court, a decision was taken to improve the harbor's defensive measures. In 1690 an edict was sent to the governor of Gaza and Jerusalem, Murtaḍa Pasha, commanding him to protect Jaffa and its harbor by sending an adequate number of *timar* and *zeamet* holders on regular shifts of duty to the site.[58] Such measures did not suffice, however, and a decade later the government had to resort to other means. In 1703 new cannon were brought and stationed in the small fortress. This caused some uproar by local customs officials and clerks who used the fortress as a convenient depot and working place. The new guns needed a lot of space, and the officials were told to leave the fortress and find some other residence. In a hearing at the Jerusalem *sharīʿa* court, the officials (and several merchants) demanded that the new guns be placed atop the fortress walls, not in the courtyard. But the local commander refused, claiming that the walls were not strong or stable enough to carry the cannon. The qadi's decision in this matter is not on record, but it seems that whatever measures were taken, they did not suffice. Pirate raids did not stop, and Jaffa was still a favorite of corsairs in following decades.[59]

Daily tribulations, added to such corsair attacks, made life miserable for the few European merchants residing in Ramla and Acre. Some of these difficulties were caused by fear and suspicion, and by a wide cultural gap. Others were the result of the fluctuating political relations between the Ottoman Empire and their respective homelands. English merchants of the Levant Company apparently decided to give up the Palestinian littoral altogether, and preferred to stay in Aleppo, and to purchase cotton in Ramla through a local agent. This cotton was sent to Acre on barges or boats, and loaded on three or four English ships every year. The Dutch ran a similar operation, and they too bought about four shiploads of cotton a year.[60] The only ones to choose Ramla and Acre as a permanent base were the French, who resided there from the beginning of the century, and only left for short periods when conditions became unbearable.[61]

The small *nation* in Ramla sent letters to France complaining of corruption, mistreatment by the authorities and the population, and difficulties in establishing trade contacts. They were forced to pay high custom rates and to bribe local officials regularly. Their negotiations with farmers and local merchants were carried out using an unfamiliar and unstable set of weights and measures. Some of these problems were debated in the Jerusalem *sharīʿa* court in 1623:

> [It appears that] the affairs of the inhabitants of Ramla and Jaffa have been confused, and they are much given to investigating and checking about weights and measures and their use for commerce at this time. The current state of affairs is that when they weigh merchandise "against" buyers (*idha iktālū ʿala al-nās*) they get the right price, whereas if they weigh correctly, or in favor of the client, they receive less than the price intended for the product. It was therefore checked in the ledger of affairs (*dīwān al-umūr*) for the general public, and it was found that the *mudd* [heavy weight measure] in Ramla and in the port of Jaffa is precisely twice the *mudd* in Jerusalem, so that one Ramla *mudd* is worth two Jerusalem *mudd*s. When the Jerusalem *mudd* was checked, it was found to weigh exactly thirteen and one third *raṭl*s of rice, and the Jerusalem *raṭl* was found to weigh 840 *dirham*, as the specialists and *waqf* officials in Jerusalem have established. In accordance with this an edict has been published on 14 Ṣafar 1033 (7 December 1623).[62]

The reasons for this confusion are not explained, but it may have been the natural deterioration of metal weights used by the merchants in Ramla and Jaffa. Reading this record, though, we may begin to understand the kind of difficulties encountered by French merchants and the differences in culture between them and their hosts. The local system of coins, weights and measures, complex and incoherent even to local inhabitants, was undoubtedly suspect from the start in a Frenchman's eye. Attempts by Ramlan merchants to get the right price by weighing "against" clients only made things worse, and led to a feeling of mistrust and suspicion among the French. These feelings find expression in letters sent to the chamber of commerce in Marseilles, and in reports sent by consuls to the ministry of foreign affairs in Paris.[63]

The feeling of mistrust was reciprocated. When the Druze emir Fakhr al-Din II, aided by the Christian princes of Toscana, attempted to conquer the districts of Palestine at the beginning of the century, rumors about a new crusade, never far from the surface, began to circulate again. Such rumors had a crucial influence on relations between Christians and Muslims in the area. Thus Jean Lempereur, who was appointed consul in Jerusalem in 1623, found himself isolated from the governors and officials of the city by a wall of suspicion, and was finally arrested and deported.[64]

In the second half of the seventeenth century, following a period of withdrawal caused by the Ottoman-Venetian war, and by internal difficulties in France itself, the French merchants returned to Palestine. Trade was revived and even grew for a while. One of the reasons for the growth in trade was worsening relations between the French merchants and the governor of Sayda in Lebanon. The French trading community was forced to leave Sayda, and many of the traders found refuge in Acre and Ramla. The newcomers encountered many new difficulties, and some were even prepared to go back to Sayda, and to suffer the harshness of the governor there, instead of the going through the hardships and misery of life in Acre or Ramla. As one trader who decided to return to Sayda said: "It is enough to have suffered one year in such a miserable place, where we have lost so many of our colleagues." Yet it was in this dark period that the foundations were laid for a permanent French presence, and for the continued export of cotton, ashes for soap-making and, occasionally, wheat.[65]

Another factor which contributed to the growth in trade was the new policy promoted by the palace and the government in France. In 1661 Colbert was appointed minister of commerce. His main goal was developing France's trade and industry in order to compete with England. Trade with the cotton-rich Levant was therefore a cornerstone in his policy, and French ambassadors to the Sublime Porte were instructed to demand concessions for traders and to press for the appointment of consuls in these regions of the Ottoman Empire. As a result, many of the dragomans and officials who stood in the way of French merchants in port towns were removed and replaced by others. The defence of ports against corsair raids was improved, and trade flourished again. The amount of cotton imported from the Levant into France grew steadily, and at the beginning of the eighteenth century exports and imports between France and the Levant were balanced. In 1721 French imports from the Levant were calculated as 531,293 French pounds (livres), while the exports were 532,216 livres.[66]

A few years earlier, in the mid-seventeenth century, in order to encourage imports for industrial purposes and help the burgeoning textile industry in France, custom fees on cotton bought in the Levant were reduced. At the end of the century, however, with France's Carribean colonies gaining in economic importance, the state council (*conseil d'etat*) decided to erect barriers against Levant cotton imports, and to make trade with the eastern Mediterranean much less profitable for both traders and manufacturers. On 11 December 1691 a new, unexpected edict was published, raising custom fees on cotton yarn to an unprecedented high, and at the same time lowering customs on Carribean cotton to about ten percent of its former level. The French infrastructure in Lebanon and Palestine was on the verge of collapse.

But, as the French government soon learned, trade with the Levant was even more crucial for France than it estimated. It soon became clear that the damages sustained by the French textile industry were much more severe than the profits made in America. The owners of textile factories, concentrated in and around the city of Lyon, were desperate. In letters and petitions to the king and the council they pleaded that they need cotton yarn spun in the Levant, because they do not possess the technical knowledge to process Levant cotton and spin it into yarn strong enough for their machines to weave. The cotton imported from America, on the other hand, can be spun and woven, but "is not of a quality suitable for the factories in Lyon."[67] As a result of the new French policy, trade with the Levant was indeed reduced, but the wheels of France's textile industry almost ground to a halt along with it. Faced with repeated requests, the council yielded and in 1700 another edict was declared, annulling the former edict and lowering taxes on Levant cotton to their former rates.[68] In the wake of this decision, trade with the Levant ports was soon back to normal, and Marseilles' registers indicate that from this point on most of the cotton imported into France was "coton de Jerusalem" and a smaller share is described as "coton de Rame" or "coton d'Acre." The volume of trade throughout the first years of the eighteenth century was slowly rising.[69]

In an article on international competition and the Ottoman textile industries in the sixteenth and seventeenth centuries, Benjamin Braude claims that the leaders of the Ottoman Empire were uninterested in catering to economic needs of private subjects and enterprises not entirely congruent with those of the state. Such state interests were often perceived very narrowly as supplies for the army and for other security forces. European industries could not claim a technological advantage over local ones at the time. Indeed, sometimes the opposite was true. Local industries were more advanced and of higher quality. But there was no merchant or entrepreneurial stratum of the kind prominent in England. No social group had risen to fight for a more aggressive economic policy, to equip local industry to cope with the challenges of rising costs and commodity dumping by foreign merchants. The state's main concern was taxation and allocation, and open borders for commodities were perceived as a means to increase income. Production by local craftsmen, on the other hand, was heavily taxed. Ottoman trades and crafts were thus at a marked disadvantage.[70]

Summing up the conditions of Jerusalem's foreign trade, we can conclude that it fits the above description. In comparison with the dynamic approach of French authorities to trade with the Levant, and even in comparison with the active cohesion of industrialists in Lyon, governors and traders in Jerusalem, and in the Ottoman Empire in general, were oblivious to the big picture, and failed to see the advantages of concerted action. They made no attempt to manage the trade, failed to defend the vital interests of local commerce and agriculture, and did nothing when the volume of trade subsided for a while. Although the revenues to be gained from foreign trade were tremendous, there was no attempt to provide better conditions for French traders, or to stimulate trade with France and its competitors. Provincial governors repeatedly saw foreign merchants as a nuisance and a potential security threat, and often blamed them for assisting corsair raids.

THE LONG ROAD TO PERIPHERALIZATION

This description can be perceived as part of a wider unfolding process: the assimilation of Ottoman economy into the world's emerging economic system. It is usually accepted that this process of "peripheralization," through which large areas of the world became an economic periphery totally dependent on the industry and technology of Western Europe, had reached its apex in the mid-nineteenth century. Even if we do not accept the neo-Marxist premises of such a description of the process, the way it is seen to have unfolded, with an economic core emerging in Europe, and a periphery in ever-widening circles around it, provides an invaluable insight into the situation in the Levant area in later centuries. The initiation of this process is one of the issues that bewilder researchers of Ottoman economic history. When did the empire as a whole, and more specifically the eastern shores of the Mediterranean, become so deeply involved with the European world economy? When did they become a dependent periphery of the industrialized world?[71]

Determined efforts by the French government and its traders and representatives in the area, coupled with the dismissive attitude of local merchants, had initiated a slow but constant process of change in the local economy. More and more primary resources and agricultural products were exported to Europe throughout the century. At the same time the volume of import of finished products from Europe increased steadily, some, perhaps, were products made in Europe from Levant materials, such as wool and cotton, and redirected into the area.

During the seventeenth century, however, this process was only in its very early stages. The volume of trade was not very significant, and as we have seen, at this point in time French merchants, like the English and Dutch, were more dependent on production in the Levant than vice versa. Local manufacture was still equipped to output products of a quality that factories in Europe were unable to imitate. The failure of the French state council to decrease trade with the Levant and to redirect cotton trade to its own American colonies demonstrates the problems faced by the French textile manufacture, still dependent on Ottoman production techniques. Yet it may be safely assumed that consumption habits of the local population were not yet based on European commodities, and that imports were mostly luxury items: small quantities of expensive fabrics, guns, spices, paper and foreign currency.

In the previous century the Ottoman government tried to prevent contraband exportation of raw materials to Europe. Now, at least as far as the government was concerned, trade flowed without hindrance. Ottoman rule did not strive to prevent trade, but to collect its revenues, even at the cost of losing control over exported quantities. European traders made nice profits. Capitulations agreed to by the central government in Istanbul guaranteed the traders reduced tax payments and safe transportation, and made it possible for them to conduct business in the hostile atmosphere prevalent in some provinces.

At the same time local taxation systems appear to have lost their guiding principles. Collection was decentralized and became more arbitrary. The Ottoman center gave up control of internal trade and of local merchant and craftsmen unions. The prices of merchandise sold in the markets were decided by the merchants themselves with no government interference. The same was true for monetary systems. A large part of the coins in use were foreign, and the Ottoman government made almost no attempt to control their flow or their value. All these symptoms indicate a marked decrease in government involvement in provincial economy, and perhaps even in the economy of the imperial center. This growing vacuum was filled by a marked increase in the importance of market forces.

Keyder and Islamoğlu, two economic historians of the Ottoman Empire, claim that when the state lost its ability to control external and internal trade and to oversee monetary and fiscal systems, it also lost the ability to direct the economy and to reproduce the economic basis of government. In other words, loss of control over the economy also meant losing the capability to maintain the Ottoman Empire as a closed economic system perpetuated by the ruling elite. As a result of this weakness, this isolated economic system went through a phase of disarticulation which led to penetration by the Western world economy, and eventually to peripheralization.[72]

In the district of Jerusalem decentralization and the breakup of central control led in two different directions: on the one hand, a measure of liberty and prospects of development for private enterprises and market economy, and on the other, increased exploitation of the population by local forces. In this second respect the decentralization of Ottoman rule did not lead to a weakening of power altogether. From the subjects' point of view decentralized rule doubled the pressure of government and its local agents. Instead of one government there were now several—the sultan, the provincial governor, the district governor and his lackeys. In economic terms, at least, this situation led to the impoverishment of the population at large, and to a gradual weakening of the Ottoman economy.

Yet, even though some of the necessary conditions existed, the district of Jerusalem did not become a periphery of the emerging world economy. Its economic systems were to a large extent separate from those of Europe, its port towns were only partly rebuilt, the volume of trade was relatively small and, it seems, well balanced. In terms used by adherents of world economy theory, there was as yet no real confrontation between the Mediterranean-Atlantic "world economy" and the Mediterranean shores of the Ottoman "world empire."[73]

The process was stalled for several reasons. The first has to do with the Western core itself. The European drive for industrialization was only then beginning to affect trade. In many domains, such as the soap industry or the textile industry, Western Europe had no significant advantage over the Islamic world. Aggressive capitalist and mercantilist policies have already begun to play a considerable role, and in the course of the sixteenth and seventeenth centuries caused a considerable weakening of Ottoman industries such as wool and cotton. But such policies did not destroy the basis of Ottoman industry altogether. Quite a few manufactures in various parts of the empire succeeded in competing with this pressure, and even in flourishing under these conditions.[74]

Another reason for the failure to peripheralize was the attitude of the inhabitants, specifically those of Jerusalem and its coastal plain, towards the Christian West. The trauma of the Crusades (whether historical or mythic) in collective memory, and the recent memories of Fakhr al-Din's exploits, aided by a militant church spirit revived in Northern Italy earlier in the century, all led to suspicion. Stories were recounted of renewed attempts by Christian armies to subdue the Ottoman Empire and to conquer the Holy Land. These fears have been the cause of repeated insults directed at Christian merchants, and of hostility towards their consuls and representatives. In such an atmosphere traders found it very difficult to promote their business and had to content themselves with a precarious status and a mission fraught with danger.

The main cause, however, for the failure of European trade to take over commerce and industry in these parts had to do with decentralization itself. The temporary weakness of central rule, the empire retreating into itself, the concentration of all available resources in order to defend itself on several fronts, all these left the district with no focal point of its own. In the second half of the century, the central government in Istanbul attempted to obliterate local dynasties, but failed in the attempt to replace them by competent governors appointed by the center and to recentralize rule. In the course of the century no substitute center of gravity was created in Palestine and its vicinity. Local notables had indeed acquired a high economic and social status, but had very little political power, and for most of the century they were not capable of imagining themselves as a group with political clout. Merchants and craftsmen did not cooperate outside their guilds and unions, and did not form a cohesive force united in its outlook. The hazy outlines of such a center led by the notables were only beginning to emerge at the end of the seventeenth century, but they too were effaced by the Naqīb al-Ashrāf revolt.

All this considered, it was almost impossible for the local population to maintain a coherent economic policy. Since land was usually divided into small lots, and very few were concentrated in the hands of one person or one family, foreign merchants had to deal with many small-scale farmers and merchants, with different aims and policies. Buying commodities on a large scale for one set price was unimaginable. French traders had to maneuver to the best of their ability in the economic quicksands of the district. In this atmosphere no large-scale or long-term contracts could be negotiated.

The obvious weakness of the economic center, and its inability to concentrate and regulate trade, or at least to direct it in a more concentrated beam, as it were, was in some ways an advantage for foreign traders. French and English merchants did not have a powerful cartel to contend with, and could, to some extent at least, dictate the terms of trade. On the other hand, the difficulties involved in trying to gather a substantial shipment of one commodity were so great, that even old hands, merchants familiar with local conditions, were unable to purchase or sell large quantities. In this respect the seventeenth century was once more an interim period between late-sixteenth-century decentralization, which entailed a lessening of control over landholding and trade, and the rise of local power brokers a century later. These new rulers attached emphasis to tax farms (which in several cases merged into very large personal estates) and the recuperation of coastal towns and ports. Both were events that, in the local sphere, accelerated the pace of peripheralization.

Chapter 7

Worlds Apart

WOMEN IN A MEN'S WORLD

The lives of women in Ottoman Jerusalem should not be seen as a monolithic, uniform pattern, unchanging through time. They were, quite naturally, bound up with those of men in corresponding socioeconomic groups. When hard times or harsh rulers deprived men of their status and property, women were also affected. When fallahin were allowed to buy and sell land, village women prospered too. In this sense there was no real difference between the sexes. Yet the changing patterns of gender roles did not necessarily follow the curve of political and economic events. Here the effects of such changes traced a path of their own, spanning a longer *durée*. To see what women's lives were like in seventeenth-century Jerusalem and how they were reflected in historical sources, we should turn to the texts and documents.

Women in Jerusalem did not write about themselves, at least not until the middle of the nineteenth century. In the attempt to reconstruct their cultural life and social position, we must rely on other sources of information. One such important source is travel literature. Another is the *sijill* records kept by the Muslim *sharī'a* court. These two types of material evoke images of women so different from one another as to suggest a deeper underlying cultural cause. Describing these different images we may attempt to uncover some of the stereotypes and biases they reflect. The contradictory attitudes of the two sources thus become both a means for understanding women's history in the period and an end in itself—an attempt to assess the different contributions of two types of sources to the history of the Ottoman provinces.

WOMEN IN TRAVEL LITERATURE

Many of the travelers to the Holy Land in the seventeenth century made few observations regarding society and culture outside their own minority communities, but a few were more curious about their surroundings. Some of these early amateur ethnographers tried to describe the different cultures they encountered in the East but failed miserably in the attempt.[1] Others, mostly Frenchmen, seem to have attained a deeper level of insight. One of these, the French author Eugène Roger, was a Franciscan monk with some knowledge of early modern medicine. Roger was appointed in or around 1630 to serve as court physician to the Lebanese *amīr* Fakhr al-Din II, a local Druze ruler of the Lebanon. He served the *amīr* for a few years before moving to Jerusalem in 1634 to practice medicine there. On several occasions during his stay he treated Muslim women of high status, usually hidden from his view behind a partition or door while he took their pulse.[2] Roger's observations are echoed by other travelers. Laurent d'Arvieux spent twelve years in the area, from 1653 to 1665, as secretary to the Ṭurabāy governing family in the district of Lajjūn, not far from Jerusalem.[3] Antoine Morison, a French monk, traveled through Jerusalem and the Arabic-speaking provinces later in the century.[4]

The lot of women in the Orient according to Roger is much worse than that of women in Europe. Muslim women in the Levant are treated as chattel for men to buy and sell. A man can buy as many as he desires, on condition that he can provide for them in keeping with their position in society. The only exceptions to this rule are widows who may buy husbands for themselves, usually on condition that they escort them on the arduous road to Mecca for the *ḥajj*. Girls are often married off at the age of seven or eight, Roger relates, well before puberty. In most cases the parents choose the husband, and the couple meet for the first time during the wedding ceremony itself.[5] The bride usually has no information about her future husband; the groom relies on the descriptions of women in the family who have seen the girl in the bathhouse. D'Arvieux, basing his experience on his observations of bedouin society, recounts that since young Arab men and women have no opportunities to communicate with each other, falling in love is based on fantasy, such as the man imagining how a specific girl looks under her veil, or on the stories of others. Prospective bridegrooms devise ways to see their intended brides, sometimes hiding near a well, where women would uncover their faces when there are no men around. A girl seeking to encourage a boy might dare to "accidentally" drop her veil for a moment, making it seem as though she were trying to adjust it.[6]

As part of the marriage agreement a bride-price is paid by the husband to the bride's parents, who use some of it to prepare a dowry of clothes and housewares. Sometimes it is paid in merchandise or livestock. Before the wedding parents may buy their daughter a set of jewels: necklaces, rings, anklets and bracelets.[7] All these "strange" customs, states Roger, are also practiced by the local Christians. D'Arvieux adds that daughters are appreciated as a special source of income for their parents. The observations imply that for women issues of marriage and family are dominated by the cruel and merciless practices of the market which demean the sanctity of matrimony: fathers sell their daughters into marriage and resell them in case of divorce, and even a woman can buy a husband. When a married couple divorces, the mother takes the daughters and the father takes the sons "unless a different transaction was previously agreed between them."[8]

Yet marriage is considered a sacred matter among Muslims, or as Morison puts it: "une alliance qui a quelque chose de saint."[9] The marriage contract, locally called *iktoub*,[10] is prepared by the qadi. Those who cannot afford an official written contract find witnesses for an oral one stating the terms of the marriage.[11] The wedding ceremony is gay and colorful. In Jerusalem, even inside the city, the parents would adorn a camel with flowers and greenery. It is followed by others carrying the dowry. Bedouin drivers lead these camels around decorated tents, playing flutes and tambourines, and the procession is cheered on by women's ululations. A banquet awaits the numerous guests after the ceremony. Both women and men are invited, but each group is entertained separately. D'Arvieux adds that at the end of the wedding ceremony the bride and the groom are usually sequestered in a room, following which the groom returns with a kerchief stained with his bride's blood.[12] Divorce, of course, is a much more mundane affair, as Roger explains. Men need no excuse to dissolve the marriage and can do so whenever they wish without providing a reason. Women cannot do the same. A woman seeking a divorce applies to the qadi and must prove one of a specific limited number of legal grounds, in order to annul the marriage.

When wedding ceremonies are over, the travelers recount, the wife moves into her husband's house. She is in charge of all household duties. Married women rarely leave their homes, and when they do, their daughters and female slaves precede them to warn of their arrival. Bedouin women wear small bells in their hair to announce their approach.[13] The cause for these precautions is the legendary jealousy of Muslim husbands, claims d'Arvieux. It is enough to mention a horned ram in their presence to make them suspicious of being cuckolded. To avoid this, men take care and refer to sheep in general terms when discussing their herds. Women suspected of having betrayed their husbands are murdered by their brothers or fathers who are held responsible for the behavior of their female relatives even after the marriage.

Women do not learn to read or write. "All around the Holy Land," writes Roger, "there is not a woman or a girl who knows the shape of one letter, nor one who can give any sort of valid explanation of their laws."[14] They spend most of their time embroidering kerchiefs and shirts. This lack of education is apparently mirrored in their wild appearance and in their cosmetic rituals: their hair and hands are dyed with henna, their eyes painted in blue-black kohl. Their faces, hands and breasts are often tattooed in patterns of leaves, flowers and other symbols, to which they add new shapes and colors every year.[15]

Women's main social activity outside the house is visiting the *ḥammām* now and then to bathe with other women. Sometimes they meet to visit the cemetery or to join a funeral procession. Funerals have thus become festive occasions. Women abandon themselves to an ecstasy of wailing songs and dances in slow monotone. An old woman would recite an ode while the rest stand in a semicircle facing her, repeating her words and dancing a rhythmic dance. Such morbid social gatherings repeat themselves every Thursday, when women visit the graves of their loved ones and adorn them with flowers. Having completed their task, they often roam the city in large groups, chatting among themselves and making an ear-splitting din. The only amusement bedouin women may enjoy, says d'Arvieux, echoing Roger's words, is chatting among themselves under their tents.

Roger's thorough description, complemented by d'Arvieux, Morison, and other travelers, draws a grim portrait of the lives of Muslim (and Christian) women in seventeenth-century Palestine. They are uneducated and ignorant, have few rights, and are usually confined to the four walls of their house. For a fleeting moment of distraction they turn the grief and lamentation of a funeral into a festive occasion. Although Roger's description is much more detailed and informed than most, other Western travelers describe much the same unhappy plight.[16]

WOMEN IN COURT RECORDS AND LOCAL SOURCES

While local sources—mainly *sijills* and *fatāwa* collections—supply a great deal of raw material, they do not provide a basis for statistical study of women's status. At best, they reflected the situation within the city walls with partial accuracy, and even there only for certain social strata. We have almost no way of knowing which social groups chose to conduct their personal affairs elsewhere. Perhaps more crucial is the fact that many of the important facets of women's lives do not reveal themselves statistically, through a multitude of records, but are better discovered in specific documents dealing with controversial or problematic issues. Given such conditions, quantitative research may lead us to the wrong conclusions.

As mentioned earlier, court records were also clearly biased, and, as a result, silent on many issues where social norms did not coincide with the written law upheld by the court. Matters concerning such diverse issues as puberty, virginity, relations between wives and concubines, were seldom brought to court. Male-dominated families tended to keep issues related to women within the private domain. Other details, such as whether a specific woman wore a veil, seemed too trivial to record.[17] In some cases the authorities, represented by the qadi and his officials, may have conspired with their subjects to hide certain facts. The *sijill*, for example, records no murders of daughters, wives or sisters who were suspected of shaming their male relatives through promiscuous sexual behavior. Though it is possible that no such murders were committed, there are some indications that this was not the case. A clue to this silence might be found in the relative abundance of reports of accidents involving women and girls in the city and the surrounding villages. In cases of unnatural death a team of investigators was sent to the scene. But when the victim was female, the evidence supplied by (usually male) relatives was deemed sufficient, even when the circumstances surrounding the death were unusual as in the following case:

> Zāyid ibn Mutāwiʿ from the village of Bayt Iksa [7 km. west of Jerusalem] arrived in court, and informed the qadi that his daughter, Banwa, had died. She had been standing on the roof of his house in the village and, as God willed it (*bi-qaḍā' Allah wa-qadrihi*), she suddenly fell. While falling, she toppled a large boulder that dropped on her head and killed her. The father requested that an inquest be held, so that he could bury his daughter.
>
> The qadi appointed his secretary, Abu al-Fath al-Dayri, the writer of this record, who traveled to the village with ʿUthmān Çelebi, an official of the Khāṣikiyya *waqf*,[18] to which the village belongs. They were joined by ʿAbd al-Qadir the *juqdār* (*cokdar*), and by Muḥammad ibn Ibrahim the *muḥḍir* (*muhzır*) in the *sharīʿa* court.
>
> When they arrived in the village an inquest was held in the presence of those mentioned above, as well as Sheikh Dīb, Sheikh Muḥammad ibn ʿAlayān, Ahmad ibn Zayid, and a group of inhabitants of the village. The girl Banwa was found lying lifeless near her

> father's house. All those present were interrogated concerning the cause of her death. All of them repeated her father's story and claimed that no one in the village was to blame for it. This evidence was heard and noted, and when the team returned to court, its members filed a detailed report, asking the qadi to write it down in the *sijill*. It was recorded in accordance with their request, on 10 Rajab 1100 [30 April 1689].[20]

Reports of this kind, about women who slid into wells, fell off roofs, or were buried by stone avalanches, are fairly numerous, certainly more so than similar cases involving men. This may suggest that women worked on roofs, near wells, or in small stone quarries more than men did, but it is more likely that these incidents represent attempts to avoid murder charges where questions of "family honor" were concerned. There might be several other issues where the *sijill*'s silence is misleading, or where the records hide more than they reveal. Yet the *sijill*'s meticulous recording of other types of cases involving women, where the ruling was sometimes clearly in their favor and against male adversaries, lends more credibility to its testimony and provides a strong basis for research.

At first glance it seems as though direct evidence in the *sijill* corroborates Roger's account. In several cases dealing with matters of morality in the city, the court's attitude to women is stern and deprecatory. The mere presence of a woman in a secluded room alone with men who are not her closest relatives is cause enough for serious punishment:

> On the night of 11 Muḥarram 1091 [11 February 1680], an inquiry was held in a room in Ya'qubiyya [the Armenian quarter in Jerusalem]. Present were the city's *subashi*, Hasan *bashsha* the *juqdar*,[21] and several others.
>
> The room was found shut and bolted from without, and was opened in the presence of all whose names are signed below. Several people were apprehended: Muḥammad ibn 'Abdallah, the Egyptian artisan, a convert to Islam; 'Awad ibn Jābir and his wife Umm al-Hanā' bint Abi al-'Awn; as well as the two Christians, Mikha'īl ibn 'Abbūd and Jiryis ibn Ḥannā. They all sat inside the room, Umm al-Hanā' sitting next to her husband.
>
> Umm al-Hanā' and the child sitting in her lap were identified by her father and by another witness, and the men were all interrogated about the circumstances of their presence in the room with a woman at night. Muḥammad the convert explained that the room was his lodging, and that Mikha'īl and Jiryis came by to have a chat with him. Umm al-Hanā' explained that she and her husband rented the adjacent yard and that her husband went to the neighbors to ask

> for a light to rekindle the fire. She went out to look for him, and as she approached this room someone pushed her inside and bolted the door behind her. They remained in their places until the inquiry. Her husband and the others told the same story.
>
> Next morning they were all brought before the qadi. Presented with the facts, the qadi found it hard to believe their story, and decided to punish them for their sins. Muḥammad the convert and ʿAwad were punished by whipping (*taʿzīr*) and were later forced to follow a town crier (*dalāl*) who denounced their sordid, vile deeds, to deter others from following their example.[22]

The court was intolerant when rules of separation were breached, even when there was no proof to sustain the allegation that an unlawful act was actually committed. For all we know Umm al-Hanā' may have participated in an orgy (although this is unlikely if a child was present). She may have come for a quiet talk with the neighbors, or just to look for her husband. No proof was needed, however, and none provided. The scribe did not deem it necessary to tell future readers of the record the exact nature of the crimes committed, and the qadi required no further proof or witnesses, precisely because the situation itself—a woman sitting after dark in a strange room with men she was not related to, even in the presence of her husband—was a breach of law. It would appear that women were confined to their own rooms and seldom went outside.

And yet, a second look at the evidence in the *sijill* suggests a different outlook on women and their place in society, and raises some doubts about travelers' descriptions. Within the restrictive social and cultural system described by travelers, women had a world of their own, and enjoyed many liberties. Even the most observant Western travelers failed to capture and encapsulate this complicated system of gender relations.

Marriage contracts were signed in the *sharīʿa* court. All inhabitants of the city itself were required to register their marriages there, as pointed out in several *fatwas* written at the time. Village marriages were registered in a different manner, by the *timar* holder or by a *waqf* official in charge of the village. These functionaries were also paid a marriage tax (*rasm ankiha*) for this registration. It seems likely, therefore, that they kept some sort of ledger to record marriages, and tried to prevent evasion of payment. Unfortunately we have no evidence of such records outside the city.[23]

Records kept in the city show that marriage and divorce, as conducted in accordance with Islamic law, allowed women some leverage. A woman who reached the age of majority could demand the annulment of her marriage if it was conducted without her consent. If married before puberty, she had the right to cancel the marriage contract upon reaching puberty or mental maturity, as defined by Muslim jurisprudence. Muslim women, and at times even Christian women, could file complaints against parents or brothers who forced them to marry against their will. Sometimes cases reached the qadi only when a disappointed husband sued his wife, demanding to consummate the marriage:

> Ibrāhīm ibn Rizqallah, the Christian[24] ironsmith, sues Maryam bint ʿĪd ibn Tuqmān, a grown girl aged sixteen, whose puberty is proved by menstruation, as attested to by the women Qādiriyyā bint ʿAyā and Āmina bint Dhū al-Nun. She was identified in accordance with the law by Sheikh ʿAbd al-Rahmān ibn Riḍwān, and by Muḥammad ibn Ṣāliḥ.
>
> In his plea to the court, the plaintiff claimed he was offered the girl's hand by her father, whom she had given permission to arrange a marriage contract on her behalf (*bi-l-wikālā ʿanhā*), and in accordance with her wishes. In return the plaintiff paid a *mahr*[25] of forty-five *ghūrush*. He now demands the consummation of the marriage.
>
> Maryam, the defendant, denied the allegation. She had not given her father permission, did not consent to the marriage offer, and does not want to be married to the plaintiff, she said. The qadi then asked Ibrāhīm to produce legal evidence proving that Maryam had given her father permission to marry her off and that she had accepted the marriage. Ibrāhīm admitted he had no such proof and demanded that Maryam take an oath. Maryam complied, swearing "by the almighty God who transmitted the gospels to Jesus son of Mary"[26] that she did not give her father permission, and does not want this marriage.
>
> Taking all this into consideration, the qadi notified the plaintiff that his betrothal was not valid, and that the marriage contract is null and void. Inscribed in the *sijill* on the 14th of Shaʿbān 1066 (7 June 1656).[27]

In spite of her youth, and perhaps deserted by her own family (no family members signed as witnesses), Maryam bint ʿĪd demanded the abrogation of a contract made by her father, and dared to reject her husband before the local qadi. Many other similar cases involving Muslim and Christian women are registered in the *sijills* of Jerusalem and Nabulus. The girl also defended herself in court without representation by an agent or proxy (*wakīl, vekil*). This was common in Jerusalem, as in other towns of the Ottoman Empire, and suggests a measure of independence and freedom of movement for women that escaped the eye of foreign travelers.[28]

It is worth noting that in many of these cases, qadis chose to believe women, ruling against the male parties. This may have reflected *sharʿī* practice, since the onus of proof is usually on the plaintiff. But needless to say, had qadis wanted to prevent women from obtaining justice, they could easily have found a way around these stipulations.

Collections of legal opinions from this period include a large number of queries concerning the rights of women to abrogate a marriage.[29] In many cases the questions were about young girls married off by their relatives. Sometimes the contract was signed at birth, to uphold a prior promise, or was part of an exchange between two families—each family's son marrying the other family's daughter. Others inquired about women who had reached puberty and were married off without their knowledge or consent. The *mufti* was sometimes asked to offer his opinion on marriages agreed to by the girl's mother, brothers, cousins or legal guardian without her consent. The large numbers of appeals to the *mufti* may suggest that abrogation of marriage by women was not a well-entrenched norm, and that women probably had to fight to get what was theirs by law. On the other hand, they demonstrate that women dared walk this seemingly dangerous path, appealed to *mufti*s and qadis, and were rewarded by having their marriages abrogated.

In most cases the girl's parents took the *mahr* (sometimes referred to as *ṣadāq*) paid by the prospective husband, sometimes using it to purchase furniture and household goods needed by the young couple in their new home. Part of the *mahr* may have been set aside for the bride's pre-wedding beauty preparations, such as the bath, hairdressing and henna. But even in this area, where custom prevailed, a bride had the right to demand the *mahr* payment for herself. In a short legal opinion, one of many on the subject, the *mufti* Khayr al-Din al-Ramli was asked: "In the case of a man who paid a *mahr* of eighty-five *ghurūsh* to the bride's father, twenty [also to her father] for her clothing, and five to her uncle. Does the whole sum belong to her, or to all the above?" "All is hers," Khayr al-Din replied curtly, "and God knows best" (*wa-Allahu aʿlam*).[30] Cases of women demanding that the money be paid into their hands are recorded in the *sijill* as well, and parents were usually instructed by the qadi to return the money to their daughters.[31]

Women had the right to demand divorce for a variety of reasons: the disappearance of a husband for a long period of time; the husband's impotence; abuse and mistreatment; or even any treatment not befitting her status in society. Sometimes women demanded the addition of a special clause to the marriage agreement signed in court, in which the husband vowed to divorce his wife if certain conditions were not met.[32] Many divorce cases were brought before the Shāfiʿī qadi (in such cases it was specifically stated that the Shāfiʿī qadi was presiding). We do not know whether in these cases women plaintiffs were Shāfiʿī by origin, and came to court knowing that their *madhhab* would be more lenient in these matters, or whether they chose to switch over temporarily to this particular school because of its liberal attitude in dissolving marriage ties.[33]

When no convincing legal reason for divorce could be brought up, marriages were often dissolved by mutual consent (*khul'*). In many cases the wife renounced her claim to the *mahr*, or to that part of it designated as "delayed *mahr*" (*mu'ajjal*), which is supposed to be paid to the wife if the husband dies or if he chooses to divorce her:

> In the *sharī'a* court, Ṣāliḥ Bey, son of the late *amīr* Mūsa, former governor of Jerusalem, representing his aunt, Ṣiffiyya *khānim*, requested ḥājj 'Alī al-Khurūji, who represents her husband Isḥaq Bey, the *za'īm*[34] in Jerusalem, to release the lady Ṣiffīyya from her marriage bond.[35] In return, he promised, a sum of four hundred *ghurūsh* would be deducted from the delayed *mahr* of one thousand *ghurūsh*. Lady Siffiyya, he declared, is also willing to waive her claim to a divorce allowance (*nafaqat 'idda*) and all other rights stipulated in the marriage agreement.
>
> Ḥajj 'Alī agreed to the request and its conditions, and by the power vested in him by Isḥaq Bey, released lady Ṣiffiyya from the marriage. By so doing, he divorced the lady from her husband in a legal manner. . . . The rest of the delayed *mahr* [six hundred *ghurūsh*] was then paid by 'Alī Bey to Ṣāliḥ Bey, and the latter declared, in the name of the lady Ṣiffiyyā, that she has no further claims from Isḥaq Bey.[36]

It appears, then, that issues of marriage and divorce were not as one-sided and male-oriented as Roger and his fellow travelers would have us believe. The marriage contract was a deal, a business transaction, as Roger described it, but it was also a two-sided affair, in which the wife had almost as much say as her husband. Marriage certainly lacked all semblance of Catholic sacrament, and was hardly reminiscent even of the postmedieval Jewish concept of marriage as a very meaningful religious event. The rites of marriage suggested a happy occasion, but the role of religion and allusions to sanctity were limited. Divorce was quite frequent and usually taken in stride; marriage ties were dissolved with relative ease by both sides.

For local society marriage was an agreement involving both economic and social considerations: the husband pledged to see to his wife's economic welfare and sexual needs. His side of the bargain included taking his bride from her father's custody or protective sphere into his own. The wife, for her part, was to bear and raise the children. Village women were expected to participate in the family's agricultural tasks, but as a rule women's economic activities were not seen as part of the marriage obligations, and it was assumed that the wife's property and financial gains were intended for her own use. An agreement was signed and guarantees posted in the form of *mahr* and dowry. When, for some reason, the marriage did not achieve its intended goals, there were few qualms about dissolving it, and in most cases the wife returned to her parents' house.

As for seclusion, in sharp contrast to the accounts of the travelers, the *sijill* describes women who are not confined to their homes. Women left their houses and visited female neighbors, friends and relatives. They conducted business affairs in an admirable manner that often discloses an understanding of the city's commercial world and a grasp of the economy.[37] Peasant women often worked in fields and quarries, of course, sometimes even outside the village. Some, in village and city alike, were often engaged in large-scale land transactions. A substantial part of the transactions in recorded sales deeds involved women buying and selling property. In many cases women represented themselves in court, rather than being represented by a *wakīl* or a male member of their family.

Some of these transactions may be explained by the fact that women were entitled to inherit part of their parents' possessions according to the *sharīʿa*. *Sharīʿa* laws of inheritance are relatively complicated. In principle, individuals cannot bequeath their property as they see fit. Most of the deceased person's estate is divided according to a very detailed proportional formula which takes into consideration the relation of prospective heirs to the deceased and their gender. According to this formula a woman is entitled to half the amount inherited by a male in the same relation to the deceased. A daughter is entitled to half the amount inherited by a son, a sister to half her brother's share.[38]

In her research on Egypt in the nineteenth century, Judith Tucker has found that women did not inherit land. Although most land was officially *miri* (owned by the state), the fallahin considered it private property to be passed on to their heirs. In this case fathers disregarded the law, and bequeathed their land almost exclusively to their sons.[39] In the district of Jerusalem, some two hundred years earlier, land definitions were much the same. People tended to regard their land as private property even when it was officially considered government land. Here too, in many instances, daughters or wives did not get their share, and in several cases were compelled to request the qadi's assistance,[40] but in most cases women did in fact receive their allocated share of the inheritance, including land and property.[41]

Women also received money and property as *mahr* when they married, or as delayed *mahr* when they were divorced by their husbands. Some preferred to sell their property and to engage in moneylending. In several cases they lent large sums of money to the Jewish and Christian communities, perhaps because it was easier to demand interest on loans outside the Muslim community, where profit from interest was frowned upon.[42]

But all this cannot account for the volume of trade carried out by women. Not just selling, but often buying, renting and investing in land and merchandise. They bought houses, fields, vineyards and orchards, sold merchandise of various kinds, and drafted sophisticated contracts in the process. In some cases women joined together to defend their inheritance rights.[43] As in other regions of the Ottoman Empire, an agent or representative often represented a woman in court. But this device was used more as a convenience than as a means for further seclusion of women. Women from all levels of society often came to court themselves to present their claims to the qadi.

According to Suraya Faroqhi, the number of women and men buying land in Anatolia grew considerably during the seventeenth century. Such a trend, which was also apparent in Jerusalem at the time, may have stemmed from a change in agrarian relations. Land, which was controlled firmly by the state and monitored through frequent surveys in the sixteenth century, was not as carefully controlled in succeeding years. State lands reverted into the hands of villagers and notables, who regarded them as freehold. People in and around Jerusalem bought and sold property in large quantities. In many cases women sold to other women, recording their transactions in the *sijill*:

> In the *sharī'a* court, Rūmiyya bint Aḥmad al-'Attār from the village of Jibāliya bought from Zahiriyya bint Shihāb al-Dīn al-Jibāli, and the latter sold unto her, what is hers, forms part of her property, to which she has the right of usufruct, and her hand is laid upon.[45] The property sold is twelve of twenty-four *qirāt*,[46] of the vineyard in the village of Bayt Lahiyya in the vicinity of the city of Gaza. . . . This vineyard includes various trees, among them pomegranates, grapevines and palm trees. The price is ten *ghurūsh*, paid in court by the buyer to the seller.[47]

As typical of Jerusalem and Nabulus as it is of Gaza, this record conveys a spirit of confidence and freedom in women's dealings inside a male-dominated and male-centered world. The property in this case, as in many others, is situated far away from both women's residences, implying that such deals were for business purposes, not necessarily an attempt to enlarge the family's estate. It is worth noting that both women represented themselves in court (although they could have sent a *wakīl*). This fact confirms the assumption that women in both positions—seller and buyer—

often conducted business by and for themselves. Otherwise a husband or father would have come as a representative, since physical presence in court was not required in such transactions.

Formal entry into specifically male professions was almost impossible. No doubt high-ranking women exerted a considerable deal of influence on the conduct of government affairs, as women in the imperial harem did at the same period.[48] Yet there were no women in military or government occupations, no women were appointed governors or deputies, of course, and none fulfilled any sort of formal administrative duty, even at the lowest levels. In the *sijill*s of Jerusalem and Nabulus for this period, no women are mentioned as *timār* holders (a rare occurrence anywhere in the Ottoman Empire), although some women have been charged with managing *timār*s as legal guardians of their minor sons. Often a young son inherited his father's *timār* while still too young to administer it himself. In such cases his mother would sometimes temporarily assume control of the fief.[49]

Religious professions were just as difficult to penetrate. A few exceptions existed, however, suggesting that these were not considered an exclusive male domain. In one or two cases women were given the task of reciting chapters of the Qur'an in a mosque, usually as a result of a specific stipulation made by the founder of a *waqf*. In other cases women of prestigious families or daughters of famous deceased religious scholars were considered part of the notable elite and given allowances from the *ṣurra* grant from Istanbul to the ulema of Jerusalem, and from the *jizya* revenues of Jerusalem.[50]

Though there are no direct indications in the *sijill*, it seems probable that in contrast to Roger's description, women received a measure of education to guide them through the complex economic and legal facets of their lives. This is suggested by the famous Ottoman traveler Evliya Çelebi, who visited Jerusalem in the second half of the century. Unlike Roger, Evliya Çelebi was impressed by the women he met, and in particular by their upbringing and education. Women in Jerusalem were probably not very different in these respects from women in other, more central regions of the Ottoman Empire, as described by Haim Gerber and R. C. Jennings in their researches on Bursa and Kaiseri, and by Leslie Peirce in her study of the imperial harem.[51]

COURT SCRIBES AND TRAVELING ETHNOGRAPHERS

How, then, are we to measure the different contribution and the relative importance of these two kinds of sources? Should we adopt a distant, nonjudgmental view that considers all sources biased and therefore transmitting a subjective reality, or is there some way of evaluating historical evidence and measuring such sources against each other?

The books and diaries written by travelers in the seventeenth century were described by their authors as documents which reflected an empirical reality. They all carry descriptive names, very similar to each other, such as *Journey to the Holy Land*, or *Voyage dans la Palestine*, hinting at the outset that the reader is about to read an "objective" report on things observed in faraway lands. Lack of bias or objectivity, however, were not their most notable qualities. The beliefs, predispositions and biases of these travelers were a distorted, if fascinating, mirror for the sights they saw. Furthermore, their observations were directed at a certain reading audience and were expected to conform to the images and demands of that audience, to confirm its worldview. In addition to all this, as Roger Chartier has shown,[52] the process of editing and publishing itself, by the author or by subsequent editors, frequently changed the emphasis and content of such books, removing them even further away from the original "reality" they witnessed. In this sense the historian should be wary of using them as "fact quarries."[53]

The records of the Jerusalem *sharīʿa* court, the *sijills*, are more difficult to assess. Maintaining the very rigid structure of official documents, with their flowery language and customary wordings, these records often deliberately conceal more than they intend to reveal, and create an artificial barrier of formality between the text and the reader. It is also difficult to measure the veracity of some of the *sijill*'s information. Court action was all too often used as a formal legal device: a lawsuit would sometimes be filed, for instance, just to test a *waqf* deed and make sure it was watertight and immune from challenge by other interested parties. In such circumstances the reader may assume he/she is looking at an authentic legal case unfolding in court, while the participants all knew they were staging a play the results of which were determined in advance.

Furthermore, those engaged in the task of compiling the *sijill*s were part of a very clearly defined social group. They were all Muslim males, with some sort of religious education or affiliation. As such, the qadi, chief scribe and other court officials tended to prefer members of their own social group to others, whether women, minorities, soldiers, or even members of the governing elite.

But beside the clear bias in their outlook, court records preserve documentary qualities which make them a deeper reflection of reality. *Sharīʿa* court records are not mere verdicts based on the *sharīʿa* or some other code of law. They include by definition the testimonies of many people, frequently frowned upon by the court; they were not written for the public at large, but rather for the court officials themselves, and were primarily meant to serve as notes for further reference. Neither was there one common thread of narrative to bind the records together. They were not intended to present a consistent worldview or a thorough description. They were very rarely personal, and contained as concise as possible a description of the goings-on in court. They were rarely edited after the initial summing up of the case, and remained in a relatively crude form, revealing facts that might have been erased had an editor gone over the text. Sometimes, in fact, records were stricken out with a few swift strokes of the scribe's pen, but are still readable. As a result, the *sijill* depicts a reality that is much more chaotic, varied and colorful (and consequently less superficial) than that described by the travelers.

A SEPARATE NETWORK

In women's history, as in other historical fields, we should therefore accord the *sijill* a higher rank on the documentary scale than travel texts. If that is the case, we should now turn to the travelers' works and look for their motivations in describing women the way they did. This should be done not in order to denigrate the travelers' accounts and show their inaccuracies, but rather in order to bring to the fore the cultural dimensions embedded in these texts and to present their vantage point, a view that did not confine itself to the writings of travelers but found its way into their culture and eventually into the local culture as well.[54]

The basis for this particular inclination of many travelers may have arisen from their own conceptions of Western women. European travelers had no other yardstick by which to measure what they saw around them; the status of women in their own societies was the only parallel on which they could draw to understand another culture. In the region they visited, systems of social control depended heavily on a strict separation of the sexes in the internal sphere, and on rigid laws of dress and conduct in external spheres. All "private" contact between men and women who were not very close relatives or married to each other was forbidden and severely punished.

In the eyes of a seventeenth-century French or English spectator, who in most cases did not understand the principles of Islamic law, and in whose culture women were free to move as they pleased between the internal and external spheres (interpreted by the travelers as private and public, or female and male, to match their own definitions[55]), this state of affairs was seen as blatant discrimination against women. They were forbidden entry into the male world, and were cut off from men's social life as a whole. This, however, was an inaccurate view of a culture that refused to present itself openly to the outsider. As a matter of fact, these women were part of a separate social, economic and cultural network, at times richer and more advanced than that of their female contemporaries in the West.[56]

This network was set apart from corresponding male systems, yet was just as intense. The interaction of women with the surrounding world was channeled through closed circuits to which men had almost no access. In the travelers' world separation was a negative value, meaning that women were barred even from the most basic freedoms appropriated by male members of society. But although "separate" was clearly not "equal," and in many respects women were still marginalized, this separation actually tended to reduce oppression. It is true that women wore veils, that they were not free to come and go as they pleased, that they could be punished for being in the company of strange men. But this segregation also allowed them to maintain their private property, to conduct business and to represent their own interests in court. For some women even the veil paradoxically represented a kind of liberty, an ability to see and be invisible at the same time.[54]

Ironically, it may have been the impact of Western social norms on local society that undermined the status of women in later centuries. Muslim norms of separation remained as strict and as culturally dominant as before, but women's freedom within their own networks was curtailed to fit Western cultural codes (true or imagined) assigning women the role of "ladies" who should not engage in commerce; what Judy Mabro calls "the idea of refinement," a relatively new concept even in Western Europe. These ideas, which gained currency in the Arab world in the mid-nineteenth century were translated into economic and social practices which prevented women from expanding their role in society and the economy. The Western Christian image of marriage as a sacred institution, rather than as a partnership agreement, was introduced into Middle Eastern culture, and later accepted as a local norm in the higher echelons of society. It too had a negative impact on the status of women, limiting their access to court to seek dissolution of marriage. The secularization of education in the nineteenth century, which drew women away from Islamic law, may have reduced their knowledge of that law and limited their access to divorce, at least for a time.[58]

Evidence from seventeenth-century Jerusalem and from other provinces demonstrates clearly that like any other historical subject, including the realm of Islamic law itself, women's history changed over time and from place to place. Women's lives in "traditional" Islamic societies today do not necessarily resemble those of previous centuries. It is no doubt true that, all things considered, women's status in the district of Jerusalem in the seventeenth century was considerably lower than that of men of the same social stratum. But the normative system was not entirely asymmetrical; women were not condemned to a life of seclusion and marginality while men went about their business. Both sides were part of a restrictive system based upon separation of the sexes. This system provided women a certain leeway, a relative measure of freedom to act in their separate networks, provided they kept their distance. The public eye of the law, as well as the eyes of neighbors and relatives, made sure the lines were not crossed by either sex. It is precisely because of the relative freedom women had in their own networks that any infringement of the delicate balance was punished, regardless of the actual sin or crime committed.

Conclusion

There were no great upheavals or dramatic turns in seventeenth century Jerusalem. The wars were short and inconsequential, and most local power games unfolded behind the scenes. But the calm surface was deceiving, belied by the storm that erupted at the end of the century—the people's revolt of 1703. In this respect the revolt is part of the previous century, and a culmination of several processes which took place in preceding decades. It destroyed the old leadership, and released sentiments of rage and pain pent up for many years. These events and their aftermath cannot be understood outside the historical context leading to the revolt.

Located neither on the frontline, nor near the imperial center, the district was not a part of the empire that government attention focused on. Though holy and revered in Muslim eyes, it was a typical Ottoman subprovince, and its history reflects that of other regions in the empire, especially those with a majority of Arabic speakers. Jerusalem and its periphery did not constitute an imminent danger to the security of the Ottoman Empire, and consequently was not often submitted to the kind of abrupt change and panic-stricken activity seen in other regions of the empire in times of war or revolt. Ottoman rule here was continuous and relatively stable. In this respect Jerusalem may provide a better example than other regions of the pristine shape of Ottoman intentions, policies, and statecraft, as they found expression in provincial administration.

After the conquest, Ottoman rule in the Arab provinces was consolidated through local governing households. Some of them were established by governors who were typical products of the central *devşirme* system, while others were local tribal chiefs, or military slaves recruited and trained in the households of officers and men of state. Such governors founded their own lineages, and attempted to secure government positions for sons and slaves, preferably in the area they chose as their home. The emerging governing elite also established and strengthened its ties with the notables of the district, led by the heads of religious institutions. Ties thus established benefited both sides. The governors found a loyal ally to help secure and legitimize their rule in order to entrench themselves in the area and bequeath their positions and possessions to their sons. The notables, for their part, basked in the governors' protection, and were able to put their special privileges as members of the *askeri* class to full use.

As the years of the seventeenth century wore on, the central government withdrew from day-to-day administration of the area, and enclosed itself in a cocoon of the capital's affairs. The provinces were often neglected, or left to the provincial, or even the district governor to oversee. In time district governors mastered the sort of political dexterity needed to maintain their positions, and retain the favor of provincial governors, the central bureaucracy, and the sultan. In Palestine several households became lineages, and these lineages combined through marriage and economic transactions to form one extended dynasty controlling several districts at once. Thus they were able to shrink or expand their dominions to accommodate the center's pressures.

Their knowledge of the area, its problems and its inhabitants, and their ability to incorporate the local notable elite in administrating the district, paved the way for widening circles of the population to identify with the locally based ruling elite. Evidence for the first part of the century suggests that Jerusalem during that period had a relatively stable and coherent social structure, and that various parts of that society found a *modus vivendi* with the government and with other components of society. Perhaps more than in any previous period the bedouin were incorporated into the social fabric, both economically and politically.

The situation began to change in the 1660s. A central government invigorated by the policies of the new grand vezir Mehmet Köprülü, sought to reestablish its control in the provinces. Local governing dynasties were gradually eliminated, their households dispersed, and new governors were appointed by the center. Just like their predecessors, the new governors learned how to manipulate the economic and political ambiguity that was still very much in existence in the region, in order to continue exploiting the population. Unlike the old guard, however, they did not know, nor did they care about the intricate web of local social relations. Having come to tidy up the stables, as it were, they distanced themselves from the notables, their only possible local allies in administrating the district, and having impaired the special relationship painstakingly built with the bedouin over the last decades, they stood aloof from village, tribe and city population alike.

Exploitation and the heavy tax load, hitherto borne with much hardship by the taxpaying subjects, now became all but unbearable. The pride and reputation of local notables, the traditional leaders of society, were hit hardest. Forsaken by the new governors, they joined the growing camp of the oppressed and the economically exploited. As the seventeenth century drew to a close, frequent petitions were sent jointly by notables and other representatives of the population to the sultan's palace in Istanbul, to complain about injustice, irreligious behavior and corruption in local government. In most cases the plaintiffs were disappointed, their complaints received dismissive responses, and the new governors were allowed to carry on. What the local notables saw as rude and cruel behavior on the part of the government's representatives, was apparently understood at the imperial center as a measure of harshness necessary to establish law and order in mutinous territory. When the revolt finally broke out at the beginning of the eighteenth century, the local populace saw it as an outcome of these harsh new centralizing policies, while from the central government's vantage point it was construed as the culmination of long years of anarchy of exactly the kind that new policies sought to rectify.

Long-term processes such as these provide an insight into the state of affairs in the empire as a whole. From a provincial perspective the impression of decline attributed to the first half of the seventeenth century (the so-called "sultanate of the women") so prominent in the writings of central government bureaucrats, was attenuated, and in some cases entirely missing. The early years of the century may have been a period of political or military decline in the Ottoman center, but subjects in distant provinces saw things differently. It was only in the last decades of the century, when the empire regained a sense of pride, confidence and self-esteem, that the subjects in the provinces felt a change for the worse. This change, a consequence of reforms in government, and of a renewed effort of centralization, brought about a series of revolts in the Arab provinces in the last decades of the eighteenth century.

Another all-imperial research concern which finds expression in this region is the study of integration into the emerging world economy, with its Western European core. The economic system characteristic of most parts of the Ottoman Empire in the previous century can be described as a closed economic structure satisfying most local demand for basic products by local supply. This system was centrally controlled from Istanbul: taxes were defined, assessed and collected; prices were regulated; foreign trade was limited to luxury items and to the emerging firearms technology. At the turn of the sixteenth century the tide began to change. Central control dissipated, and the system became more flexible, not as rigidly regulated from above. The new economic spirit of laissez-faire made it possible for local markets to open up to Europe and its commercial advances. But contrary to our expectations, this new spirit, which should be attributed more to decentralization than to deliberate policy, did not induce a serious measure of dependency on foreign trade, and did not lead to peripheralization. On the contrary, for various reasons the economy of France, the leading European power to have established trading depots in the Palestinian and Lebanese littoral, was more dependent on continued supply from the Levant than vice versa.

Furthermore, such an attempt to establish commercial contacts in seventeenth-century Palestine, on the grand scale required in order to turn the region into an economic periphery, was doomed to fail. The same trend of economic decentralization responsible for the openness towards Europe became an insurmountable obstacle when European merchants tried to reach agreements on a larger scale with local key figures. Ironically, it was the lack of any dominant power that barred the way to peripheralization. In the district of Jerusalem, as elsewhere, there were no merchants, governors or leaders with enough authority to steer the economy in any single direction. Only when rule was centralized, or in the hands of very influential local rulers such as Fakhr al-Dīn II in Lebanon, or Ḍahir al-ʿUmar and al-Jazzār in northern Palestine a century later, did European efforts to penetrate and control local economy find a foothold in the region. All in all the importance and influence of commerce with Europe during the 1600s was negligible, and the influence of European merchants on local economy, local politics or local culture, was hardly felt.

Finally, when we consider the history of Jerusalem as a province of the Ottoman Empire, we may conclude that the paradigm of rise and decline, so dominant in Ottoman historiography, cannot assist us in trying to interpret Ottoman provincial history. Theories seeking to replace this paradigm with one that sees the Ottoman Empire in alternating cycles of centralization and decentralization, are better capable of interpreting the events and processes of the seventeenth century. A period of decentralization at the beginning of the century ushered in a series of changes in the government, the social structure, and the economic and cultural atmosphere. The subsequent attempt to recentralize the government brought some of these trends to an abrupt end, leading to frustration and violence.

But although these notions are better suited to explain and interpret Ottoman history, to a certain extent they too are still prisoners of the former decline paradigm. They contain an implied assumption that decentralization is tantamount to decline. The Ottomans, we are told, managed to survive for so long because they could adapt. When the going got tough, the central government folded its petals and decentralized, until the time came to regain full control. Such periods of centralization are often seen as times of improvement, in which the Empire resumed its ascent.

From the center's point of view this may be so. Centralization seems to reflect a stronger, more effective government, and therefore at least a measure of security for the subjects. But in the provinces, in the empire's backyard, as it were, things were very different. In Jerusalem it was the period of decentralization that brought about a relative improvement in security and the quality of life for various groups in local society. On the other hand, the attempt made by the central government to centralize rule in the second half of the century, the effort to eliminate local dynasties and appoint new governors, brought about a rift between the government and its allies in the region, continued destruction of the countryside and a total breakdown of trust between ruler and ruled. For local inhabitants, this indicated rapid decline.

Conditions throughout the century may have been unpropitious for a centralizing reform, such as that carried out more than a century later in the *tanzimat* period. The *devşirme* system, the imperial factory that turned out generation after generation of well-trained, talented, disciplined governors and administrators, reached its apex in the previous century. Now its wheels ground to a halt. No new governing elite was created in the center. Its place as the main repository for administrators was taken by the households of provincial rulers, and by warlike elements such as the bedouin or mountain village populations.

But in order to avail itself of this new source of manpower the central government had to relinquish a measure of its authority, to do away with some of its former privileges and prerogatives. Under these conditions, however, any attempt to recentralize the government based on administrators dispatched from the center, was doomed to fail. As long as the central government accepted these new rules of the game, albeit reluctantly, its suzerainty was accepted, and in most cases its dues were paid. The trouble began when, under the influence of a new, dynamic vezirate, the Ottoman imperial center attempted to regain full control. The lack of properly trained governors and administrators, and the measure of autonomy gained by the provinces thus far, made the task impossible. By shattering the delicate social and political balance of the region, it destroyed any vestiges of legitimation, and postponed the hope of restoring centralized rule for a very long time. From this perspective the rise of local potentates in Palestine, as in other parts of the Ottoman empire, at the beginning of the eighteenth century, is as much a consequence of the failure of centralization efforts in the second part of the seventeenth century, as it is a consequence of the empire's renewed cycle of decentralization in the eighteenth century.

Notes

INTRODUCTION

1. P. M. Holt, *Egypt and the Fertile Crescent, 1516–1922* (Ithaca, 1966), 33–45; Andrew Hess, "The Ottoman Conquest of Egypt and the Beginning of the Sixteenth-Century World War," *International Journal of Middle East Studies* (1973): 55–76. Yitzhaq Ben-Zvi, *Eretz-Yisra'el ve-yishuva Bi-yemey hashilton ha-Othmāni* (Jerusalem, 1979), 3–14; Stanford Shaw, *History of the Ottoman Empire and Modern Turkey* (Cambridge, 1976), I:83–85.
2. Holt, 38-40; Ben-Zvi, *ibid*.
3. Ehud Toledano, "Sanjaq Yerushalayim ba-me'ah ha-tet zayin—hityashvut kafrit u-megamot demografiyot," in A. Cohen, *Prakim be-toldot Yerushalayim be-reshit ha-tkufa ha-'Othmānit* (Jerusalem, 1979), 61–62.
4. Amnon Cohen and Bernard Lewis, *Population and Revenue in the Towns of Palestine in the Sixteenth Century* (Princeton, 1978), 18–26, 33–4, 43, 170.; W. D. Hütteroth and Kamal Abdulfattah, *Historical Geography of Palestine, TransJordan and Southern Syria in the Late Sixteenth Century* (Erlangen, 1977). It should be stressed here that all assessments of population in the period under discussion are inaccurate. Some of these assessments are based on *tapu-tahrir* surveys made by the Ottomans several times in the sixteenth century, but these surveys were conducted for other purposes and were never intended to be more than approximations of population and revenue in the surveyed area.
5. Hütteroth and Abdulfattah, 101, 104; Cohen and Lewis, 42.
6. Amnon Cohen, *Economic Life in Ottoman Jerusalem* (Cambridge, 1989), 119–126; Idem and Elisheva Simon-Pikali, *Yehudim be-bet ha-mishpat ha-Muslemi* (Hebrew; Jerusalem, 1993).
7. Amnon Cohen, *Palestine in the Eighteenth Century* (Jerusalem, 1973), 312–325.

1. ZOOMING IN

1. On the religious, pilgrimage-oriented nature of travel prior to the eighteenth century, and the beginnings of secularization, see Billie Melman, *Women's Orients: English Women and the Middle East, 1718–1918* (Ann Arbor, 1992), 14–16.
2. Nathaniel Crouch, *Two Journeys to Jerusalem* (London, 1699, SOAS library), 74–75.
3. W. Forster, *The Travels of John Sanderson in the Levant* (London, 1931), 112. See also Eugène Roger, *La Terre Sainte, Ou Description topographique très particulière de la Terre de promission* (Paris, 1664), 3–4.
4. du Rozel, *Voyage de Jerusalem*, 114–15; *Journey to the Holy Land* (British Library Manuscript), fol. 141b; Crouch, 84; Henry Moundrel, *A Journey from Aleppo to Jerusalem at 1697*, in Wright Thomas (ed.), *Early Travels in Palestine* (New York, 1968); Laurent d'Arvieux, *Voyage dans la Palestine* (Amsterdam, 1718), 39; Masson, *Histoire du Commerce Français dans le Levant au 17é siècle* (Paris, 1896); Jean Doubdan, *Le Voyage de la Terre Sainte* (Paris, 1661), 36. See also Amnon Cohen, "Ottoman Rule and the Re-emergence of the coast of Palestine," *Revue de l'Occident Musulman et de la Mediterranée* 39. 1 (1985): 164–175.
5. *Journey to the Holy Land*, fols. 141b–42b. See also Crouch, 57.
6. Ibid.
7. J. Thevenot, *The Travels of M. de Thevenot into the Levant* (London, 1687), 361.
8. The Galilee was included for most of the period in the *sanjaq* of Safad, sometimes part of the province of Damascus, and sometimes united for political reasons with the province of Sidon (Sayda).
9. Roger, 3–6; Doubdan, 38–39; Maundrel, 431–34; Sandys, *Travels, Containing a History of the Original of the Turkish Empire* (London, 1670), 150; Crouch, 9; du Rozel, 30–32.
10. *Journey to the Holy Land*, fols. 141b–42b. See also: du Rozel, 24, 32, 114–5.
11. Forster, 48. See also ibid., 112; Morison, 223–24.
12. Morison, 224; Forster, 48, 112.
13. Forster, 100.
14. Doubdan, 40; *Journey to the Holy Land*, fol. 141.
15. Ibid.
16. Heyd, *Ottoman Documents on Palestine*, 102–5, 107–16; du Rozel, 36.
17. Morison, 224; d'Arvieux, 124–26.
18. This refers to the site of Nabi Musa, the burial place of Moses, which according to Muslim tradition is on the way to Jericho. Moses is known in Islam as *kalīm allah* (the one who conversed with God).

19. The Khasikiyya *waqf* was the main charitable endowment in Jerusalem, established by Khasiki Hurrem Sultan (Roxellana), wife of Süleyman the Magnificent, in 1552. Tax payments from several villages, including Bayt Iksa and Bayt Liqya, belonged to the *waqg*.
20. (*fa-na'muru man lahu wilāyat ta'dībihim wa-l-khurūj min haqqihim bi-ta'dībihim*). This refers apparently to the officials of the *waqf*.
21. *Jerusalem Sijill* (*JS*) 183:103 (awā'il Rabī' al-thāni 1091/May 1680). See also Heyd, *Ottoman Documents on Palestine*, 98–99.
22. Max Weber, *The City* (London, 1958), 65–85. A different view of Western cities is suggested by Braudel, who sees the village and the city in early modern Europe not as two separate entities, but rather as a continuum of social and economic activities. See F. Braudel, *Civilization and Capitalism 15th–18th Century*, vol. I: *The Structure of Everyday Life* (London, 1981), pp. 479–89. I would like to thank Professor Halil Inalcik for introducing me to the complexities of this issue. His explanations, as well as a lecture he presented at the CIEPO conference in Jerusalem in 1990, serve as a basis for this debate.
23. Weber, *The City*, 82.
24. G. Von Grunebaum, "The Structure of the Muslim Town," in idem, (ed.), *Islam: Essays in the Nature and Growth of a Cultural Tradition* (London, 1965), 141–58.
25. Ira Lapidus, *Muslim Cities in the Later Middle Ages* (Cambridge, Mass., 1967), 107–13.
26. Ira Lapidus, "Muslim Cities and Islamic Societies," in idem, (ed.), *Middle Eastern Cities* (Berkeley and Los Angeles, 1969), 73.
27. Janet Abu-Lughod, "The Islamic City—Historic Myth, Islamic Essence, and Contemporary Relevance," *International Journal of Middle East Studies* 19 (1987): 155–59.
28. Ibid., 160. See also A. Hourani, "The Islamic City" in *The Emergence of the Modern Middle East* (London, 1981), 19–35. It seems that many of Abu Lughod's assumptions already appear in this essay, which is actually the foreword of: A. Hourani and S. M. Stern, *The Islamic City* (Oxford, 1970). The book itself is the outcome of a symposium held in Oxford in 1965.
29. Ibid., 161–62.
30. Ibid., 162–69.
31. Suraya Faroqhi, *Men of Modest Substance: House Owners and House Property in 17th-Century Ankara and Kayseri* (Cambridge, 1987) p. 220–221. See also André Raymond, "Islamic City, Arab city: Orientalist Myths and Recent Views" *British Journal of Middle East Studies*, 21 (1994) 3–18.
32. Crouch, 72–73.

33. *Sūbāshi* (Turk. *subaşi*—an officer in charge of public order). The city's *sūbāshi* was usually a high-ranking officer in the district's administration.
34. Crouch, 72–73.
35. Başbakanlik Arşivi (BBA), Zeyl-i Mühimme, 11:98, no. 434 (awākhir Rajab 1108/ 21 November 1697); Forster, 122; *Journey to the Holy Land*, fol. 143.
36. In Ottoman terminology the *mi'mār* bashi (*mimar başı* in Turkish) was both an architect and an engineer; these two professions were not differentiated at the time. In times of war, the *mi'mār bashi* was sent to the front and put in charge of constructing fortifications, and planning battle engines and demolitions. See Mehmet Zaki Pakalin, *Osmanli Tarih Deyimleri ve Terimleri* (Istanbul, 1946), II:534.
37. About the *dhirā'* (usually referred to as *arşın* in Turkish, see Midhat Sertoğlu, *Osmanlı Tarih Lugatı* (Istanbul, 1986), 19.
38. *Jerusalem Siljill (JS)*, 107:247, no. 1093 (20 Rab' awwal 1033/ 12 January 1624); see also: ibid., 98:108, no. 624 (29 Shawwāl 1024/ 21 November 1615).
39. *JS*, 107:351, no. 1518 (Rab' al-thāni 1033/ January–February 1624).
40. *Public Records Office* (PRO), SP97, p. 94 (16 May 1624). About Ottoman views of the wall and its function, see also Amnon Cohen, *Economic Life in Ottoman Jerusalem* (Cambridge, 1989), 4.
41. *Jsijill*, 107:538 (24 Şafar 1033/ 21 December 1623); no. 802 (28 Şafar 1033/ 21 December 1623). See also ibid., 98:108, no. 624 (29 Shawwāl 1024/ 21 November 1615).
42. A. Rabbath, *Documents inédits pour servir à l'histoire du Christianisme en Orient* (Paris, 1905–1911; repr. New York, 1973), 344–45. See also Minna Rozen, *Horvot Yerushalayim* (Hebrew; Tel-Aviv, 1981), 47
43. Doubdan, 330–31: "que les religieux faisaient une citadelle pour battre la ville en ruyne, et que par ce moyen ils se rendraient bien-tôt les maistres."
44. On relations between Jews and Christians in Jerusalem, and on rare instances of intellectual contact between them, see Minna Rozen, *The Jewish Community in Jerusalem in the Seventeenth Century* (Hebrew; Jerusalem, 1984) 75–92. On relations with the Muslim community, see ibid., 64–74.
45. See Cornell H. Fleischer, "The Lawgiver as Messiah: The Making of the Imperial Image in the Reign of Süleyman," in Gilles Veinstein (ed.), *Soleiman le Magnifique et son temps* (Paris, 1992), 164–69
46. *Tapu-tahrir* surveys were carried out by the Ottomans once every several years in all Ottoman territories until the seventeenth century. These surveys assessed the taxable land and property, and the amount of tax to be paid by each village, tribe or guild. On *Tapu-tahrir* surveys

and their implementation in Palestine, see Amnon Cohen and Bernard Lewis, *Population and Revenue in the Towns of Palestine in the Sixteenth Century*, (Princeton, 1978), Amy Singer, "Ottoman Officials and Palestinian Peasants: Rural Administration in the Sancak of Jerusalem in the Mid-Sixteenth Century," unpublished Ph.D. disseration, Princeton University, 1989, and also idem, *Palestinian Peasants and Ottoman Officials: Rural Administration around Sixteenth Century Jerusalem* (Cambridge, 1994).

47. Cohen and Lewis, 34–41.
48. See, for example, Jews buying houses from Muslims in the Risha neighborhood—*JS*, 107:324, no. 1401 (20 Rabīʿ al-Thāni 1033/ 10 February 1624); Fakhr al-Din ibn Zakariyya, son of the Mufti, buying part of a house in the Jewish quarter—ibid., 125:120, no. 511 (3 Ramaḍān 1045/ 10 February 1636); Muammad al-ʿAsali, a prominent merchant, buys a house in the Jewish quarter—153:65 (Dhu al-Ḥijja 1085/ March 1674). In this connection, see also Cohen and Lewis. A similar situation existed in eighteenth century Aleppo, where quarters usually consisted of one majority ethnic or religious group, but people of all sects resided practically anywhere. In Aleppo the process of separation was apparently not in an active phase. See Marcus, *The Middle-East on the Eve of Modernity: Aleppo in the Eighteenth Century* (New York, 1989), 315–322.
49. See Marcus, 314–15.
50. On the residence of the ʿAsalis, see *JS*, 177:19 (awāsiṭ Jumāda al-ākhira 1085/ Mid-August 1674); 191:139 (awākhir Rajab 1100/ Mid-May 1689); 191:163 (awākhir Shaʿbān 1100 mid-June 1689). Residence in Bab Hutta: 85:28, no. 39 (awākhir Shaʿbān 1013/ mid-January 1605); 85:266, no. 1549 (18 Rajab 1014/ 29 November 1605); 168:92 (9 Rajab 1078/ 25 December 1667); 177:2 (awākhir Shawwāl 1085/ end of January 1675); 177:97 (Muḥaram 1086/ April 1675) and many more. On local notable families, see chapter 3.
51. Moshe Perlmann, "A Seventeenth-Century Exhortation Concerning al-Aqsa," *Israel Oriental Studies* 3 (1973): 286–91.
52. By "secular" I refer to activities not directly related to religion, not to any denial of faith.
53. *Ağa* is a title of an Ottoman officer, covering a wide range of duties and ranks.
54. The qadi in Jerusalem was one of the senior qadis in the Ottoman Empire, who bore the title of *molla*. His jurisdiction—the district of Jerusalem—was termed *mevleviyet*.
55. Evliya Çelebi, *Seyahatname*, IX:463. Evliya is mistaken in some of the definitions he offers. The *muhzır başı*, for example, was mainly in charge of summoning people and accompanying them to court. See

Pakalın, II:572. It is not clear whether these heads of guilds mentioned at the end are the nine missing *ağa*s in the description, or whether perhaps other officers of lesser positions were not mentioned.

56. On the *muhtasib,* see Pakalın, II:572; Cohen, *Economic Life,* 11–12. The role of the *muhtasib, shaykh al-suq,* and *sheikh al-tujjar* is discussed further in chapter 6.
57. Most of the quotations and examples from the *sijill* in this and in other chapters attest to the considerable variety of issues in the *sharī'ā* court.
58. Here are just a few examples picked at random from one volume of the *sijill* (vol. 146, 1650–1651): p. 265—a firman from Istanbul; p. 283—notables are summoned; p. 321—issues concerning the governors funds; p. 335—the governor's letter of appointment; p. 359—an investigation team dispatched to carry a survey of the water supply to the city; p. 365—a criminal case; p. 385—debt payment; p. 392—a sales deed. It appears that the qadi's authority, relative to that of the governor, was greater than in Aleppo a century later. See Marcus, *The Middle East on the Eve of Modernity,* 80.
59. These are some examples of records in the *sijill* referring to market activities: *JS,* 107: no. 612—appointing the head of a guild; no. 145—trade problems; 171:190—hoarding wheat to inflate prices; 171:421—a brawl in the marketplace; p. 590—friction between villagers and townsmen; 171:661—demand to uphold the rights of a guild; 201:313—exploitation of artisans; *Nābulus Sijill* (*NS*), 1:142—libel lawsuits between merchants. See many other examples of activity in the market in chapter 6.
60. On the Khasikiyya *waqf* see S. H. Stephan, "An Endowment Deed of Khasseki Sultan, Dated the 24th of May 1552," *The Quarterly of the Department of Antiquities in Palestine* 10, (1944): 170–94; Oded Peri, "The Waqf as an Instrument to Increase and Consolidate Political Power: The case of Khasseki Sultan Waqf in Late Eighteenth Century Jerusalem," in G. R. Warburg and G. Gilbar (eds.), *Studies in Islamic Society: Contributions in Memory of Gabriel Baer* (Haifa, 1984) 47–62. For a discussion of the term "Khasiki Sultan," see Pakalın, I:754. Marcus claims that in the eighteenth century the Ottoman state had no notion of welfare, and the poor and needy in Aleppo had to rely on the charity of private individuals. In this regard Jerusalem presents a clear contrast: the main welfare establishment was endowed and kept by the state, and the qadi, a representative of the state, allocated rations in court. A similar situation existed in Nabulus, where the qadi would order several charities to attend to the needs of the poor.
61. The word *takīya* describes both a Sufi prayer room or monastery, and a welfare store.

62. Abd al-Ghani al-Nabulsi, *Kitāb al-Ḥadra al-Unsiyya fi 'l-Riḥla al-Qudsiyya*, 1100h. (Bibliotheque Nationale, Mss. Arabes 5960), fol. 61a.
63. *Bimāristan* is a Persian word meaning hospital or mental institution.
64. The *ghurūsh* referred to at this period (unless stated otherwise) is the Dutch Reichstaler (sometimes called *ghurūsh asadi*, referring to the imprint of a lion on its face). See chapter 5.
65. *JS*, 125:77, no. 326 (6 Sha'bān 1045/ 15 January 1636).
66. Ibid. 107:145 (20 Shawwāl 1032/ 17 August 1623); 107:155, no. 660 (Ṣafar 1033/ December 1623); 107:337, no. 1468 (Rabī' al-Thāni 1033/ January–February 1624); 146:392 (Rajab 1062/ June–July 1652); 201:356 (12 Rabī' al-Thāni 1114/ 5 September 1702). Ralph Hattox, *Coffee and Coffee Houses: The Origins of a Social Beverage in the Medieval Near East* (Seattle and London, 1985), 92–98. See also 'Adil Mannā'. "Mered Naqīb al ashrāf Bi Yerūshalāyim, 1703–1705" (The Naqīb al-ashrāf Revolt in Jerusalem, 1703–1705). Hebrew. *Cathedra* 53 (1989): 62–63; Muḥammad Adnan Bakhit, *The Ottoman Province of Damascus in the 16th Century. (Beirut, 1982), 156; Rozen, Horvot Yerushalayim*, 111. On Drugs and their use, see also d'Arvieux, 12–14.
67. Braudel, *Civilization and Capitalism*, 267–71.
68. The terms *salāmlik* (*selamlik*) and *haramlik* (*haremlik*) were sometimes used in this Turkish form, but in most cases only the private part of the house was referred to as a separate sphere, called the *harim*.
69. Leslie P. Peirce, *The Imperial Harem: Women and Sovereignty in the Ottoman Empire* (New York, 1993), 7–12. On the evolution of the harem as an abode of privacy in Western travel accounts, see Billie Melman. *Women's Orients: English Women and the Middle East, 1718–1918* (Ann Arbor, 1992).
70. See Roger, 300–301.
71. For cases of "accidents" involving the mysterious death of women, see *JS*, 183:227 (awāsiṭ Rajab 1091/ mid-August 1680); 191:67 (3 Jumāda al-Ākhira 1100/ 25 March 1689); p. 116 (10 Rajab 1100 30 April 1689); *NS*, 1:83, no. 2 (2 Dhu al-Ḥijja 1066/ 21 September 1656).
72. Examples of inheritance: *JS*, 125:65, no. 256 (Rajab 1045/ December 1635 - January 1636); 125:121, no. 512 (9 Ramaḍān 1045/ 16 February 1636); 125:177, no. 767 (Shawwāl 1045/ March–April 1636) 125:178, no. 768 (same date); 125:179, no. 770 (same date); 177:66 (14 Dhu al-Ḥijja 1085/11 March 1675); 183:200 (Jumāda al-Ākhira 1090/ July–August 1679). Other records may also indicate the contents of a house. See report of a theft, 168:62 (27 Ramaḍān 1078/ 11 February 1668). On furniture in Jewish houses, see Rozen, *Haqehila Hayehudit*, pages 249–50; Ya'ari, *Masa'ot*, 281. On contents and furniture in (mostly

upper-class Ottoman) harems, see also Billie Melman, *Women's Orients*, 150–53.

73. Braudel, *Civilization and Capitalism*, I:285–94.
74. See d'Arvieux, 18; Ya'ari, *Masa'ot*, 337.
75. In addition to the above-mentioned inheritance records, see Ya'ari, *Masa'ot*, 33.
76. Books in inheritance records: *JS*, 125:177, no. 767 (Shawwāl 1045/ March–April 1636); 183:4 (awāsiṭ Dhu al-Ḥijja 1090/ mid-January 1680). See also: Ya'ari, *Masa'ot*, 354.
77. The Naqīb al-Ashrāf revolt will be discussed in the following chapters, mainly in chapter 3. See also Manna', "The Naqib al-Ashraf Revolt," 54–56, 62–66.

2. RISE AND FALL OF LOCAL DYNASTIES

1. I would like to thank Halil Inalcik for pointing out the importance of the Celali revolts in this process.
2. On the *devşirme* system, see Stanford Shaw, *History of the Ottoman Empire and Modern Turkey* (Cambridge, 1976), 112–15; On systems of governor appointments, see Halil Inalcik, *The Ottoman Empire: The Classical Age*, 104–18; Gibb and Bowen, I:137–54; Norman Itzkowitz, *The Ottoman Empire and Islamic Tradition* (Chicago, 1980). On changes in the system, see Inalcik, "Centralization and Decentralization," 27, 29–30.
3. Metin Kunt, *The Sultan's Servants—The Transformation of Ottoman Government, 1550–1650* (New York, 1983). The summary presented here and in the following paragraphs is based on most of this book.
4. On the allocation of *çiftliks*, see ibid., 85–87.
5. Ibid., 70–72.
6. Several detailed essays on the two families—Farrūkh and Ṭurabāy—shed some light on their origins and histories. 'Adel Mannā', basing his research on the Jerusalem *sijill*, describes the first two generations of the Farrūkhs—Farrūkh himself, the founder of the small dynasty, and his son Muḥammad, both of whom held the position of governor in Jerusalem and Nabulus on several occasions. He describes the contacts between the Farrūkhs and the Ṭurabāys, and an ambivalent relationship with the beduins in the region: 'Adel Mannā', *Mishpāḥat Farrūkh: shilṭōna u-fō'ola (The House of Farrūkh: Its rule and Deeds)* (M. A. Thesis, The Hebrew University of Jerusalem, 1978). A summary of this work is published as an article: "Moshley Yerūshālāyim mi-beyt Farrūkh (The Farrūkh Governors of Jerusalem) in: Amnon Cohen

(ed.) *Peraqim be-tōldōt Yerūshalāyim be-rēshit hateqūfa ha-ʻōthmānit (Chapters in the History of Jerusalem at the beginning of the Ottoman Period)* (Jerusalem, 1979) pp. 196–232. See also: Minna Rozen, *Ḥōrvōt Yerūshalāyim (The Ruins of Jerusalem)* (Tel-Aviv, 1981).

Moshe Sharon, Adnan Bakhit and Abd al-Rahim abu Husayn wrote on the Ṭurabāys, who ruled the district of Lajjun for several generations. Their work is based mainly on Ottoman sources and on the accounts of the French aristocrat d'Arvieux, who was in the Ṭurabāy's employ for several years: Adnan Bakhit, "al-Usra al-Ḥārithiyya fi Marj bani ʻAmr (The Harithite family in Marj Bani ʻAmr)" *Al-Abḥāth*, vol. 27 (1980), 55–78; idem, *The Ottoman Province of Damascus in the Sixteenth Century* (Beirut, 1982), 208–216; Moshe Sharon, "The Political Role of the Beduins in Palestine in the Sixteenth and Seventeenth Centuries" in M. Maoz (ed.) *Studies on Palestine During the Ottoman Period* (Jerusalem, 1975). The Ṭurabāys are also discussed by Abd al-Rahim Abu Husayn, *Provincial Leadership in Syria, 1575–1650* (Beirut, 1985), 183–198. These works stress the family's bedouin origin, its special relationship with the Ottomans from the beginning of the sixteenth century, and its prolonged war against Fakhr al-Din II. The Riḍwān family is often mentioned by Uriel Heyd in his book *Ottoman Documents on Palestine.*

7. Mehmed Süreyya, *Sicill-i Osmani* (Istanbul, 1308–11), IV:374–75; Heyd, *Ottoman Documents*, 41–42. Heyd points out that the governor of Gaza was the only governor in Palestine whose salary exceeded half a million *akçe* a year, and was therefore the only one among them eligible for the post of *beylerbey* (province governor). This may explain why Kara Mustafa received the governorship of Gaza after a tour of duty as province governor.
8. Süreyya, *Sicill-i Osmani*, II:401–2; Heyd, *Ottoman Documents*, 50, 186, 105–6, 137; Mannaʻ, "Moshley Yerushalayim Mi-Beyt Farrukh," 197; Rafeq, *The Province of Damascus, 56.* Iḥsān al-Nimr, *Tārikh Jabal Nābulus*, I:79.
9. Muḥibbi, I:187; II:134–36.
10. Süreyya, *Sicill-i Osmani*, II:133–134; Muḥibbi, II:16. See also Heyd, *Ottoman Documents*, 186. Heyd suggests that Hasan was called "Arap" because of his dark skin color.
11. Muḥibbi, II:88–89; Abd al-Karim Rafeq, *Bilād al-shām wa-Miṣr min al-fatḥ al-ʻuthmāni* (Damascus, 1968), 225.
12. *JS*, 171:659 (Shaʻbān 1081/ December 1670 - January 1671)
13. The title *amīr al-darbayn* refers to the Ṭurabāys' task of guarding the coastal road (via Maris) and the stretch of road from Damascus to Jerusalem that passes through the Jordan valley and Jenin. On doubts concerning their origins, see Abu Husayn, *Provincial Leadership*, 184–85.

14. Heyd, *Ottoman Documents*, 45–46, 50–52, 56–57, 94–95; Sharon, "The Political Role of the Beduins," 26–30; Abu Husayn, *Provincial Leadership in Syria*, 187, 191; Bakhit, *The Ottoman Province of Damascus*, pp. 208–12; D'Arvieux, 74–78. On the Ṭurabāys' bedouin connections and requests for camels by the Ottoman authorities, see also d'Arvieux, 20, 106–7; *Başbakanlık Arşivi* (*BBA*), Mühimme Defteri (MD), 69:183, no. 368 (20 Rabi' al-Awwal 1000/ 6 January 1592); 69:34, no. 40 (29 Jumāda al-Ūla 1000/ 14 March 1592); Abu Husayn, 191.
15. Abu Husayn, 187–88; Bakhit, *The Ottoman Province of Damascus*, 56–66.
16. Abu Husayn, 189–90; Bakhit, "The Harithite Family," 68–69; Heyd, 45, 52–53, 109–10.
17. Muḥibbi, I:221; Sharon, "The Political Role of the Bedouins," 28–29; Bakhit, "The Harithite Family,", 70–77; Abu Husayn, 192–97.
18. Halil Inalcik, Fariba Zarinebaf and Karen Barkey, *BBA Provincial Appointment Registers* (to be published): "Liva-i mezburda mutasarrıf olan Turabay oğlu Ahmedin şekaveti zuhur edüp"; see also Muḥibbi.
19. Sharon, "The Political Role of the Bedouins," 29; Muḥibbi; Bakhit, "The Harithite Family," 77–78.
20. Manna', "The Governors of Jerusalem"; Rozen, *The Ruins of Jerusalem*, 23–49; idem, *Ha-qehila Ha-Yehudit Be-Yerushalayim* (The Jewish Community in Jerusalem in the Seventeenth Century) (Tel-Aviv, 1985), 30–57.
21. Manna', "The Governors of Jerusalem," 203–7; Rozen, *The Ruins of Jerusalem*, 23–26.
22. Manna', "The Governors of Jerusalem," 209–15; Rozen, *The Ruins of Jerusalem*, 26–49.
23. Muḥibbi, IV:108–10; Iḥsān al-Nimr, *Tārikh Jabal Nābulus wa-l-Balqā'* (History of Jabal Nabulus and the Balqa'), I.
24. *NS*, 1:40, 43, 67, 101, 158, 163. Many other records and firmans that do not deal directly with issues of government refer to 'Assāf as governor.
25. *JS*, 168:16 (25 Rajab 1078/ 10 January 1668); 168:42 (26 Rajab 1078/ 11 January 1668); 171:185 (awākhir Jumāda al-Ākhira 1080/ end of November 1669); 171:639 (6 Sha'bān 1081/ 19 December 1670); 171:659 (Sha'bān 1081/ December 1670), etc. At the beginning of the seventeen nineties another governor named 'Assaf was *sanjaq bey* of Jerusalem and 'Ajlun, and *amīr al-ḥajj*. See Karl Barbir, *Ottoman Rule in Damascus, 1708–1758* (Princeton, 1980), 46–47. And also: *BBA*, MD, 98:79, no. 242 (awāsiṭ Rabī' al-Awwal 1100/ mid-January 1689); 99:162, no. 522 (awākhir Rabī' al-Thāni 1101/ February 1680); 102:125, no. 521 (Awā'il Jumāda al-Ūla 1103/ January 1692); 104:178 (awā'il Rabī' al-Thāni 1104/ mid-December 1692); 104:214 (awāsiṭ Sha'bān 1104/ April 1693). If

Muḥibbi's account of 'Assaf's death, corroborated by the *sijill*, is to be believed, then this could not be the same person. There is a slim chance, though, that news of 'Assaf's death was false and that he later reappeared. If this is true, it may provide another explanation for the pen strokes on documents pertaining to 'Assaf's death and to his inheritance.

26. Mannā', "The Governors of Jerusalem," 202–4.
27. Ibid, 207, 211.
28. Ibid.
29. *NS*, vol. 1, p. 40 (10 Rajab 1066/ 4 May 1656).
30. JS, 171:639 (6 Sha'bān 1081/ 19 December 1670).
31. Ibid., p. 659 (Sha'bān 1081/ January 1671).
32. Heyd, *Ottoman Documents*, 50–52.
33. Mannā', "The Governors of Jerusalem," 211–15; idem, "The Farrūkh Family," 44; Ahmad al-Khalidi, *Lubnān fi 'ahd al-amir Fakhr al-Din al-Ma'ni al-thāni (Lebanon in the Reign of Fakhr al-Din II)* (Beirut, 1636), 106, 111–12, 124–25; Bulus Qar'ali, *Fakhr al-Din al-Ma'ni al-thāni ḥākim Lubnān wa-dawlat Tuskāna 1605–1635* (Fakhr al-Din and the State of Tuscany) (Rome, 1938) II:126–28; Abu Husayn, *Provincial Leadership*, 87–110; P. M. Holt, *Egypt and the Fertile Crescent, 1516–1922* (Ithaca and London, 1966), 115–19.
34. N. J. Coulson, *Succession in the Muslim Family* (Cambridge, 1971), 40–47. According to the *sharī'a* most of the inheritance is fixed and cannot be altered by a will. Each of the deceased's relatives—children, parents, brothers, sisters, and other kin—is entitled to a share of the inheritance, in accordance with the number of heirs, their relation or proximity to the deceased, and their sex. As a rule a male receives twice the amount given to a female in the same proximity to the deceased.
35. *NS*, 1:43, no. 3 (15 Rajab 1066/ 9 May 1656).
36. *JS*, 171:659 (Sha'bān 1081/ December 1670 - January 1671).
37. Manna', "The Governors of Jerusalem," 208, 211; Rozen, *The Ruins of Jerusalem*, 23; Inalcik, Zarinebaf and Barkey, "Liwa Lajjun."
38. On the Ṭurabāy's Bedouin heritage, see: d'Arvieux, 106–7.
39. Dror Zeevi, *Slavery in the Ottoman Empire in the 19th Century—Social and Judicial Aspects (Hebrew)*, unpublished M.A. thesis, Tel Aviv University, 1985, 104–8; Metin Kunt, "Kullarin Kullari," *Boğaziçi Üniversitesi—Hümaniter Bilimler* 3 (1975): 27–42; Süreyya, *Sicill-i Osmani*, 374–75.
40. Kunt; Manna', "The Governors of Jerusalem". Another of Riḍwān's *mamlūks*, Kiwān Bey, was sent to Damascus, where he (and later his son) became *amir al-ḥajj* several decades later.

41. On the system of education in the sultan's palace, see Norman Itzkowitz, *Ottoman Empire and Islamic Tradition* (Chicago and London, 1972), 59–60; Inalcik, *The Ottoman Empire*, 78–79.
42. Muḥibbi, I:187–88.
43. Muḥibbi, II:16, 88; ʿArif al-ʿArif, *Tarīkh Ghazza* (History of Gaza) (Jerusalem, 1943), 178. Travelers from the West who visited Gaza during Ḥusayn Pasha's reign confirm this description of a remarkably generous and noble person. See Martin M. Meyer, *History of the City of Gaza* (New York, 1907), 97–98.
44. Muḥibbi, III:271; IV:108.
45. Carter Findley, *Bureaucratic Reform in the Ottoman Empire* (Princeton, 1980), 31–40.
46. Farrūkh himself, of course, began as a *mamlūk* in the service of Bahrām Pasha. Other mentions of *mamlūks* see Ovadia Salameh, "Slavery and Waqf in Jerusalem, in the Early Ottoman Period" (Hebrew), unpublished seminar paper presented to the Hebrew University, 1989, 9–10, 13; *JS*, 107:351. no. 1504 (18 Dhu al-Ḥijja 1032/ 13 October 1623); Rozen, *The Ruins of Jerusalem*, 93; *BBA*, MD, 96:125, no. 627 (Awā'il Shaʿbān 1089/ September 1678).
47. On other sets of political marriage in these local dynasties, see Muḥibbi, I:189; al-Khalidi, 129; On marriage in and outside the social class, see Findley, *Bureaucratic Reform*, 32–33.
48. This can be perceived in many *sijill* records in Jerusalem and Nabulus. Some are quoted in this chapter.
49. On military bands and battle standards, see al-Khalidi, 9. As for sports and hunting, Muḥibbi, I:187, recounts that the forefather of the Ridwan family, Kara Shahin Mustafa Pasha, received his nickname Shāhīn (falcon) or Abu Shāhīn, because, being very fond of this hunting method, he was frequently seen with a falcon on his wrist.
50. d'Arvieux, 54.
51. On the transfer of *'imārat al-ḥajj* to Damascus, see Rafeq, *The Province of Damascus*, 53–58. Rafeq notes the attempt to remove command of the *ḥajj* caravan from the Palestinian districts to the Damascene center, but does not mention the subsequent failure of this attempt, and the success of the southwestern *sanjaqbeys* in regaining control of this lucrative task.
52. In this context *faqīh* probably means a reciter of the Koran.
53. *NS*, 1:38, no. 2 (8 Rajab 1066/ 2 May 1656). On the *ulak* rapid messenger service, see Midhat Sertoğlu, *Osmanlı Tarih Luğatı* (Istanbul, 1986), 348.
54. Muḥibbi, II:89: "lam yajni dhanban ghayr anna zamānahu * qad fuwwiḍa al-ahkām li'l-ḥussād * Hābūhu wa-hūwa muqayyad fi sijnihi * wa-kadha al-suyūf tuhābu fi al-aghmād."

55. *BBA*, MD, 102:202 (awākhir Rabīʿ al-Thāni 1103/ mid-January 1692); 104:103, (awā'il Rabīʿ al-Awwal 1104/ mid-November 1692); 106:120, no. 417 (awāsiṭ Shawwāl 1106/ May–June 1695); 111:508, no. 1761–62 (awāsiṭ Rabīʿ al-Thāni 1112/ September–October 1700); 111:574, no. 2022 (awā'il Muḥarram 1113/ March 1702); 110:154, no. 544 (awā'il Shawwāl 1113/ March 1702); *JS*, 201:1 (awāsiṭ Dhu al-Ḥijja 1112/ October 1698). On the abandonment of villages, see ʿAdel Mannaʿ, "The Naqib al-Ashraf Revolt," 53.
56. Mannaʿ, "The Naqib al-Ashraf Revolt," 55–62.
57. Ibid., 63–68.
58. Rifaat Abou el-Haj, *The 1703 Revolt and the Structure of Ottoman Politics* (Istanbul, 1984), 88–93.
59. On the transfer of *imārat al-ḥajj* to Damascus, see Rafeq, *Bilad al-Sham,* 225.

3. THE SUFI CONNECTION

1. Shaw, *The Ottoman Empire,* 225–29; Abou el-Haj, *The 1703 Revolt*; P. M. Holt, *Egypt and the Fertile Crescent,* 88–90; Rafeq, *The Province of Damascus,* 81–85. On the Naqib al-Ashraf revolt of 1703 in Jerusalem, see above, pp. 60–61.
2. Abou El-Haj, *The 1703 Revolt,* 13–14, 88–93. See also Holt; Mannaʿ, "The Naqib al-Ashraf Revolt," 54–56.
3. Gibb and Bowen, I:198–99, 256–57.
4. Albert Hourani, "Ottoman Reform and the Politics of Notables" in idem, *The Emergence of the Modern Middle East* (London, 1981), 40–41.
5. Ibid., 42.
6. Ibid., 44.
7. Ibid., 44–45.
8. Ibid., 45–51
9. Ibid., 66.
10. Inalcik, "Centralization and Decentralization," 37–39.
11. Ibid., 37–38.
12. Ibid., 44–45.
13. Barbir, *Ottoman Rule in Damascus,* 68–73.
14. For examples of the use of the term *ayan* and its definitions, see Gibb and Bowen, I:198–99; Inalcik, "Centralization and Decentralization," 30–38; idem, "Military and Fiscal Transformation," 327–29; McGowan, "Research of Land and Agriculture," 60; Hourani, "Politics of Notables," 44–45.
15. *JS*, 146:285 (19 Jumāda al-Ūla 1062/28 April 1652). Another example will be discussed at length later in the chapter *NS*, 1:169, no. 1 (awā'il

Sha'bān 1067/15 May 1657). On honorific titles in the *sijill* of Aleppo, see Marcus, *The Middle East on the Eve of Modernity,* 57.

16. Use of the terminology suggested by Lybyer does not mean acceptance of his division into "ruling" and "military" institutions based on ethnic and religious lines. The two elites were far more complex in their constitution, as well as in their self-image, than ethnic and religious divisions suggest.
17. See Hourani, "Politics of Notables," 45–49.
18. Abd al-Ghani al-Nābulsi, *Riḥlati ila al-quds (al-ḥaḍra al-unsiyya fi al-riḥla al-qudsiyya* (al-Qāhira, Maktabat al-qāhira bi-al-ṣanādiqiyya, n.d.), 13, 15, 19, 40, 52, 73. See also the manuscript: *kitāb al-haḍra al-unsiyya fi al-riḥla al-qudsiyya* (Mss. Arabes no. 5960, Bibliothèque Nationale, Paris), fols. 52b, 62.
19. Evliya Çelebi, *Seyahatname,* IX:488.
20. Muḥibbi, Ulema who studied in Cairo: I:87, 297, 489, 500; II:134–6, 172, 238, 437; III:110, 266, 340, 356, 411, 412, 413, 475, 482; IV:315.
21. Ibid.
22. Ibid., II:433; III:340. On connections between *ashrāf* and Sufi orders see *JS,* 98:93, no. 525 (17 Shawwāl 1024/9 November 1615).
23. Muḥibbi: Muḥammad al-Dajjāni, III:356 'Abd al-Qādir al-Ghazzi, II:437; the 'Alamis, II:219, IV:78. Other Sufi ulema: Ḥafiz al-Din b. Muḥammad al-Surūri, I:500; Darwīsh ibn Sulaymān al-Dajjāni, II:156; Ṣāliḥ ibn 'Ali al-Ṣafadi, II:238; Muḥammad b. Sāliḥ al-Dajjāni, III:475; Muḥammad b. abi al-Luṭf, III:482; Muḥammad al-Dayri al-Qudsi, IV:313. See also Muḥammad Khalīl al-Murādi, *Silk al-durar fi a'yān al-qarn al-ḥādi 'ashar* (Baghdād, Maktabat al-muthanna, n.d.): Abu al-wafā al-'Alami, I:71; Aḥmad b. Ṣaliḥ al-'Alami, I:117.
24. Roger, 284–92.
25. Ibid., 288: "Les seigneurs, Bachas et Sanjacqs ont d'ordinaire un de ces derviches avec eux, et lors qu'ils vont en campagne ils les logent dans leurs tents et pavillions."
26. For the status of *ṭariqas* in Damascus, see Bakhit, *The Ottoman Province of Damascus,* 214.
27. *JS,* 107:284, no. 1225 (5 Rabī' al-Thāni 1033/28 December 1623).
28. Ibid., 107:302, no. 1304 (6 Rabī' al-Thāni 1033/28 December 1623). For other cases of *waqfs* dedicated by governors and ulema to the Sufis, see ibid, 85, no. 1549 (18 Rabī' al-Thāni 1014/2 September 1605); 107, no. 550 (Ṣafar 1033/November–December 1623); 107:571 (same date). In addition to their income from *waqfs,* Sufis were also helped by their benefactors to receive allowances for performing ritual and traditional prayer tasks: see ibid, 107:247, no. 1092 (10 Muḥarram 1033/November 4, 1623).

29. Ibid., 107:161, no. 671; 191:107 (awākhir Jumāda al-Ākhira 1100/April 1689). See also 107:175, no. 720 (19 Ṣafar 1033/21 December 1623).
30. Muḥibbi, II:88 (Ḥusayn Pasha b. Riḍwān); 134–136 (Khayr al-Din al-Ramli); IV:212 (ʻUmar b. ʻAbd al-Qadir al-Ghazzi).
31. W. A. S. Khalidi, "al-ʻAlami", *Encyclopedia of Islam*, 2nd edition, I:352.
32. Ibid. Building a mosque on the site of the Ascension provoked protests from Christians residing in Jerusalem, who considered this part of their own heritage.
33. *JS*, 107. no. 571 (Ṣafar 1033/November–December 1623). Sheikh Asʻad is referred to as *"al-mufti al-aʻẓam bi-dār al-salṭana al-sanīyya."*
34. *JS*, 107. no. 688 (1033/1623); 107:301, no. 1302 (10 Rabīʻ al-Thāni 1033/10 January 1624); 107:312, no. 1376, (Rabīʻ al-Thāni 1033/January 1624); 107:404, no. 1750 (Jumāda al-Ūla 1033/February–March 1624); 107:405, no. 1754 (same date); 125:40, no. 177 (13 Rajab 1045/22 December 1635); 125:52, no. 213 (12 Rajab 1045/22 December 1635).
35. On ʻAlamis receiving *ṣurra* payments, see *JS*, 98:76, no. 437 (12 Shawwāl 1024/4 November 1615); 125:80, no. 336 (Shaʻbān 1045/ January–February 1636); Iḥsān al-Nimr, *Tārīkh jabal Nābulus wa-al-Balqāʼ*, I:88.
36. *JS*, 107: no. 974 (Rabīʻ Awwal 1033/December 1623 - January 1624); 125:80, no. 336 (Shaʻbān 1045/January–February 1636); 201: no. 423 (19 Shawwāl 1114/8 March 1703).
37. *JS*, 177:145 (22 Rabīʻ Awwal 1086/16 July 1675).
38. *JS*, 98:108, no. 264 (29 Shawwāl 1024/11 November 1615). It should be mentioned, though, that in another record of the same year another *sayyid*, Zakariyya, is mentioned as *naqīb al ashrāf*: ibid., 98:46, no. 437 (12 Shawwāl 1024/5 November 1615). Mannāʻ, "The Naqib al-Ashraf Revolt," 56.
39. *JS*, 107: no. 446 (Muḥarram 1033/November 1623).
40. Ibid, no. 1091 (18 Rabīʻ Awwal 1033/9 January 1624).
41. Ibid, 125:67, no. 265 (Rajab 1045/December 1635 - January 1636); 125:80, no. 336-337 (Shaʻbān 1045/January–February 1636); 146:285 (19 Jumāda al-Ūula 1062/April–May 1652) Compare with the status of *naqīb al ashrāf* in Damascus: Bakhit, *Damascus in the 16th Century*, 215. Bakhit claims that the *naqīb* in Damascus had no special status throughout the 17th century.
42. Mannāʻ, "The Naqib al-Ashrāf Revolt," 72–73.
43. *JS*, 85:55, no. 244 (8 Shawwāl 1013/27 February 1605); 85:309, no. 1368 (Rabīʻ al-Thāni 1033/January 1624); 85: no. 439 (Muḥarram 1033/October–November 1223). On the position of *raʼīs al-tujjār* (*bazar başı*) in sixteenth-century Jerusalem, see Amnon Cohen, *Economic Life in Ottoman Jerusalem*, 77, 85, 104, 109.

44. *JS*, 125:201, no. 865 (29 Shawwāl 1045/6 April 1636); 146:285 (19 Jumāda al-Ūla 1062/28 April 1668).
45. *JS*, 168:56 (Ramaḍān 1078/ February-March 1668); 168:57, (20 Ramaḍān 1078/ 5 March 1668); 168:273 (ghurrat Muḥarram 1079/ 11 June 1668); 168:401 (Jumāda al-Thāniya 1079/November 1668); 191:64 (Jumāda al-Ūla 1100/February-March 1689).
46. ʿAbd al-Ghanī Al-Nābulsī, *Riḥlatī ilā al-Quds (Al-Ḥaḍra al-unsiyyā fi al-riḥlā al Qudsiyya)* (Cairo, n.d.), 21; *JS*, 183:156 (10 Jumāda al-Ūla 1091/8 June 1680).
47. *Sekban* were military units recruited ad hoc, mainly from among the peasants, and sometimes discharged when the war was over. Many unemployed *sekban* units rebelled against the central government and ravaged the Anatolian countryside.
48. Karl Barbir, "From Pasha to Effendi: The Assimilation of Ottomans into Damascene Society, 1516–1783," *International Journal of Turkish Studies* 1. 1 (Winter 1979–80): 69–71.
49. *JS*, 191:177 (8 Ramaḍān 1100/26 June 1689). For another dimension of this issue, local groups integrated into the military elite, see ibid., 168:354, (5 Jumāda al-Ākhira 1079/10 November 1668) and subsequent records.
50. *Bashsha* (*beççe*) is a title for a junior officer in the sultan's inner service. The title, literally meaning "swallow chick," was given to particularly swift and agile youths. See Pakalin, I:184.
51. *Müteferrika*—member of a special corps of the sultan's external service, staffed by slaves as well as sons of *ümera*.
52. *NS*, 1: 169, no. 1 (awā'il Shaʿbān 1067/May 1657). Other documents presenting a similar pecking order: *JS*, 146:285 (19 Jumāda al-Ūla 1062/28 April 1652); 183:158 (7 Jumāda al-Ūla 1091/5 June 1680).
53. Robert Darnton, "A Bourgeois Puts His World in Order: The City as a Text," in *The Great Cat Massacre and Other Episodes in French Cultural History* (New York, 1984), 107–40.
54. Ibid., 120.
55. Marshal S. Hodgson, *The Venture of Islam* (Chicago, 1974), I:105–11.
56. The *ṣurra* (*sürre*) was an annual gift of money sent from Istanbul to various places in the empire, including Jerusalem. Those entitled to receive it were certain high-ranking ulema, members of established families, etc. *Ṣurra* grants were relatively small.
57. Doubdan, 327–335.
58. Ibid.
59. *JS*, 146:283 (19 Jumāda al-Ūla 1062/ 28 April 1652).
60. Ibid., 285 (same date).

61. For an interesting discussion of salaries and grants of money as status symbols, see Darnton, "A Bourgeois Puts His World in Order," 120–22.
62. *JS*, 183:117 (Ṣafar 1091/ March 1680); *NS*, I:243, no. 1 (27 Jumāda al-Ūla 1066/ 24 March 1656).
63. Inalcik, "Fiscal and Military Transformation," 331–33; idem, "Centralization and Decentralization," 41. This description obviously applies to eighteenth-century notables. See Marcus, *The Middle East on the Eve of Modernity*, 57–58.
64. On local leasing of *timar* and *waqf*, see chapter 5.
65. See Mannā', "The Naqib al-Ashrāf Revolt," 68–74.
66. BBA, *MD*, 104:103 (awā'il Rabī' al-Awwal 1104/ mid-September 1692); 106:120, no. 417 (awāsiṭ Shawwāl 1106/ end of May 1695); *JS*, 201:299 (22 Muḥarram 1115/ 7 June 1703); ibid., p. 311 (awāsit Rajab 1110/mid-January 1699), and many others. See also chapter 2.
67. 'Ādel Mannā', "The Naqib al-Ashrāf Revolt," 56–57; Silahdar Findiklili Mehmed aga, *Silahdar Tarihi* (Istanbul, 1928) 242; Rozen, "Mered naqīb al-ashrāf" (The Naqīb al-Ashraf Revolt) 77–78.
68. Mannā', "The Naqib al-Ashrāf Revolt," 68–74.
69. Rafeq, *Bilād al-Shām wa-Miṣr*, 221; Holt, *Egypt and the Fertile Crescent*, 88–90; Abou al-Haj, *The 1703 Revolt*, 88–93.

4. DESERT, VILLAGE AND TOWN

1. See Heyd, *Ottoman Documents*, 63–78. Heyd suggests that the decline of janissaries and *sipahis* can be traced back to the mid-sixteenth century (p. 63). This state of affairs stems, according to Heyd, from the weakness of several sultans and from the demise of the *devşirme* system as a result of pressures from without. On the reasons for the disappearance of the *devşirme*, see above, pp. 36–39.
2. On janissaries in commerce and daily life, see *JS*, 98:94, no. 531 (23 Shawwāl 1024/15 November 1615); 107, no. 696 (17 Ṣafar 1033/ 2 August 1623); 107, no. 974 (Rabī' Awwal 1033/ December 1623 - January 1624); 107:264 (27 Rabī' Awwal 1033/ 18 January 1624); 107:300, no. 1351 (2 Rabī' al-Thāni 1033/ 23 January 1623); no. 380 (awāsiṭ Muḥarram 1033/November 1623); 125, no. 453 (6 Sha'bān 1045/15 January 1636). *NS*, 1:36 (5 Rajab 1066/ 29 April 1656); p. 56 (22 Sha'bān 1066/ 15 June 1656); 1:135 (awākhir Rajab 1067/ Beginning of May 1657); 1:138 (16 Shawwāl 1067/ 28 July 1657).
3. In most cases this term (*al-takalif al-'urfiyya*) refers to taxes and impositions by local governors or by the central government, in addition to the regular taxes mentioned in the *kanun* names and in *tapu-tahrir* registers. On taxation, see chapter 6, pp. 145–154.

4. For janissary inheritance lists, see *JS*, 107:264, 284, 300, 318; *NS*, 1:53, 66. For a janissary as translator (*turjumān*), see *JS*, 171:188 (28 Jumāda al-Ākhira 1080/ 23 November 1669).
5. See Kunt, *The Sultan's Servants*, 79.
6. *BBA*, MD, 73:475, no. 1048 (17 Ramaḍān 1003/ 26 May 1595); 92:13, no. 57 (awā'il Ramḍān 1067/ mid-June 1657).
7. Farrūkh Bey and Kiwān Bey, both *mamlūks* of the Riwḍān family, were given *timars* and ranks, on their way to becoming district governors. See chapter 2, p. 40.
8. This case is contained in a series of records: *JS*, 168:354 (5 Jumāda al-Ākhira 1079/ 10 November 1668); 356 (10 Jumāda al-Ākhira 1079/ 15 November 1068); 171:396 (12 Muḥarram 1081/ 1 June 1670). See also 201:380 (awākhir Jumāda al-Ākhira 1114/ mid-November 1702).
9. In yet another parallel dispute, the relatives reached a compromise with the families of the executed assassins. Both sides agreed to waive demands for compensation and resume their lives, but this intriguing affair is beyond the scope of this chapter.
10. *JS*, 183:239 (awākhir Rajab 1091/ end of July 1680). On attempts to turn *timars* into private property and bequeath them to sons, see chapter 5, pp. 128–129.
11. *JS*, 183:183 (Jumāda al-Ūla 1091/ June 1680)/ 183:218 (8 Rajab 1091/ 4 August 1680); 183:227 (awāsiṭ Rajab 1091/mid-August 1680). See also Gerber, *The Social Origins*, 20.
12. See Heyd, *Ottoman Documents*, 63, 67–68, 70–72, 76. *NS*, 1:31, no. 2 (Jumāda al-Ūla 1066/ February–March 1656); 1:337, no. 1 (awākhir Jumāda al-Ūla 1068/ March 1658). *BBA*, MD, 98:80, no. 243 (awāsiṭ Rajab 1100/ May 1689); 106:120, no. 417 (awāsiṭ Shawwāl 1106/ May–June 1695). Evliya Çelebi, *Seyahatname*, IX:462.
13. The declining status of this once feared institution was reflected in the attitude of people in the city towards them. In one case a *sipahi* filed a complaint against a Christian residing in the city for allegedly calling him "a leech and a bugger" (*ya 'alaq, ya manyuk*).
14. Halil Inalcik, "Military and Fiscal Transformation in the Ottoman Empire, 1600–1700," *Archivum Ottomanicum* 4 (1980): 299–300; Ihsan al-Nimr, *Tārikh Jabal Nābulus*, I:85; Al-Khalidi, *Lubnān fi 'ahd al-Amīr Fakhr al-Dīn*, 186–192.
15. Ibn Khaldun, *The Muqaddimah: An Introduction to History*, (Trans. Franz Rosenthal (New York, 1958), 247–287.
16. Uriel Heyd, *Ottoman Documents on Palestine* (Oxford, 1960).
17. Ibid., 91–92.
18. Ibid., 94–96.
19. Ibid., 96–98.

20. Ibid., 90–91.
21. Moshe Sharon, "The Political Role of the Bedouins in Palestine in the Sixteenth and Seventeenth Centuries," in M. Ma'oz (ed.) *Studies on Palestine during the Ottoman Period* (Jerusalem, 1975), 17–19.
22. Ibid., 26–30. Ṭurabāy is a Mamluk name and Sharon wonders about its origin, but the clan itself, and its bedouin background are well known. See also 'Adnan Bakhīt, "Al-Usra al-Ḥārithiyya fi Marj bani 'Amr" (The Harithite family in Marj Bani 'Amr), *Al-Abḥath* 18 (1980): 55–78.
23. Ibid.
24. 'Ādil Mannā', "Moshley Yerushalayim mi-beyt Farrūkh" (The Farrūkh Governors of Jerusalem), in Amnon Cohen (ed.), *Prakim be-toldot Yerushalayim be-reshit hatkufa ha-Othmanit* (Chapters in the History of Jerusalem at the Beginning of the Ottoman Period) (Jerusalem, 1979), 202.
25. Ibid., 209–215.
26. Ibid. and records on pp. 217–224.
27. Haim Gerber, *The Social Origins of the Modern Middle East* (Boulder, Colorado, 1987), 60. This is by no means the only example. See also Ihsan 'Abbās, "Hair Ad-Din Ar-Ramli's Fatāwa: A New Light on Life in Palestine in the Eleventh/Seventeenth Century" in Ulrich Haarman and Peter Bachman (eds.) *Die Islamische Welt Zwischen Mittelalter und Neuzeit* (Beirut, 1979) pp. 10–11 – 'Abbās conforms to the general view on bedouin. Some tribes obeyed Khayr al-Dīn's *fatāwa*, other tribes frequently cooperate with villagers. Women who quarrelled with their husbands sometimes find shelter with them. Yet in the end they are described as the disruptive element *par exellence* in the region.
28. Heyd, *Ottoman Documents*, 93–94.
29. Ibid., 98–99.
30. Sharon, "The Political Role of the Bedouins," 20n.50, 23n.70.
31. Heyd, *Ottoman Documents*, 98–99, and n. 10.
32. *BBA*, MD, 104, no. 162 (awāsiṭ Jumāda al-Ākhira 1104/ end of February 1693). On a similar function of the *amir al-'Arab* at the beginning of the century, see Bakhit, *The Ottoman Province of Damascus*, 202–4.
33. Mannā', "The Farrūkh Governors of Jerusalem," 200–201; *BBA*, MD, 98:172, no. 579 (awāsiṭ Jumāda al-Ūla 1100/ beginning of March 1689); 114:1, no. 1 (beginning of Rabī' al-Thāni 1114/ end of July 1702); *JS*, 153:1 (6 Dhu al-Ḥijja 1067/ 15 September 1657).
34. *JS*, 98:108, no. 624 (29 Shawwāl 1024/ 21 November 1615). On the notables mentioned in this record, see chapter 3.
35. Aḥmad ibn Muḥammad al-Khālidi, *Lubnān fi 'ahd al-amīr Fakhr al-Dīn al-Ma'ni al-thāni* (Beirut, 1936), 189–93. Al-Khālidi mentions that

Ibn Farrūkh also had with him a force of *sakmāniyya* (an Arabic version of the Turkish word *sekban*, local forces). These are not mentioned in other sources at this stage, although in the late seventeenth century they frequently appear in *sijill* records. There is no way of knowing who these *sakmāniyya* were. They may have been forces from Anatolia, but they could also be bedouin recruited as a special force. On Fakhr al-Dīn II and his exploits, see also chapter 2, p. 49.

36. *Archives Nationales*, Affaires Etrangères, serie bIII, 34:308. At the end of the letter the trader informs the minister that the pirates were later found out to be French—Captains Dedon and Daleste.
37. See Daniel Panzac, "International and DOmestic Maritime Trade in the Ottoman Empire during the 18th Century" *International Journal of Middle East Studies* 24 (1992) pp. 189-206.
38. See a detailed description of the economy in chapter 6. See also: *Histoire du Commerce de Marseille* (Paris, 1954), IV:92–94; V:395; François Charles-Roux, *Les Echelles de Syrie et de Palestine* (Paris, 1928), 9.
39. Heyd, *Ottoman Documents*, 95–96. See also ibid., 81. Amnon Cohen, *Yehudim Be-Shilton Ha-Islam*, 208–9.
40. *BBA*, MD, 102:212, no. 817 (awā'il Shawwāl 1103/ mid-June 1692); 115:137, no. 563 (awākhir Jumāda al-Ākhira 1118/ beginning of October 1706).
41. *JS*, 107:102 (11 Dhu al-Ḥijja 1032/ 6 October 1623); Cohen, *Economic Life in Jerusalem*, pp. 37, 55. According to Cohen, the meat supplied by bedouin was considered of a better quality than that supplied by villagers.
42. *JS*, 98:94, no. 531 (23 Shawwāl 1024/ 15 November 1615). See also *JS*, 107, no. 1066 (Rabīʿ Awwal 1033/ December 1623 - January 1624); *NS*, 1:45, no. 2 (16 Rajab 1066/ 10 May 1656). For supplies of horses and camels by the Ṭurabāys, see d'Arvieux, 106–7.
43. *BBA*, MD, 88:61, no. 155 (11 Rajab 1047/ 29 November 1637). See also 69:22, no. 40 (29 Jumāda al-Ūla 1000/ 14 March 1592); 69:30, no. 57 (4 Jumāda al-Ākhira 1000/ 18 March 1592); 69:98 no. 201 (21 Jumāda al-Ākhira 1000/ 17 April 1592)/ 78:82, no. 215 (13 Shaʿbān 1018/ 11 November 1609); 89:41, no. 108 (17 Rajab 1052/ 11 October 1642). On the terms *cebeci, arabaci, cebehane, mukabeleci, baş çavuş* and *serdar*, see Sertoğlu, 16–17, 35–36, 61, 62, 229, 312.
44. *JS*, 125:164, no. 729 (Shawwāl 1045/ March-April 1635); 125:170, no. 746 (Shawwāl 1045/ March-April 1635).
45. *BBA*, MD, 101:73, no. 227 (awā'il Rajab 1102/ beginning of April 1691). The decree instructs the governor of Damascus to put an end to this shameful practice.

46. On the rise in exports from Acre: *Histoire du Commerce de Marseilles,* IV:92–94; on exports from Gaza: *Journey to the Holy Land,* fol. 140b; Nathaniel Crouch, *Two Journeys to Jerusalem,* 84. On the quarrel between merchants in Acre and Sidon, see *Chambre du Commerce de Marseille,* serie J880 (Lettres de la Nation et des Deputés, 1657–1742), letter dated 25 October 1679; J772 (Acre, d'Esquissier), letters dated 9 September 1687 and 27 November 1687; J883 (Rame), letter dated 3 August 1690.
47. Iḥsān al-Nimr, *Tārikh Jabal Nābulus,* II: 288–293.
48. *JS,* 107 no. 1077 (Rabīʿ awwal 1033/ December 1633 - January 1624); 107:309, no. 1368 (Rabīʿ al-Thāni 1033/ January–February 1624); 201:418, (19 Shawwāl 1114/ 8 March 1703); *NS,* 1:129, no. 3 (awā'il Rabīʿ al-Thāni 1067/ end of January 1656). For a detailed and interesting description of the soap manufacturing process, see Cohen, *Economic Life in Ottoman Jerusalem,* 81–85;
49. *JS,* 107: no. 102 (11 Dhu al-Ḥijja 1032/ 5 October 1623). Later on in the same year the Balaqina tribesmen presented their claim for compensation from their assailants and received payment: Ibid., no. 231 !awākhir Dhu al-ḥijja 1032/ October 1623).
50. On drought in the same year, see ibid., no. 145 (20 Shawwāl 1032/ 17 August 1623). For another incident in which bedouin and villagers joined forces, see *JS,* 171:592 (24 Juamāda al-Ākhira 1081/ 8 November 1670).
51. Fernand Braudel, *The Mediterranean and the Mediterranean World in the Age of Philip II,* 2 vols. (London, 1972). On the hilly areas, see I:53–56; on mountains, 25–40; on plains, 85–100; on seas and shores, 103–67.
52. Ibid., I:180. See also I:176–80.
53. Dale F. Eickelman, *The Middle East: An Anthropological Approach* (Englewood Cliffs, N.J., 1981), 65.
54. For early functionalist theories, see Talcott Parsons, *The Social System* (Glencoe, Ill., 1951). For later developments in this school, see Robert K. Merton, *Social Theory and Social Structure* (Glencoe, Ill., 1957). For a critique of Parsons and early functionalist theory, see ibid., 19–84.
55. Immanuel Wallerstein, "The Rise and Future Demise of the World Capitalist System: Concepts for Comparative Analysis," *Comparative Studies in Society and History* 16.4 (September 1974): 390.
56. On the premises of this school—symbolic interaction—see Herbert Bloomer, *Symbolic Interactions: Perspective and Method* (Englewood Cliffs, N.J., 1969).
57. Clifford Geertz, "Thick Description: Toward an Interpretive Theory of Culture," in idem, *The Interpretation of Cultures* (New York, 1973), 3–30.

58. On the Ṭurabāy court, see d'Arvieux, 12, 50, 72. On marriages with other governing families, see Mannā', "The Farrūkh Governors of Jerusalem," 199.
59. One record mentions a fallah from a village in the district of Gaza who married a bedouin girl and was held hostage by Ibn Ridwan in order to ensure the good behavior of her tribe. See Mannā', "The Farrūkh Governors of Jerusalem" 204. *JS* 107:354 no. 1518 (Rabī' al Thāni 1033/January 1623).
60. Muḥibbi, I:88; II:134–36. For bedouin in court, see *JS*, 107, no. 231 (awākhir Dhu al-Ḥijja 1032/ end of December 1623); 107:329, no. 1438 (Rabī' al-Thāni 1033/ January–February 1624); 171:592 (24 Jumāda al-ūla 1081/ 9 October 1670). On Ridwan Pasha's relations with the bedouins, see also Meyer, *The City of Gaza*, 98.
61. Heyd, *Ottoman Documents*, 85, doc. 38; Sharon, "The Political Role of the Bedouins," 23n. 70; *JS*, 107:102 (11 Dhu al-Ḥijja 1032/6 October 1623); 171:592 (24 Jumāda al-Ūla 1081/ 9 October 1670). See also *BBA*, MD, 70:133, no. 260 (27 Jumāda al-Ākhira 1001/ 1 April 1593); 201:347 (11 Rajab 1114/ 1 December 1702).
62. According to al-Ramli's *fatāwa*, many peasants abandoned their villages as a result of injustice and mistreatment by the government, and found refuge with nomadic tribes. See Amin Seikali, "Land Tenure in 17th century Palestine: The Evidence from the al-Fatāwa al-Khairiyya," in Tarif Khalidi (ed.), *Land Tenure and Social Transformation in the Middle East* (Beirut, 1984), 406.
63. See also: Bakhit, "The Harithite Family," 78.

5. LAYERS OF OWNERSHIP

1. See Kenneth M. Cuno, "The Origins of Private Ownership of Land in Egypt: A Reappraisal" *International Journal of Middle East Studies*, 12 (1980): 245–46.
2. Halil Inalcik, "Military and Fiscal Transformation in the Ottoman Empire, 1600–1700," *Archivum Ottomanicum 6* (1980): 283–337.
3. On the shift from *timār* to *iltizām* in the Ottoman empire, see Inalcık, "Military and Fiscal Transformation," 327–29. On the gradual disappearance of *timārs*, see also Karl K. Barbir, "From Pasha to Effendi: The Assimilation of Ottomans into Damascene Society, 1516–1783," *International Journal of Turkish Studies* 1.1 (Winter 1979–80): 73; McGowan, "Land and Agriculture," 57–59. On a similar process in Palestine, see Amnon Cohen, *Palestine in the 18th Century*, 294–95.
4. The basic tenets of world economy theory in relation to the Ottoman Empire are summarized in Immanuel Wallerstein, "The Ottoman

Empire and the Capitalist World Economy: Some Questions for Research," *Review* 2, pt. 3 (1979): 389–401; and in Huri Islamoğlu and Çağlar Keyder, "Agenda for Ottoman History," *Review* 1, pt. 1 (Summer 1977): 31–55. For a partial revision of these concepts, see Chris Wickham, "The Uniqueness of the East," in Jean Baechler, John A. Hall and Michael Mann (eds.), *Europe and the Rise of Capitalism* (Oxford, 1988), 66–100.

5. Wickham, 66–70.
6. Inalcik, "Ottoman Methods of Conquest," *Studia Islamica* 2 (1954): 107–9; Stanford Shaw, *History of the Ottoman Empire and Modern Turkey* (Cambridge, 1976), I:26; Inalcik, *The Ottoman Empire—the Classical Age*, 104–18; Gibb and Bowen, *Islamic Civilization and the West*.
7. Inalcik, "Ottoman Methods of Conquest," 112–13.
8. On the principles of the *waqf* institution, see W. Heffening, "Waqf" *Encyclopedia of Islam*, 1st edition, (London and Leiden, 1931), 1096–1102; S. H. Stephan, "An Endowment Deed of Khasseki Sultan, Dated the 24th of May 1552," *The Quarterly of the Department of Antiquities in Palestine* (Jerusalem and London) 10 (1944): 173–74. On *waqfs* in the Ottoman Empire, see Haim Gerber, "The *Waqf* Institution in Early Ottoman Edirne," in Gabriel Warburg and Gad Gilbar (eds.), *Studies in Islamic Society: Contributions in Memory of Gabriel Baer* (Haifa, 1984), 29–30; Haim Gerber, *The Social Origins of the Modern Middle East*, 20, 22–24. On *waqf* systems in Palestine and Syria, see further Jean Paul Pascual, *Damas à la fin du XVIé siècle d'après trois actes de waqf Ottomans* (Damascus, 1983); Muḥammad As'ad al-Imām al-Ḥusayni, *al-Manhal al-ṣafi fi al-waqf wa-aḥkāmihi* (Jerusalem, 1982). I would like to thank sheikh As'ad al-Imām al-Ḥusayni for his detailed explanations of problems pertaining to the *waqf* institution.
9. It should be noted, though, that several times in Islamic and Ottoman history, governments decided to obliterate *waqfs* or to change their designation, ignoring the *waqfiyya* stipulations and circumventing the tenets of *shar'i* law.
10. Shaw, *The Ottoman Empire*, 121; Inalcik, "Centralization and Decentralization," 30; idem, *The Ottoman Empire—The Classical Age*; Metin Kunt, *The Sultan's Servants*, 79–80; Inalcik, "Military and Fiscal Transformation," 327–29. Gerber, *The Social Origins of the Modern Middle East*, 53–56.
11. Abdul Rahim Abu Husayn, *Provincial Leadership in Syria, 1575–1650*, (Beirut, 1985), 187, 191. See also idem, "The *Iltizām* of Mansur Furaykh: A Case Study of *Iltizām* in Sixteenth Century Syria," in Tarif Khalidi (ed.), *Land Tenure and Social Transformation in the Middle East* (Beirut, 1984), 249.

12. Evliya Çelebi, *Seyahatname*, 222. On *arpalık*, see: Inalcık "Centralization and Decentralization," 30–31. A *has* was defined as an estate yielding more than 100,000 *akçe* a year. *Has* estates allocated to district governors were in most cases larger, usually over 200,000 *akçe* a year. See: Gibb and Bowen, I:48–49, 149.
13. Haim Gerber has reached a similar conclusion from *fatāwa* books and *sijills* concerning Bursa in the seventeenth century: *The Social Origins of the Modern Middle East*, 50–53.
14. *NS*, 1:31, no. 2 (16 Jumāda al-Ūla 1066/13 March 1656).
15. The villages sampled are: Al-Sawiyya, Al-ʿAzariyya, Bayt Ḥanīna, Bayt Ṣurīk, Bayt Ṣafāfa, Bayt Illu, Bayt Ṣaḥūr, Bayt Imrīn, Bayt Liqya, Bethlehem, Jabarīyya, Dayr Istya, Dayr Ḥāmid, Dayr Dibwān, Dayr Sudān, Khirbat al-Lawz, Ṭayba, Jericho, Lifta, Mikhmās, Sabāstiya, Silwān, Sanūr, ʿAtāra, ʿAyn Sina, ʿIsāwiyya, Furaydīs, and Qaqūn. Villages in the sample, mentioned in several volumes of the *sijill*, were checked against the *mufaṣṣal* registers for Jerusalem and Nabulus, dated 1596–97/1005 (which I was able to check through the kindness of Prof. Amnon Cohen). The assumption that most villages did not change their status is also borne out in Amnon Cohen's book, *Palestine in the Eighteenth Century*, 294–95. Cohen points to a possible decline in the number of *timars*, but there are no clear indications in the *sijill* for such a trend. There may have been some lessening of imperial control over the number of *timars* and their allocation. See also Gerber, *The Social Origins of the Modern Middle East*, 20–21. On *tapu-tahrirs* and their accuracy, see also Amy Singer, "Tapu-Tahrir Defterleri and Kadi Sicilleri: A Happy Marriage of Sources," *Tārih* 1 (1990): 95–125.
16. Inalcik, "Centralization and Decentralization," 30–31.
17. On the *arpalık* as a system, see Inalcik, "Centralization and Decentralization," 30–31; Kunt, *The Sultan's Servants*, 75–76, 86. On Jerusalem and other Palestinian districts as *arpalık*, see *BBA*, Mühimme Defterleri, 81:27, no. 61 (3 Rabīʿ al-Awwal 1025/ 21 March 1616); 98:79, no. 242 (awāsiṭ Rabīʿ al-Awwal 1100/beginning of January 1689); 105:7, no. 22 (awākhir Shawwāl 1105/ mid-June 1694); 108:29, no. 93 (awākhir Jumāda al-Ūla 1108/ mid-December 1696); 108:340, no. 1418 (awā'il Dhu al-Ḥijja 1107/ beginning of July 1696); 111:253–54, no. 893, 897 (awāsiṭ Rabīʿ al-Thāni/ beginning of October 1699); 111:581, no. 2945 (awāsiṭ Muḥarram 1113/ end of June 1701); 111:615, no. 2158 (awā'il Ṣafar 1113/ mid-July 1701); 114:79, no. 360 (awāsiṭ Dhu al-Qaʿda 1114/ beginning of April 1703); *JS*, 107, no. 802 (28 Ṣafar 1033/ 21 December 1623); 146:321 (awāsiṭ Jumāda al-Ūla 1062/ end of April 1652); 171:580, (awā'il Jumāda al-Ūla 1081/ end of September 1670); 201:411 (Shawwāl 1114/ February–March 1703; 201:300 (16 Shaʿbān 1114/5 January 1703). *NS*,

1:32, no. 3 (Jumāda al-Ūla 1066/February-March 1656) 1:34, no. 3 (same date). Halil Inalcik Fariba Zarinebaf and Karen Barkey, *Başbakanlık Arşivi Provincial Appointment Registers* (to be published), 71-73.

18. *JS*, 107, no. 436 (27 Muḥarram 1033/ 10 November 1623); no. 429 (Muḥarram 1033/ November 1623); no. 802 (28 Ṣafar 1033/ 21 December 1623). On provincial appointments, see Inalcik, Zarinebaf and Barkey, 71. On the Farrūkh and Riḍwān dynasties, see chapter 2.
19. *NS*, 1:108, no. 2 (end of Muḥarram 1067/ mid-November 1656).
20. Though the defendant's rank and status are not stated, the title implies that he too was a member of the governing elite, probably a *sipahi*.
21. Turkish *muhzırbaşı*—the official in charge of court procedure and summoning people to court.
22. Turkish *çavuş*—an officer of the imperial messenger corps.
23. On *rijāliyya*, see Cohen and Lewis, *Population and Revenue*, 18, 153. Their claim that this was a tax collected from Kurdish inhabitants of Nabulus does not fit this case.
24. On *khamīsiyya*, see ibid., 151n. 18—a tax for holding fairs on Thursday. See also Ihsan ʿAbbas, "Hair Ad-Din Ar-Ramli's Fatāwa: A New Light on Life in Palestine in the Eleventh/ Seventeenth Century," in Ulrich Haarman and Peter Bachmann (eds.), *Die Islamische Welt Zwischen Mittelalter und Neuzeit* (beirut, 1979), 15. ʿAbbas describes it as a "Thursday gift."
25. On marriage tax (*rasm ankiḥa*), see B. Lewis, "ʿArus Resmi," EI_2, I:679.
26. Probably a tax paid to the *subashi* as an additional income.
27. On *bād-ı hava*, see Cohen and Lewis, 74. The name literally means "wind of the air" or windfall, and was intended to denote unexpected income from fines, prizes, etc. It became a useful name for an assortment of illegal taxes.
28. *JS*, 168:10 (16 Rajab 1078/ 1 January 1668).
29. *Çorbacı* (Arabic *jurbaji*)—commander of a janissary unit. See Sertoğlu, 76. Since a *çorbacı* was not often a pasha, the actual title might have been *bashsha* (Turkish *beççe*).
30. *Bölükbaşı* (Arabic *blukbāshi*)—commander of a janissary unit, similar to *çorbacı*. See: Sertoğlu, 57.
31. *JS*, 183:215 (8 Rajab 1091/ 4 August 1680). See also *BBA*, MD, 92:13, no. 57 (beginning of Ramaḍan 1067/ mid-June 1657).
32. *Bashsha* (*beççe* in Turkish) is a title given to members of the sultan's slave corps. See chapter 3, n. 50.
33. On the *waqf* of *Khāsiki Sultan* (*Haseki Sultan* in Turkish), created for and named after Kanuni Süleyman's wife, Roxellana (Haseki Hurrem Sultan), see chapter 1, p. 27.
34. *JS*, 107, no. 696 (17 Ṣafar 1033/ 10 December 1623).

35. The *qit'a Miṣriyya* was an Ottoman *para* coin minted in Cairo. The usual rate of exchange was thirty *qit'a Miṣriyya* for one *ghurūsh*.
36. *JS* 80:518, no. 2915 (12 Dhu al-Ḥijja 1008/ 24 June 1600). The record further reveals that the income from the village is divided so that the Khasikiyya *waqf* gets 6,000 *qit'a*, which is considered the village's *'ushr* (land tax) and *waqf* al-Malik al-Mu'ayyad gets 4,000, which is considered the village's taxes for crops, olives and kharāj. On leasing to *sipahis*, see *JS*, 168:52 (27 Jumāda al-Ūla 1078/ 2 November 1668); leasing to an *'ālim*—107: no. 871 (Rabī' al-Awwal 1033/ December 1623) and 201:312 (awāsiṭ Jumāda al-Ūla 1114 beginning of October 1702); leasing to a former supervisor—107:256, no. 1129 (21 Rabī' al-Awwal 1033/ 12 January 1624); leasing to a governor and a local notable—*NS*, 1:163, no. 2 (awā'il Rajab 1067/ end of April 1657); leasing to janissaries—1:138, no. 2 (6 Rabī' al-Thāni 1067/ 22 January 1656).
37. *BBA*, MD, 89:35, no. 90 (28 Ramaḍān 1052/ 20 December 1642). See also 89:13, nos. 34, 35, 36, 37 (10 Rabī' al-Awwal 1052/ 8 June 1642); 89:16, no. 41, 42, 43; p. 63, no. 152 (1 Muḥarram 1053/ 22 March 1643).
38. See Chapter 6, p. 159–61.
39. *JS*, 183:239 (awākhir Rajab 1091/ end of August 1680). On renewal of *berats* and minor *sipahis*, see also 171:396 (12 Muḥarram 1081/ 1 June 1670); 201:78 (7 Muḥarram 1113/ 15 June 1701); 201:300 (23 Muḥarram 1115/ 9 June 1703); *BBA*, MD, 110:223, no. 997 (awāsiṭ Jumāda al-Ākhira 1109/ end of July 1697).
40. This is also reflected in Khayr al-Dīn al-Ramli's *fatāwa*, which deny the legal right to ownership to grant-holders. They could neither sell nor bequeath the land. See Seikali, "Land Tenure in 17th Century Palestine," 403.
43. Ö. L. Barkan, *XV ve XVI Asırlarda Osmani Imparatorluğunda Zirai Ekonominin Hukuki ve Mâli Esasları* (Istanbul, 1943); Gabriel Baer, *Mavo le-Toldot Ha-Yeḥasim Ha-Agrariyim Ba-Mizraḥ Ha-Tikhon* (Tel-Aviv, 1971), 16; Bakhit, *The Province of Damascus* 166; Cuno, "The Sources of Land Ownership in Egypt," 246.
42. Mantran et Sauvaget, *Règlements Fiscaux Ottomans, les Provinces Syriennes* (Beirut, 1951), 35–42; Ö. L. Barkan, *Hukuki ve Mali Easasları* vol. I, 221; See also W. D. Hütteroth and K. Abdelfattah, *Historical Geography of Palestine, Transjordan and Southern Syria in the late 16th Century* (Erlangen, 1977); Ihsan 'Abbas, "Hair ad-Din ar-Ramli's Fatāwa," 14–15. According to one of al-Ramli's *fatāwa*, timariots had no right to uproot trees planted by farmers, even if he thought that by doing so he could make the land more productive.
43. Barkan, *Hukuki ve Mali Esasları*, 221; Mantran and Sauvaget, 8. See also Halil Inalcik, "Islamization of Ottoman Laws on Land and Tax,"

in Christa Fragner and Klaus Schwarz (eds.), *Festgabe au Josef Matuz: Osmanistik—Turkologie—Diplomatik* (Berlin, 1992), 101–18.

44. One possible indication for the tendency to increase private property by changing land designation can be seen in the great rise in quantities of olive oil and grapes during the sixteenth century. See Singer, *Ottoman Officials and Palestinian Peasants*, 84–85.
45. Mehmet Ertuğrul Düzdağ, *Şeyhülislam Ebüssuud Efendi Fetvaları Işiğinda 16 asır Türk Hayatı* (Istanbul, 1972), 167. For other examples of Ebüssuud's attempts to define property rights and reconcile the *sharī'a* with Ottoman land law, see Inalcik, "Islamization of Ottoman Laws," 101–7.
46. Ibid.
47. Al-Ramli, *Al-Fatāwa al-Khayriyya*, 94–95.
48. Ibid., 94–95, 168–70. See also Seikali, "Land Tenure in 17th century Palestine," 402–3. Seikali suggests that some of the *fatwas* were intended to counter the trend of treating *waqf* as *milk*.
49. A sample of sales deeds in the *sijill*: *NS*, 1:26, no. 3 (12 Jumāda al-Ākhira 1066/ 7 April 1656); 1:30, no. 1 (same date); 1:39, no. 4 (8 Rajab 1066/ 2 May 1656); 1:40, no. 2 (10 Rajab 1066/ 4 May 1656); 1:46, no. 4 (Awail Sha'bān 1066/ end of May 1656); 1:47 (same date); 1:62, no. 2 (10 Ramaḍān 1066/ 2 July 1656); 1:77, no. 3 (awāsiṭ Dhu al-Qa'da 1066/ beginning of September 1656); 1:81, no. 3 (awākhir Dhu al-Ḥijja 1066/ mid-September 1656); 1:82, no. 4 (same date). In the *Jerusalem Sijill*, see most of the examples in this and other chapters. On land sale *sijill* records in Anatolia, see Gerber, *The Social Origins of the Modern Middle-East*, 22–24.
50. In sale transactions, bequests and leases, most property was divided at the time into twenty-four equal shares called *qirāt*. Smaller parts were counted in fractions of *qirāts*.
51. *NS*, 1:77, no. 3 (awāsiṭ Dhu al-Qa'da 1066/ beginning of September 1656).
52. *JS*, 191:97 (awākhir Jumāda al-Akhira 1100/ mid-April 1689). For another record on the same matter, see ibid., 98 (same date). *Al-Fatāwa* al-Khayriyya, I:111.
53. Ibid., 168:15 (19 Rajab 1078/ 4 January 1668).
54. Suraya Faroqhi, *Towns and Townsmen of Ottoman Anatolia* (Cambridge, 1984), 265–66.
55. *JS*, 125:121, no. 512 (9 Ramaḍān 1045/ 16 February 1636); 125:177, no. 767 (Shawwāl 1045/ March–April 1636); 168:42 (20 Rajab 1078/ 5 January 1668); 171: no. 653 (Sha'bān 1081/ December 1670 - January 1671). The record is cancelled by pen strokes, but its contents are interesting); 201:445 (14 Ramaḍān 1114/ February 1702). There are many other records in each volume. *NS*, 1:40, no. 2 (1066/1656); 1:81, no. 3 (awākhir

Dhu al-Qaʿda 1066/ mid-September 1656); 1:92, no. 3 (awāʾil Muḥarram 1067/ end of October 1656).

56. Ihsan Abbas, "Hair ad-Din ar-Ramli's *Fatāwa*," 6; Samir Seikali, "Land Tenure in 17th Century Palestine," 401.
57. *JS*, 183:164 (Rabīʿ awwal 1091/ April 1680).

6. AN ECONOMY IN TRANSITION

1. A. Singer, "Tapu Tahrir Defterleri and Kadi Sicilleri," 95–125.
2. Ibid. See also Cohen and Lewis, *Population and Revenue*, 3–12; Ö. L. Barkan, "Research on the Ottoman Fiscal Surveys," in M. A. Cook (ed.), *Studies in the Economic History of the Middle East* (Oxford, 1970).
3. Bruce McGowan, "The Study of Land and Agriculture in the Ottoman Provinces within the Context of an Expanding World Economy in the 17th and 18th Centuries," *International Journal of Turkish Studies* 2. 1 (Spring-Summer 1981): 57–58.
4. McGowan, "The Study of Land and Agriculture," 59. On leasing *timars* and *waqfs*, see chapter 5, pp. 122–129.
5. On the *akçe* as money of account, see Cohen and Lewis, *Population and Revenue*, 43–44.
6. On the value of Ottoman coins, see Gibb and Bowen, *Islamic Society and the West*, II:51–54; Heyd, *Ottoman Documents*, 120; Amy Singer, *Ottoman Officials and Palestinian Peasants*, xi. See also list of coins in Ben-Zvi, *Eretz-Yisrael ve-yishuva*, 466; Minna Rozen, *Ha-qehila ha-yehudit* 237.
7. *JS*, 80:26, no. 247 (2 Shawwāl 1007/28 April 1599).
8. In seventeenth-century Palestine, *khawājā* was the common title for notables who were not of *askeri* status. Later on, in the nineteenth century, it was used to designate non-Muslim notables.
9. The title *muʿallim* usually refers to master craftsmen, who were authorized to teach and initiate young apprentices.
10. The *muḥtasib* was appointed by the local government to oversee market activities, check weights and measures, and apply the laws and regulations of the marketplace. See Amnon Cohen, *Economic Life in Jerusalem*, 11–18. On the ʿAsali family, see above, chapter 3. On the Duhayna family, see A. Cohen, *Economic Life in Jerusalem*, 30–34.
11. *JS*, 85:55, no. 244 (8 Shawwāl 1013/27 February 1605). The *dinār* is apparently the old Ottoman coin known as *altın*. The value of the *altın*, at first more or less equivalent to the Venetian Ducat, was frequently devalued during the sixteenth century. *Sharīfi* (*Şerifi*) and *Ibrāhīmi* are kinds of *Altın* coins.
12. For information about the value of the *kuruş*, see *JS*, 28, no. 199 (14 Shaʿbān 100/12 March 1599); 85:47, no. 207 (awāsiṭ Ramaḍān 1013/

beginning of February 1605); 107:266, no. 1162 (27 Rabīʿ al-Awwal 1033/19 January 1624); 171:185 (awākhir Jumādā al-Ākhirā 1080/end of November 1669); 177:48 (20 Dhū al-Qaʿdā 1085/15 February 1675). On the frequent use of Dutch *löwen rikstalers* and Spanish *reals* towards the end of the century, see *JS*, 191:76 (awā'il Jumāda al-Ūla 1100/ end of February 1689). See also the frequent references to *kuruş* (*ghurūsh*) in this and other chapters.

13. Ö. L. Barkan, "The Price Revolution of the Sixteenth Century," *International Journal of Middle East Studies* 6 (1975): 3–28; Halil Inalcik, "The Ottoman Economic Mind and Aspects of the Ottoman Economy," in M. A. Cook (ed.) *Studies in the Economic History of the Middle East* (Oxford, 1978), 215.
14. Al-malik al-Ashraf Qayitbāy, the last great Mamluk sultan, ruled the sultanate from 1468 to 1496.
15. McGowan, "Land and Agriculture," 57, 59; Gibb and Bowen, *Islamic Society and the West*, I:37, 43; Mantran and Sauvaget, *Règlements fiscaux*, 8.
16. Alan Makovsky, "Sixteenth Century Agricultural Production in the Liwa of Jerusalem: Insights from the Tapu Defters and an Attempt at Quantification," *Archivum Ottomanicum* 9 (1984): 102; Amy Singer, *Palestinian Peasants and Ottoman Officials*, 32–45. On changes in the agrarian system, see chapter 5.
17. McGowan, "Land and Agriculture," 58; Inalcik, "Military and Fiscal Transformation," 314–5; Metin Kunt, *The Sultan's Servants*, 79–82. On restricted use of *avarız* taxes in the sixteenth century, see A. Singer, *Ottoman Officials and Palestinian Peasants*, 96–97.
18. *Yerliyya* (literally, "local") units were provincial janissary forces fashioned to fit the mould of imperial janissary battalions.
19. *BBA*, MD 106:120 no. 417 (awāsiṭ Shawwāl 1106/May-June 1695).
20. *Selamlık*—named after the public part of the house where male guests are usually entertained. See Inalcik, "Military and Fiscal Transformation," 320.
21. *Muşahara*—a monthly gift.
22. *Bad-ı hava* (literally, "wind of the air") is a general term for all irregular and occasional revenues. See above, chapter 5, p. 124 and Lewis and Cohen, *Population and Revenue*, 74–75.
23. *Defter* is a notebook or register. Here the term probably refers to the *tahrir* surveys, which were meant to define the amount of money to be collected from each household.
24. *BBA*, MD, 76:120, no. 417 (awāsiṭ Shawwāl 1106/May–June 1695).
25. *JS*, 153 (awāmir):15 (awākhir Jumāda al-Ūla 1067/March 1657). In the version of the edict copied into the *sijill*, the village is not mentioned by name.

26. *JS*, 125:80, no. 336 (Shaʿbān 1045/January–February 1636); 169:51 (3 Muḥarram 1080/3 June 1669); 169:71 (20 Ṣafar 1080/20 July 1669); *BBA*, MD, 110:490, no. 2213–2214 (awā'il Ramaḍan 1110/ beginning of March 1699). On the allocation of taxes in the sixteenth century in the district itself see Cohen and Lewis *Population and Revenue*, 95–104.
27. *JS*, 169:51 (3 Muḥarram 1080/3 June 1669); 169:71 (20 Ṣafar 1080/20 July 1669).
28. This small fortress was built by the Ottomans in the seventeenth century to guard water cisterns that supplied Jerusalem and to defend travelers on the road from Jerusalem to Hebron. Heyd, *Ottoman Documents on Palestine*, 146–49, 190.
29. Huri Islamoğlu and Çağlar Keyder, "Agenda for Ottoman History," *Review* 1.1 (Summer 1977) 44–45. The terms "Asian mode of production" or "Asiatic mode of production" refer to Marx's famous assertions that conditions in certain Asian societies have brought forth a structure of production relations that does not permit evolution through the necessary stages of history towards socialism. This term was used by Marxist historians to describe various societies in and out of Asia which failed to develop according to the Marxist outline. For an analysis of the term, its development by Marx himself and its use by later Marxist historians, see Perry Anderson, *Lineages of the Absolutist State* (London, 1974), 482–92.
30. Near the village of Salfīt, southwest of Nabulus.
31. *NS*, 1:243 (20 Jumāda al-Ūla 1066/17 March 1656).
32. *NS*, 1:47 (awā'il Shaʿbān 1066/May–June 1656).
33. See *JS*, 183:117 (Ṣafar 1091/March 1680).
34. The term *ṭā'ifā* was used to designate all kinds of groups in the city—religious minorities, army units, official and unofficial clergy, Sufi brotherhoods, etc. The entire city was divided into merging *ṭawā'if*, which were seen as the main administrative link between government and subjects/citizens in an urban setting. See Haim Gerber, *Economy and Society in an Ottoman City: Bursa 1600–1700* (Jerusalem, 1988) p. 34 and also M. E. Yapp, *The Making of the Modern Middle East, 1792–1923* (New York, 1987), 24.
35. A barber (*ḥallāq*) was also a surgeon and sometimes a pharmacist too. Their *ṭā'ifā* was considered a prestigious one.
36. *NS*, 1:64, no.1 (awākhir Ramaḍan 1066/mid-July 1656).
37. See Amnon Cohen's description in *Economic Life in Ottoman Jerusalem*, 21. See also Gerber, *Economy and Society*, 40–41.
38. This could give us a further indication of the value of coins in 1624: one *löwentaler* was worth 8.33 *dirham* of silver.

39. *JS*, 107, no. 1088 (13 Rabīʿ al-Awwal 1033/4 January 1624). On the appointment of *ṭāʾifā* sheikhs, see 107:138, no. 612 (Ṣafar 1033/December 1623); 107:248, no. 1094 (22 Rabīʿ al-Awwal 1033/13 January 1624); 170:29 (10 Shaʿbān 1079/13 January 1669); 171:602 (end of Jumādā al-Āakhira 1081/mid-November 1670); 171:692 (Rajab 1081/ November–December 1670); 183:223 (awāsiṭ Rabīʿ al-Thānī 1091/mid-May 1680). For a description of seventeenth-century appointments of guild masters see Inalcik, "The Ottoman Economic Mind," 216.
40. "Wa-lam yusāwī maʿhum fi maʿānihim wa-maghārimihim ḥasab al-ʿādā al-qadīmā kull man bāʿa wa-ishtarā min al-khuḍar bi-l-sūq yusāwi jamāʿatahu."
41. *JS*, 201:12 (awāsiṭ Rabīʿ al-Thāni 1114/August–September 1702). About price lists see also Gerber, *Economy and Society*, p. 54.
42. *JS*, 171:590 (11 Jumāda al-ākhira 1081/26 October 1670).
43. *Bashsha* (*beççe* in Turkish) was a title given to junior officers of the sultan's slave corps. Its use in this context is yet another layer of evidence for the integration of the military into local economy, or vice versa—merchants and craftsmen being able to buy military ranks.
44. *JS*, 171:590 (25 Shaʿbān 1081/7 January 1671).
45. A *raṣṣāṣ* is a dealer in lead or tin. It is not clear whether this was a description of the person's initial profession, or whether this was the family's name.
46. *Kayyāl bāshi*—official "measurer" in charge of weighing and measuring in the market. The *kayyāl bāshi* was also entrusted with weighing and assessing the taxes paid in kind. See Amnon Cohen, *Economic Life in Ottoman Jerusalem*, 107.
47. *JS*, 171:190 (4 Rajab 1080/28 November 1669). See also 169:16 (Dhu al-Ḥijja 1079/May 1669); 107:145 (20 Shawwāl 1032/17 August 1623).
48. On the importance attached to constant supply, see Inalcik, "The Ottoman Economic Mind," 215–17.
49. The edict, like many others, refers to the governors and their retinues as a *ṭāʾifā* in its own right: *"fa-ʾamara mawlānā ʿalā ṭāʾifat ahl al-ʿurf."*
50. *JS*, 201:313 (awāsiṭ Jumāda al-Ūla 1114/October 1702).
51. *BBA*, MD, 111:508, no. 1763 (awāsi Rabīʿ al-Thānī 1112/end of September 1700).
52. *JS*, 201:356 (12 Rabīʿ al-Thānī 1114/ 5 September 1702).
53. Amnon Cohen, "Ottoman Rule and the Re-emergence of the Coast of Palestine," *Revue du Monde Musulman et de la Mediteranee* 39 (1985); Ralph Davis, "English Imports from the Levant, 1580–1780," in M.A. Cook (ed.), *Studies in the Economic History of the Middle East* (Oxford, 1970), 202–3. On export prohibitions, see Heyd, *Ottoman Documents*,

130; Inalcik "The Ottoman Economic Mind," 217; Barkan, "Sixteenth-Century Price Revolution."

54. On the importance of trade in cotton and soap ashes, see *Archives du Chambre de Commerce de Marseilles (ACCM)* H196 (coton 1629–1791); J880 (Acre, Lettres de la nation et des deputés) 25 Octobre 1679; J772 (Lettres de Joseph d'Esquissier des Tourres) 27 Novembre 1688, and many others. On irregular purchases of wheat, see ibid., H105 (blé) 1702.
55. From the Hebrew translation in Joel Raba, *Eretz-Yisra'el be-te'urey nos'īm Rusiyīm* (Russian Travel Accounts on Palestine) (Jerusalem, 1986), 233.
56. Nathaniel Crouch, *Two Journeys to Jerusalem* (London, n.d.), 84.
57. *ACCM*, J883 (Rame - Lettres des vice-consuls etc. 3.8.1690). About raids on the port of Jaffa, see also *Archives Nationales*, AE bIII, v. 34, 307–8 (24 Juillet 1689); *Histoire du Commerce de Marseille*, V:395 (19.6.1689). *BBA*, MD, 100:64, no. 234 (awākhir Muḥarram 1102/November 1690). See also A. Cohen, "Re-Emergence of the Coast of Palestine," 166.
58. *BBA*, 99:132, no. 421 (awākhir Jumādā al-Ākhira 1102/ March 1691).
59. *JS*, 201:488 (19 Dhu al-Qa'da 1114/7 April 1703); 201:290 (Muḥarram 1115/ May–June 1703); Cohen, "Re-Emergence of the Coast of Palestine," 166.
60. *Public Records Office*, SP110 (Levant Company reports) bundles 10–15. Purchases of soap and cotton in Acre and Ramla, see also *ACCM*, J772 (Acre—Lettres du consul d'Esquissier, 1682–1692), lettre du 27 Novembre 1688.
61. François Charles-Roux, *Les Echelles de Syrie et de Palestine au 18é siècle* (Paris, 1928), 6–9; *Histoire du commerce de Marseille*, V:399–400; IV:96; François Charles du Rozel, *Voyage de Jerusalem* (Paris, 1864), 114–15.
62. *JS*, 107, no. 531 (14 Ṣafar 1033/ 7 December 1623).
63. *BBA*, MD, 79:408, no. 1018 (17 Shawwāl 1019/ 2 January 1611); 92:57 (awā'il Dhu al-Qa'da 1067/August 1657); 94:20, no. 90 (awā'il Dhu al-Qa'da 1073/ June 1663); 94:42, no. 216 (awāsiṭ Shawwāl 1075/ May 1665); 95, no. 554 (awākhir Dhu al-Qa'da 1075/June 1665); 100:64, no. 234 (awākhir Muḥarram 1102/ November 1690).
64. A. Rabbath, *Documents inédits pour servir à l'histoire du Christianisme en Orient* (Paris, 1905–1913; repr. New York, 1973), I:344–345. This story is told in further detail in chapter 1.
65. *ACCM*, J880 (Lettres de la nation et des deputés 1567–1742): "et c'est asses avoir souffert une anné dans un lieu sy mizerable ou nous avons perdu beaucoup de nos messieurs." See also *Histoire du commerce de Marseille*, IV:96.
66. Alfred C. Wood, *A History of the Levant Company* (Oxford: 1935) p. 161; *BBA*, MD, 94:27, no. 127 (awākhir Rabī' al-Thānī 1073/mid-December

1662); 94:20, no. 20 (awā'il Dhu al-Qaʻda 1073/mid-June 1663) 94:42, no. 216 (awāsiṭ Shawwāl 1075/beginning of May 1665); Charles-Roux, *Echelles*, 195.

67. "N'est pas d'une qualité convenable aux manufactures des Lyonois."
68. *ACCM*, H196 (coton, 1629–1791), Arrest du Conseil d'État du Roy, 1700.
69. Ibid., documents from the year 1711.
70. Benjamin Braude, "International Competition and Domestic Cloth in the Ottoman Empire, 1500–1650: A Study in Underdevelopment" *Review* 2. 3 (1979), 450–451.
71. See the special issue of *Review* devoted to these questions (*Review* 2.3) as well as Şevket Pamuk, *The Ottoman Empire and European Capitalism, 1820–1913—Trade, Investment and Production* (Cambridge, 1987); Huri Islamoğlu-Inan (ed.), *The Ottoman Empire and the World Economy* (Cambridge, 1987), and others.
72. Islamoğlu and Keyder, "Agenda for Ottoman History," 41.
73. According to this terminology a *world-economy* is defined as a single division of labor with multiple polities and cultures, while a *world-empire* is defined as a unit with a single division of labor and multiple cultural systems but with one overarching political system. See I. Wallerstein, "The Rise and Future Demise of the World Capitalist System," 390–91.
74. Braude, "International Competition and Domestic Cloth"; S. Faroqhi, *Men of Modest Substance*, 209–12.

7. WORLDS APART

1. In many cases travelers did not hesitate to describe their contempt for the land and its people. With very little understanding of Islam or local custom, the English traveler Maundrel, who visited Palestine at the end of the seventeenth century writes to one of his readers: "Their religion is framed to keep up great outward gravity and solemnity, without begetting the least good tincture of wisdom or virtue in the mind." In Thomas Wright (ed.), *Early Travels in Palestine* (New York, 1968), 505. Others described the entire country as a den of thievery, sodomy and bestiality: "There is no evil deed on this earth not performed by the inhabitants of this terra sancta or holy land which hath the name and nothing else." In Nathaniel Crouch, *Two Journeys to Jerusalem* (London, 1699, manuscript in the SOAS library), 74–75. These views persisted well into the nineteenth and twentieth centuries.
2. Eugene Roger, *La Terre Sainte, ou Description très particulier de la Terre de promission* (Paris: 1664), 296–308. The views of Roger described in the next few paragraphs are all summed up in these pages. For Western

physicians treating Muslim women, see also L. Hayes, Baron de Courmenin, *Voyage de Levant, Fait par le Commendement du Roi en l'année 1621* (Paris, 1629), 163.

3. Laurent d'Arvieux, *Voyage dans la Palestine* (Amsterdam, 1718). Apart from Roger, d'Arvieux is perhaps the most notable traveler to have written about women in this period, although his emphasis is on bedouin women of the Ṭurabāy family.
4. Antoine Morison, *Relation historique d'un voyage nouvellement fait au Mont de Sinaï et à Jerusalem* (Paris, 1705). See also Jean Doubdan, *Le Voyage de la Terre Sainte* (Paris, 1666). French travelers seem to have attained the highest degree of cross-cultural understanding and a keen interest in other societies, that is evidently lacking in most other travel accounts of the period. English travelers usually dismiss local Muslim, and even Christian society with a few sentences, and do their best to emulate their compatriots' descriptions of holy Christian monuments. Italian travelers, very prominent in the Mamluk period, left a much smaller impact on seventeenth- and eighteenth-century literature.
5. Roger, *La Terre Sainte*, 297—"Soit que le mari luy agrée ou non, il faut qu'elle y consente."
6. D'Arvieux, *Voyage dans la Palestine*, 221: "Comme les Arabes n'ont aucune communication avec les femmes ni avec les filles d'autrui, ils ne sauroient etre amoureux que par imagination, ou sur le rapport qu'on leur en fait. Ils ne leur approchent point, et ne leur voient en public que par hazard et un peu de loin."
7. See also d'Arvieux, ibid.; Morison, *Relation Historique*, 710.
8. d'Arvieux, ibid.
9. Morison, 710.
10. This term does not exist in Palestinian Arabic today. Roger may have got it wrong. Perhaps the word used was *kitāb*, or *maktūb*, or another derivation of the root *k*t*b*.
11. See also d'Arvieux, *Voyage dans la Palestine*, 222.
12. Ibid., 225–26.
13. D'Arvieux, *Voyage dans la Palestine*, 218.
14. Roger, *La Terre Sainte*, 299.
15. See also d'Arvieux, *Voyage dans la Palestine*, 214.
16. It is interesting to see how nineteenth-century English women travelers created an entirely different description of Oriental women, to serve as a model of liberty and virtue in comparison with Victorian society. See Billie Melman, *Women's Orients*, especially chapter 3.
17. About questions of privacy in a neighboring Muslim society, see Abraham Marcus, "Privacy in Eighteenth Century Aleppo: The Limits

of Cultural Ideals," *International Journal of Middle East Studies* 18, (1986): 165–67.

18. The Khasikiyya *waqf* was a large endowment made by Khaseki Hurrem Sultan (Roxellana), wife of Kanuni Sultan Süleyman (the Magnificent) in 1552, to build and provide for a mosque-madrasa-imaret complex in Jerusalem. Many villages, including Bayt Iksa, paid their taxes directly to the *waqf*. *Waqf* officials had some responsibility for maintaining law and order inside the village. See Oded Peri, "The Waqf as an Instrument to Increase and Consolidate Political Power," 47–62. See also, chapter 6.
19. *Cokdar*—(*cuhadar*), literally, carrier of the cloth, an important official in the *Kapı Kulları*. See M. Pakalın, *Osmanlı Tarih deyimleri ve terimleri* (Istanbul, 1946), I:384. The *muḥḍir* was an officer responsible for bringing people to court.
20. *JS*, 191:116 (10 Rajab 1100/30 April 1689). For other instances of accidents involving women, see ibid., 191:67 (3 Jumāda al-Ākhira 1100/25 March 1689); 183:227, (awāsiṭ Rajab 1091/ mid-Aug. 1680); *NS*, 1:83, no. 2 (2 Dhu al-Ḥijja 1066/21 September 1656).
21. *Bashsha* (*beççe*) is a Persian word meaning "swallow chick." This is the title given to a member of the *Kapı Kulları*, usually of the *acemi oğlan* (external service). See Pakalin, I:184.
22. *JS*, 183:62 (Ṣafar 1091/ March 1680).
23. *JS*, 177:172 (11 Sha'bān 1100/31 May 1689); Khayr al-Din al-Ramli, *Al-Fatāwa al-Khayriyya* (Bulaq, 1300), I. 19–21.
24. Christians and Jews, recognized by the Ottomans as autonomous communities (*millets*) had the right to maintain their own legal systems. In many cases, however, they preferred to present their case at the *sharī'a* court. Sometimes the reasons had to do with the qadi's greater authority and ability to punish and exact payment, sometimes (as in this case, probably) with laws that were better disposed toward the plaintiff. No similar cases involving Jewish women were found.
25. The term *mahr* is sometimes translated as "bride-price," implying that it was payed to the bride's relatives. Since this was not always the case in Ottoman Jerusalem, the original term seems more appropriate.
26. "*Bi-allah al-'azīm al-qādir al-qāhir alladhī anzala al-injīl 'ala 'Isa bin Maryam*."
27. *NS*, 1:55 (14 Sha'bān 1066/31 May 1689).
28. Ramli, *al-Fatāwa al-Khayriyya*, I:19–20. *JS*, 107:260, no. 1149 (Rabī' Awwal 1033/January 1624); 177:46 (6 Dhu al-Qa'da 1085/ 31 January 1675); 183:137 (Jumāda al-Ūla 1091/ June 1680); 201:325 (20 Jumāda al-Ūla 1114/12 October 1702); *NS*, 1:246, and others. The number of requests for abrogation of marriage agreements and dissolution of marriage is

particularly surprising when compared to the small number of such requests in the modern era. Compare with Aharon Layish, *Women and Islamic Law in a Non-Muslim State* (Jerusalem, 1975), 163–72. For the use of *wakil* at the time in other parts of the empire, see R. C. Jennings, "The Office of Vekil (Wakil) in 17th Century Ottoman Sharica Courts" *Studia Islamica* 42 (1979): 147–68.

29. It is almost impossible to know from the text itself whether these queries were written by women (indicating that at least some knew how to read and write), whether they were helped by literate men, or whether they presented themselves in person or sent another man or an older woman to present their case.
30. Ramli, *al-Fatāwa al-Khayriyya,* 1:28. See also p. 29 on the same subject.
31. See *JS,* 107:790 (Ṣafar 1033/December 1623).
32. See, for example, *JS,* 125:131 (Ramaḍān 1045/ February 1636). At the request of a wife the qadi adds a stipulation to the marriage agreement whereby the husband vows that if he beats his wife again, she would automatically be allowed to divorce him.
33. Husband's impotence as cause for divorce: *JS,* 107:790 (Ṣafar 1033/ December 1623); husband's absence: 107:260,(Rabīʿ Awwal 1033/ January 1624); *NS* 1:75; 246; *JS,* 183:56 (Ṣafar 1091/March 1680); 201:317 (20 Jumāda al-Ūla 1114/ 12 October 1702); mistreatment and abuse: *JS,* 125:131 (Ramaḍān 1045/ February 1636); renunciation of dower: *NS,* 1:137; *JS,* 177:68 (15 Dhu al-Ḥijja 1085/12 March 1675); 177:81 (awā'il Muḥarram 1086/ April 1675). On preconditions for marriage, including "parity of status," see Jamal J. Nasir, *The Islamic Law of Personal Status* (London, 1986), 54. On dissolution of marriage in the various schools of law, see Keith Hodkinson, *Muslim Family Law: A Sourcebook* (London, 1984), 224; Nasir, *The Islamic Laws of Personal Status,* 114. According to Nasir, "the Hanafis maintain that dissolution of marriage is the exclusive right of the husband, with the court having to intervene only in the event of a serious genital defect such as impotence or castration."
34. *Zaʿīm*—holder of a *zeamet,* a large *timār* estate.
35. The term used is *min ʿiṣmatihi,* literally, "from his protection (or custody)."
36. *JS,* 191:43 (awāsiṭ Jumāda al-Ūla 1100/March 1689).
37. For a description of women's conduct in the imperial palace along similar lines, see Leslie Peirce, *The Imperial Harem,* 6–7, 198–216.
38. N. J. Coulson, *Succession in the Muslim Family* (Cambridge, 1971), 40–47.
39. Judith Tucker, *Women in Nineteenth Century Egypt* (Cambridge, Mass., 1985), 43–46.
40. See, for example, *JS,* 107:49 (Dhu al-Ḥijja 1032/ October 1623).

41. Women heirs are most often mentioned when selling their property. See *JS*, 107: 284, 318, 324 (5 Rabīʿ al-Thāni 1033/ 26 January 1624); 125:65 (Rajab 1045/ December 1635 - January 1636); 177:85 (10 Muḥarram 1086/6 April 1675); 177:97 (Muḥarram 1086/April 1675); 183:183 (Jumāda al-Ūla 1091/June 1680); 201:380 (Awākhir Jumāda al-Ākhira 1114/mid-November 1702).
42. On moneylending, see *JS*, 183:236 (awākhir Rajab 1091/September 1680). A Jewish woman moneylender: 191: 76 (awā'il Jumāda al-Ūla 1100/ February 1689).
43. See, for example, *NS*, 1:25 (12 Jumāda al-Ūla 1066/9 March 1656).
44. Suraya Faroqhi, *Men of Modest Substance: House Owners and House Property in Seventeenth Century Ankara and Kaiseri* (Cambridge, 1987), 159–60. On women buying property in Jerusalem, see *JS*, 107, no. 471 (21 Muḥarram 1033/ 14 November 1623); 107: no. 668 (Ṣafar 1033/ November–December 1623); 107:310, no. 1369 (Rabīʿ al-Thāni 1033/ January–February 1624); 125:15, no. 71 (Jumāda al-Ūla 1045/ October–November 1635); 125: 170, no. 746 (Shawwāl 1045/ March–April 1636); 168: 57, (20 Ramaḍān 1078/ 5 March 1668); 168: 62, (Rajab 1078/ December 1667 - January 1668); 168: 92 (same date); *NS*, 1:25, no. 2 (12 Jumāda al-Ūla 1066/ 9 March 1656). This situation continued in eighteenth-century Aleppo. See Abraham Marcus, *The Middle East on the Eve of Modernity* (New York, 1989), 54. According to Marcus, 40 percent of sellers and buyers of houses in Aleppo were women.
45. This is part of the formula used in the *sharīʿa* court to ascertain that all aspects of private property were examined by the court and that the property can be sold by the person offering it for sale (*ma huwwa laha, wa-jāri fi mulkiha, wa-taḥt taṣarrufiha, wa-yadduha wāḍiʿa ʿala dhalika*).
46. For purposes of transactions or inheritance, property was divided in most cases into twenty-four parts called *qirāt*. Parts smaller than one *qirāt* were usually counted as simple fractions of a *qirāt*. One could inherit, for instance, five and one-third *qirāts* (5⅓/24) of a house or orchard.
47. *JS*, 177: 90 (14 Muḥarram 1086/ 10 April 1675).
48. See Leslie Peirce, *The Imperial Harem*, especially 186–216.
49. A similar situation existed in eighteenth-century Aleppo, see Abraham Marcus, *The Middle East on the Eve of Modernity*, 53.
50. *JS*, 177:47 (20 Dhu al-Qaʿda 1085/ 15 February 1675); 177: 91 (15 Muḥarram 1086/11 April 1676).
51. Evliya Çelebi, *Seyahatname* (Istanbul, 1935), IX:497; R. C. Jennings, "Women in Early-Seventeenth-Century Ottoman Judicial Records: The Sharia Court of Anatolian Kaiseri," *Journal of the Economic and Social*

History of the Orient 18 (1975): 53–114; Haim Gerber, Social and Economic Position of Women in an Ottoman City, Bursa, 1600–1700," *International Journal of Middle East Studies* 12 (1980): 231–44; Leslie Peirce, *The Imperial Harem*, 141.

52. Roger Chartier, "Texts, Printing, Reading," in Lynn Hunt (ed.), *The New Cultural History* (Berkeley, 1989), 154–75.
53. See a similar dilemma described by Leslie Peirce, *The Imperial Harem*, 117–18.
54. False impressions were by no means limited to the West. Muslim travelers visiting the West had their own stereotypes and misconceptions. The liberal attitude towards women in the West was interpreted as shocking sexual behavior. One Moroccan ambassador to Europe in the eighteenth century remarked:

> Their dwellings have windows overlooking the street, where the women sit all the time, greeting the passersby. Their husbands treat them with the greatest courtesy. The women are very much addicted to conversation and conviviality with men other than their husbands, in company or in private. They are not restrained from going wherever they think fit. It often happens that a Christian returns to his home and finds his wife or his daughter or his sister in the company of another Christian, a stranger, drinking together and leaning against one another. He is delighted with this and, according to what I am told, he esteems it as a favor from the Christian who is in the company of his wife or whichever other woman of his household it may be.
>
> [. . .] When the party dispersed we returned to our lodgings and we prayed to God to save us from the wretched state of these infidels who are devoid of manly jealousy and are sunk in unbelief and we implored the Almighty not to hold us accountable for our offense in conversing with them as the circumstances required.

See Bernard Lewis, *The Muslim Discovery of Europe* (New York, 1982), 288.

55. See Leslie Peirce, *The Imperial Harem*, 7–12.
56. The advantages of seclusion and segregation were more readily understood by women travelers who visited the area in later centuries. In their eyes, however, seclusion was mistakenly identified with privacy, a projection of Victorian values onto the local harem system. See Billie Melman, *Women's Orients*, 139–48.
57. See Billie Melman, *Women's Orients*, 85–87.

58. On the other hand, as Beth Baron has shown in her research on marriage in Egypt, another Western influence—the idea of romance—pulled in the opposite direction, towards greater access to divorce. See Beth Baron, "The Making and Breaking of Marital Bonds in Modern Egypt," in N. Keddie and B. Baron (eds.), *Women in Middle Eastern History* (New Haven and London, 1991), 284–87.

Bibliography

ARCHIVAL MATERIAL

*Court Records (*sijills*) in the Archive of the Jerusalem* Sharīʿa *Court:*

Vol. 80 (1008–1009h./1599–1600)
Vol. 85 (1012–1013h./1603–1604)
Vol. 98 (1024–1025h./1615–1616)
Vol. 107 (1032–1033h./1622–1623)
Vol. 125 (1045h./1635–1636)
Vol. 146 (1061–1062h./1650–1651)
Vol. 153 (1067–1070h./1656–1660, *awāmir*)
Vol. 168 (1078–1079h./1667–1668)
Vol. 169 (1079–1080h./1668–1670)
Vol. 170 (1080–1081h./1669–1670)
Vol. 177 (1085–1086h./1674–1675)
Vol. 180 (1088–1089h./1677–1678)
Vol. 183 (1091h./1680)
Vol. 191 (1100h./1688–1689)
Vol. 201 (1113–1115h./1701–1704)

Sijill *in the Archive of the Nabulus Sharīʿa Court:*

Vol. 1 (1066–1068/1655–1658)

Archives of the Prime Minister's Office in Istanbul (BBA):

Mühimme Defterleri, vols. 68–115 (998–1120h./1599–1708)
Zeyl-i Mühimme, vol. 11 (1108/1696–1697)
Maliyeden Müdevver, no. 2841 (1048/1638)

Marseilles Chamber of Commerce (Chambre de Commerce de Marseilles):

H105 (Blé, 1631–1773)
H196 (Coton, 1629–1791)

I1 (Statistiques, 1680–1683)
J772 (Lettres de Joseph d'Esquissier des Tourres, Consul, Âcre 1686–1692)
J878 (Lettres des Consuls de Jérusalem, 1699–1700)
J879 (Âcre, Lettres des ViceConsuls, 1657–1782)
J880 (Âcre, Lettres de la Nation et des Deputés de la Nation, 1657–1742)
J883 (Lettres des Vice-Consuls etc., Rame)

Archives Nationales, Paris

Affaires Étrangères:
Serie B1 (Correspondance Consulaire)—628: (Jérusalem 1699–1717)
Serie B3 (Levant et Barbarie)—1, 34–36, 125, 129
Serie B7 (Marine)—59, 205, 208

Public Record Office, London:

SP97—State Papers, Turkey
Levant Company
SP105, no. 110 (Out letters)
SP110—Aleppo, Factory and Consulate Records, bundles 10–14

BOOKS AND MANUSCRIPTS

ʿAbbās, Iḥsan. "Hair Ad-Din Ar-Ramli's Fatāwa: A New Light on Life in Palestine in the Eleventh-Seventeenth Century," in Ulrich Haarman and Peter Bachman (eds.), *Die Islamische Welt Zwischen Mittelalter und Neuzeit*. Beirut, 1979.

Abou El-Haj, Rifaat. *The 1703 Rebellion and the Structure of Ottoman Politics*. Istanbul, 1984.

Abu Husayn, Abd el-Rahim. *Provincial Leadership in Syria 1575–1650*. Beirut, 1985.

———. "The Iltizam of Mansur Furaykh: A Case Study of Iltizam in Sixteenth-Century Syria." In T. Khalidi (ed.), *Land Tenure and Social Transformation in the Middle East*. Beirut, 1984.

Abu-Lughod, Janet. "The Islamic City—Historic Myth, Islamic Essence, and Contemporary Relevance." *International Journal of Middle East Studies* 19 (1987): 155–76.

Anderson, Perry. *Lineages of the Absolutist State*. London, 1974.

Al-ʿĀrif, ʿĀrif. *Al-Mufaṣṣal fi Tārikh al-Quds*. Jerusalem, 1961.

———. *Tārikh Ghazzā*. Jerusalem, 1943.

Arnon, A. "The Quarters of Jerusalem in the Ottoman Period." *Middle Eastern Studies* 28.1 (1992): 1–65.

D'Arvieux, Laurent. *Voyage dans la Palestine*. Amsterdam, 1718.

Ayn-ı 'Ali, Kavanin-i Al-ı Osman, in M. Belin "Du Régime des Fiefs Militaires dans l'Islamism." *Journal Asiatique* 15 (1870).

Baer, Gabriel. *Mavō letōldōt ha-yeḥasīm ha-agrariyīm ba-mizraḥ ha-tikhōn* (Introduction to the History of Agrarian Relations in the Middle East). Hebrew. Tel-Aviv, 1971.

———. *Egyptian Guilds in Modern Times*. Jerusalem 1964.

Bakhit, Muḥammad Adnan. *The Ottoman Province of Damascus in the 16th Century*. Beirut, 1982.

———. "Al-Usra al-Ḥārithiyya fi marj Bani 'Amr 885–1088/1480–1677." *Al-Abḥāth* 28 (1980): 55–78.

Barbir, Karl K. *Ottoman Rule in Damascus, 1708–1758*. Princeton, 1980.

———. "From Pasha to Effendi: The Assimilation of Ottomans into Damascene Society, 1516–1783." *International Journal of Turkish Studies* 1.1 (Winter 1979–80): 69–71.

Barkan, Ömer L. *XV ve XVI asırlarda Osmanlı Imparatorluğunda Zirai Ekonominin Hukuki ve Mâli Esasları*. Istanbul, 1943. Vol. 1—Kanunlar.

———. "The Price Revolution of the Sixteenth Century." *International Journal of Middle East Studies* 4 (1975): 3–28.

———. "Research on the Ottoman Fiscal Surveys," in M. Cook (ed.), *Studies in the Economic History of the Middle East*. Oxford, 1970, pp. 163–71.

Bell, Richard. *Account of the Travels of Richard Bell from Lisbon to Jerusalem and Other Places*. London: 1669.

Ben-Zvi, Y. *Eretz Yisra'el ve-yishūva bi-yemēy hashilṭōn ha-'ottomāni* (Palestine and Its Settlement in the Ottoman Period). Hebrew. Jerusalem, 1956.

Biddulph, William. *The Travels of Certaine Englishmen into Africa Asia etc., Begunne in 1600*. Manuscript in the British Library. London, 1609.

Bloomer, Herbert. *Symbolic Interactions: Perspective and Method*. Englewood Cliffs, N.J., 1969.

Braude, B. "International Competition and Domestic Cloth in the Ottoman Empire, 1500–1650: A Study in Underdevelopment." *Review* 2.3 (1979).

Braudel, Fernand. *Civilization and Capitalism, 15th–18th Century*, vol. I: *The Structure of Everyday Life*. London, 1981.

———. *The Mediterranean and the Mediterranean World in the Age of Philip II*. 2 vols. London, 1972.

De Calahora, J. *Chronica de la Provincia de Syria y Tierra Santa de Gerusalem*. Madrid, 1684.

Çetin, Atillâ. *Başbakanlık arşivi Kilavuzu*. Istanbul, 1979.

Charles-Roux, François. *Les Echelles de Syrie et de Palestine*. Paris, 1928.

Cohen, Amnon. *Economic Life in Ottoman Jerusalem*. Cambridge, 1989.

———. "Ottoman Rule and the Re-emergence of the Coast of Palestine." *Revue de l'Occident Musulman et de la Mediterranée (ROMM)* 39 (1985): 163–75.

———. *Palestine in the 18th Century.* Jerusalem, 1973.

———. *Yehūdīm be-shilṭōn ha-Islām: Qehilāt Yerūshalāyim be-rēshīt ha-tequfa ha-'ōthmānit* (Jews under Islamic Rule: The Jewish Community of Jerusalem in the Early Ottoman Period). Hebrew. Jerusalem, 1982.

Cohen, Amnon and Bernard Lewis. *Population and Revenue in the Towns of Palestine in the Sixteenth Century.* Princeton, 1978.

Coulson, N. J. *Succession in the Muslim Family.* Cambridge, 1971.

Cox, Edward G. *A Reference Guide to the Literature of Travel*. Seattle, 1935.

Creasy, E. S. *History of the Ottoman Turks*. London, 1877.

Crouch, Nathaniel. *Two Journeys to Jerusalem*. London, 1699.

Cuno, Kenneth M. "The Origins of Private Ownership of Land in Egypt: A Reappraisal." *International Journal of Middle East Studies* 12 (1980).

Darnton, Robert. "A Bourgeois Puts His World in Order: The City as a Text." In *The Great Cat Massacre and Other Episodes in French Cultural History.* New York, 1984.

Davis, Ralph. "English Imports from the Levant, 1580–1780." In M. A. Cook (ed.), *Studies in the Economic History of the Middle East*. Oxford, 1970.

Davis, Ralph. *Aleppo and Devonshire Square, English Traders in the Levant in the 18th Century.* London, 1967.

Doubdan, Jean. *Le Voyage de la Terre sainte*. Paris, 1666.

Doumani, Beshara B. "Palestinian Islamic Court Records: A Source for Socioeconomic History." *Middle Eastern Studies Association Bulletin* 19 (1985): 155–72.

Drory, Joseph. "Yerūshalayīm ba-teqūfa ha-mamlūkit." In B. Z. Qedar (ed.), *Peraqim be-toldōd Yerūshalāyīm bi-Yemey ha-beynāyyim*. Jerusalem, 1979.

Drory, J. *Eretz Yisra'el ba-teqūfa ha-mamlūkīt* (Palestine in the Mamluke Period). Hebrew. Jerusalem, 1993.

Du Rozel, François C. *Voyage de Jerusalem.* Paris, 1864.

Duzdağ, M. E. *Şeyhülislam Ebussuud Efendi Fetvaları Işiğinda 16. Asır Türk Hayatı*. Istanbul, 1972.

Eickelman, Dale F. "Is There an Islamic City?" *International Journal of Middle East Studies* 5 (1974): 274–94.

———. *The Middle East: An Anthropological Approach*. Englewood Cliffs, N.J., 1981.

Evliya Çelebi. *Seyahatname*. Istanbul, 1935.

Faroqhi, Suraya. *Men of Modest Substance: House Owners and House Property in 17th Century Ankara and Kayseri*. Cambridge, 1987.

———. *Towns and Townsmen of Ottoman Anatolia*. Cambridge: 1984

Findley, Carter. *Bureaucratic Reform in the Ottoman Empire*. Princeton, 1980.

Foster, W., ed. *The Travels of John Sanderson in the Levant*. London, 1931.
Friedman, Yoḥanan. "Eretz Yisra'el vi-Yerūshalāyim ʿerev ha-kībūsh ha-ʿōthmāni." In A. Cohen (ed.), *Peraqīm be-tōldōt Yerūshalāyim be-rēshīt ha-teqūfa ha-ʿothmānit* (Jerusalem in the Early Ottoman Period). Hebrew. Jerusalem, 1979.
Geertz, Clifford. *The Interpretation of Culture*. New York, 1973.
Gerber, Haim. *Economy and Society in an Ottoman City: Bursa 1600–1700*. Jerusalem, 1988.
———. "The Waqf Institution in Early Ottoman Edirne." In G. R. Warburg and Gad G. Gilbar (eds.), *Studies in Islamic Society: Contributions in Memory of Gabriel Baer*. Haifa, 1984.
———. *The Social Origins of the Modern Middle East*. Boulder, Col., 1987.
———. "Social and Economic Position of Women in an Ottoman City, Bursa, 1600–1700." *International Journal of Middle East Studies* 12 (1980): 231–44.
Al-Ghazzi, Najm al-Dīn Muḥammad. *Luṭf al-samar wa quṭf al-thamar min tarājim al-ṭabaqāt al-ūla min al-qarn al-ḥādi ʿashar*. Damascus, 1981–2.
Gibb, H. A. R. and H. Bowen. *Islamic Society and the West*. Oxford, 1950–57.
Goffman, Daniel. *Izmir and the Levantine World, 1559–1650*. Seattle, 1990.
Goujon, J. *Le Voyage de la Terre Sainte*. Lyons, 1671.
Hattox, Ralph. *Coffee and Coffee Houses: The Origins of a Social Beverage in the Medieval Near East*. Seattle and London, 1985.
Hayes, L. Baron de Courmenin. *Voyage de Levant fait par le commendement du Roy en l'année 1621*. Paris, 1624.
Heffening, W. "Wakf." *Encyclopedia of Islam*, 1st edition, London and Leiden, 1931, pp. 1096–1102.
Heyd, Uriel. *Ottoman Documents on Palestine, 1552–1615*. Oxford, 1960.
Hodgson, Marshall S. *The Venture of Islam*. Chicago, 1974.
Holt, Peter M. *Egypt and the Fertile Crescent, 1516–1922*. Ithaca and London, 1966.
Hourani, Albert. *The Emergence of the Modern Middle East*. London, 1981.
———. *Europe and the Middle East*. Berkeley, 1981.
Hourani, Albert and S. M. Stern. *The Islamic City*. Oxford, 1970.
Hütteroth W. D. and K. Abdulfattah. *Historical Geography of Palestine, Transjordan and Southern Syria in the Late 16th Century*. Erlangen, 1977.
İnalcık, Halil. *The Ottoman Empire: The Classical Age*. New York, 1973.
———. "Centralization and Decentralization in Ottoman Administration." In Thomas Naff and Roger Owen (eds.), *Studies in Eighteenth Century Islamic History*. Carbondale and Edwardsville, 1977, pp. 27–52.
———. "Islamization of Ottoman Laws on Land and Tax." In Christa Fragner and Klaus Schwarz (eds.), *Festgabe au Josef Matuz: Osmanistik—Turkologie—Diplomatik*. Berlin, 1992, pp. 101–18.

———. "Military and Fiscal Transformation in the Ottoman Empire, 1600–1700." *Archivum Ottomanicum* 6 (1980): 283–337.
———. "Istanbul: An Islamic City." *Journal of Islamic Studies* 1 (1990): 1–23.
———. "The Ottoman Economic Mind and Aspects of the Ottoman Economy." In M. A. Cook (ed.), *Studies in the Economic History of the Middle East*. Oxford, 1978.
———. "Ottoman Methods of Conquest." *Studia Islamica* 2 (1954).
———. "Introduction to Ottoman Metrology." *Turcica* 15 (1983): 311–48.
Inalcik, Halil and Carter Findley. "Maḥkama: The Ottoman Empire." *Encyclopedia of Islam* 2nd edition, 4: 1–44.
Inalcik, Halil, Zarinebaf-Shahr Fariba, and Karen Barkey. *Başbakanlık Arşivi Provincial Appointment Registers*. Forthcoming.
Islamoğlu-Inan, Huri, ed. *The Ottoman Empire and the World Economy*. Cambridge, 1987.
Islamoğlu, Huri and Suraya Faroqhi. "Crop Patterns and Agricultural Production in 16th Century Anatolia." *Review* 2.3 (1979): 401–36.
Islamoğlu Huri and Keyder Çağlar. "Agenda for Ottoman History." *Review* 1.1 (1977): 31–55.
Itzkowitz, Norman. *Ottoman Empire and Islamic Tradition*. Chicago and London, 1972.
Jennings, Ronald C. "The Office of Vekil (Wakil) in 17th Century Ottoman Sharia Courts." *Studia Islamica* 42 (1979): 147–68.
———. "Women in Early 17th Century Ottoman Judicial Records: The Sharīʿa Court of Anatolian Kaiseri." *Journal of the Economic and Social History of the Orient* 18 (1975): 53–114.
Kaldy-Nagy, Giula. "Rural and Urban Life in the Age of Sultan Suleiman." *Acta Orientalia* 32.3 (1978): 285–319.
al-Khālidi, Aḥmad. *Lubnān fi ʿahd al-amīr Fakhr al-Dīn al-Maʿnī al-thānī*. Beirut, 1936.
Khalidi, W. A. S. "al-ʿAlami." *EI_2* 1: 352.
Kunt, Metin. *The Sultan's Servants—The Transformation of Ottoman Government, 1550–1650*. New York, 1983.
———. "Kulların Kullarını." *Boğazici Üniversitesi Humaniter Bilimler* 3 (1975).
Ladurie, Emmanuel le Roy. *Le Carnaval de Romans*. Paris, 1979.
———. *Montaillou*. Paris, 1980.
———. *Les Paysans de Languedoc*. Paris, 1966.
Laouste, H. *Les Gouverneurs de Damas Sous les Mamlouks et Les Premiers Ottomans (656–1156/1260–1744): Traduction des Annales d'Ibn Tulun et d'Ibn Guma*. Damas, 1952.
Lapidus, Ira. *Muslim Cities in the Later Middle Ages*. Cambridge, Mass., 1967.
———. "Muslim Cities and Islamic Societies." in idem (ed.), *Middle Eastern Cities*. Berkeley and Los Angeles, 1969.

Layish, Aharon. *Women and Islamic Law in a Non-Muslim State*. Jerusalem, 1975.

Lewis, B. *Islam in History: Ideas, Men and Events in the Middle East*. New York, 1973

———. "Ottoman Land Tenure and Taxation in Syria." *Studia Islamica* 50 (1979): 109–24.

———. "ʿArus Resmi." EI_2 1: 679.

———. "Bad-i Hawa." EI_2 1: 850

Makovski, A. "Sixteenth Century Agricultural Production in the Liwa of Jerusalem." *Archivum Ottomanicum* 9 (1984): 91–127.

Mandaville, Jon E. "The Jerusalem Sharīʿa Court Records as a Supplement and Complement to the Central Ottoman Archives." In M. Sharon (ed.), *Studies on Palestine During the Ottoman Period*. Jerusalem, 1975.

Mannāʿ, ʿAdil. "Mered Naqīb al-ashrāf Bi-Yerūshalāyim, 1703–1705" (The Naqīb al-Ashrāf Revolt in Jerusalem, 1703–1705). Hebrew. *Cathedra* 53 (1989): 49–74.

———. "Moshley Yerūshalāyim mi-Bēyt Farrūkh ve-yeḥaseyhem ʿim ha-beduim." In A. Cohen (ed.), *Peraqim be-tōldōt Yerūshalāyim be-rēshit ha-teqūfa ha-ʿōthmānit* (Jerusalem in the Early Ottoman Period). Hebrew. Jerusalem, 1979.

———. "Mishpaḥat Farrūkh, shilṭona u-foʿola" (The Farrūkh Family, Its Rule and Deeds). Unpublished M.A. thesis, Hebrew University, 1978.

Mantran, Robert and Jean Sauvaget. *Réglements fiscaux Ottomans, les provinces Syriennes*. Beirut, 1951.

Al-Maqqār, Ibn Jumʿa. *Wulāt Dimashq fi al-ʿahd al-ʿUthmānī*. Damascus, 1949.

Marcus, Abraham. *The Middle East on the Eve of Modernity: Aleppo in the Eighteenth Century*. New York, 1989.

———. "Privacy in Eighteenth-Century Aleppo: The Limits of Cultural Ideals." *International Journal of Middle East Studies* 18 (1986).

Masson, P. *Histoire du commerce Français dans le Levant au 17é siècle*. Paris, 1896.

Matthews, N. and D. M. Wainwright. *A Guide to Manuscripts and Documents in the British Isles Relating to the Middle East and North Africa*. Oxford, 1980.

Maundrell, Henry. "A Journey from Aleppo to Jerusalem at 1697." In Thomas Wright (ed.), *Early Travels in Palestine*. New York, 1968.

McGowan, Bruce. "The Study of Land and Agriculture in the Ottoman Provinces within the Context of an Expanding World Economy in the 17th and 18th Centuries." *International Journal of Turkish Studies* 2.1 (1981): 57–63.

Melman, Billie. *Women's Orients: English Women and the Middle East, 1718–1918*. Ann Arbor, 1992.

Merton, R. K. *Social Theory and Social Structure*. Glencoe, Ill., 1957.

Meyer, M. M. *History of the City of Gaza*. New York, 1907.

Morison, Antoine. *Relation historique d'un voyage nouvellement fait au mont de Sinaï et à Jerusalem*. Paris, 1705

Morone, Mariano da Maleo. *Terra Santa Nuovamente Illustrata*. Piacenza, 1669.

Al-Muḥibbi, Muḥammad Amīn. *Khulāṣat al-āthār fi aʿyān al-qarn al-ḥādi ʿashar*. Cairo, 1284/1869.

Al-Murādī, Muḥammad. *Silk al-durar fi aʿyān al-qarn al-thānī ʿashar*. Cairo, 1292–1301/1874–1883.

Al-Nābulsī, ʿAbd al-Ghanī. *Al-Haḍra al-unsiyya fi al-riḥla al qudsiyya*. Manuscript, Bibliothèque Nationale, Mss. Arabes 5960, Damascus, 1101/1690.

———. *Kitāb al-ḥaqīqa wa-l-majāz fi riḥlat Bilād al-Shām wa-Miṣr wa-l-Ḥijāz*. Manuscript, Bibliothèque Nationale, Mss. Arabes 5042, n.d.

———. *Riḥlatī ilā al-Quds (Al-Haḍrā al-unsiyyā fi al-riḥlā al-Qudsiyyā)*. Cairo, n.d.

Naima, Muṣṭafa. *Rawḍat al-Ḥusayn fi khulāṣat akhbār al-ḥāfiqayn (Tārikh Naima)*.

Al-Nimr, Iḥsān. *Tārikh jabal Nābulus wa-l-Balqā'*. Nabulus, 1961.

Pakalın, M. Z. *Osmanlı Tarih Deyimleri ve Terimleri*. Istanbul, 1946.

Pamuk, Şevket. *The Ottoman Empire and European Capitalism 1820–1913—Trade, Investment and Production*. Cambridge, 1987.

Panzac, Daniel. "International and Domestic Maritime Trade in the Ottoman Empire during the 18th Century" *International Journal of Middle East Studies* 24 (1992) 189–206.

Paris, R. *Histoire du Commerce de Marseille—Le Levant*. Paris, 1957.

Parsons, Talcott. *The Social System*. Glencoe. Ill., 1951

Peirce, Leslie P. *The Imperial Harem: Women and Sovereignty in the Ottoman Empire*. New York, 1993.

Peri, Oded. "The Waqf as an Instrument to Increase and Consolidate Political Power: The Case of Khasseki Sultan Waqf in Late Eighteenth Century Jerusalem." In G. R. Warburg and G. Gilbar (eds.), *Studies in Islamic Society: Contributions in Memory of Gabriel Baer*. Haifa, 1984, pp. 47–62.

Perlmann, Moshe. "A Seventeenth Century Exhortation Concerning Al-Aqsa." *Israel Oriental Studies* 3 (1973): 261–92.

Qar'ali, Būlus. *Fakhr al-Dīn al-Maʿnī al-thānī ḥākim Lubnān wa dawlat Tuskāna 1605–1633*. Rome, 1938.

Al-Qudsi, Ḥasan ʻAbd al-Latīf. *Tarājim rijāl al-qarn al-thāni ʻashar min ahālī Miṣr wa-l-Quds al-sharīf*. Manuscript, British Library, Or. 3047, n.d.

Raba, Joel. *Eretz Yisra'el be-tē'ūrey nos'īm Russiyim* (Russian Travel Accounts of Palestine). Hebrew. Jerusalem, 1986.

Rabbath, A. *Documents inédits pour servir a l'Histoire du Christianisme en Orient*. Paris, 1905–1913 (repr. New York, 1973).

Rafeq, Abdul Karim. *The Province of Damascus 1723–1783*. Beirut, 1966.

———. *Ghazza, dirāsā ʻumrāniyyā wa ijtimāʻiyyā wa iqtiṣādiyyā min khilāl al-wathā'iq al-sharʻiyyā*. Amman, 1980.

———. *Bilād al-Shām wa Miṣr min al-fatḥ al-ʻUthmāni ilā ḥamlat Napuliūn Bunāpart*. Damascus, 1968.

Al-Ramli, Khayr al-Dīn. *Al-Fatāwa al-Khayriyya li nafʻ al-barīya*. Cairo, 1300h./1882–3.

Rauwolf, Leonhard. *Leonhard Rauwolf, Sixteenth Century Physician, Botanist and Traveler*. Cambridge, Mass., 1968.

Raymond, André. *The Great Arab Cities in the 16th–18th Centuries: An Introduction*. New York, 1984.

Roger, Eugène. *La Terre Sainte, ou Description très particulier de la Terre de Promission*. Paris, 1664.

Rozen, Minna. *Ḥōrvōt Yerūshalāyim* (The Ruins of Jerusalem, an edited manuscript). Hebrew. Tel-Aviv, 1981.

———. *Ha-qehīlā ha-Yehūdit bi-Yerūshalāyim ba-mē'ā ha-17* (The Jewish Community of Jerusalem in the 17th Century). Hebrew. Tel-Aviv, 1985.

———. "Mered Naqīb al-ashrāf bi-Yerūshalāyim ba-shanīm 1702–1706." (The Naqib al-Ashrāf Revolt in Jerusalem, 1702–1706). Hebrew. *Cathedra* 22 (1982).

Salameh, ʻOvadya, "ʻAvadīm be-baʻalūtam shel Yehūdīm ve-Notzrīm Bi-Yerūshalāyim ha-ʻōthmānit" (Slaves Owned by Jews and Christians in Ottoman Jerusalem). Hebrew. *Cathedra* 49 (1988): 62–75.

Sandys, George. *Travels, Containing a History of the Original of the Turkish Empire*. London, 1670.

Seikali, Amin. "Land Tenure in 17th Century Palestine: The Evidence from al-fatāwa al-Khairiyya." In Tarif Khalidi (ed.), *Land Tenure and Social Transformation in the Middle East*. Beirut, 1984.

Sertoğlu, Midhat. *Osmanlı Tarih Luğati*. Istanbul, 1986.

Shapira, Jonathan. *Yesōdōt ha-sotzyologya* (The Foundations of Sociology). Hebrew. Tel-Aviv, 1983.

Sharon, Moshe. "The Political Role of the Beduins in Palestine in the Sixteenth and Seventeenth Centuries." In M. Ma'oz (ed.), *Studies on Palestine during the Ottoman Period*. Jerusalem, 1975.

Shaw, Stanford. *History of the Ottoman Empire and Modern Turkey*. Cambridge, 1976.

Silāhdar, Findıklılı Mehmed ağa. *Silaḥdār tārikhi*. Istanbul, 1928.

Singer, Amy. "Ottoman Officials and Palestinian Peasants: Rural Administration in the Sancak of Jerusalem in the Mid-Sixteenth Century." Unpublished Ph.D. dissertation, Princeton University, 1989.

Singer, Amy. *Palestinian Peasants and Ottoman Officials: Rural Administration around Sixteenth-Century Jerusalem*. Cambridge, 1994.

———. "Tapu Taḥrīr Defterleri and Kadı Sicilleri: A Happy Marriage of Sources." *Tarih* (1990): 95–125.

Stephan, S. H. "An Endowment Deed of Khasseki Sultan, Dated the 24th May 1552." *The Quarterly of the Department of Antiquities in Palestine* 10 (1944): 170–94.

Süreyya, M. *Sicilli Osmani*. Istanbul, 1308–11h.

Surius, B. *Le Pieux pelerin du voyage de Jérusalem*. Brussels, 1666.

De Thevenot, Jean. *The Travels of Monsieur de Thevenot into the Levant*. London, 1687 (French version, 1674).

Toledano, E. "Sanjaq Yerūshalāyim ba-me'ā ha-16, hityashvūt kafrīt u-megamōt demōgrafīyōt." In A. Cohen (ed.) *Peraqim betōldōt Yerushalayim be-rēshīt ha-teqūfa ha-ʿothmānīt* (Jerusalem in the Early Ottoman Period). Hebrew. Jerusalem, 1979.

———. *Mavo le-tōldōt ha-imperyā ha-ʿōthmānit* (An Introduction to the History of the Ottoman Empire). Hebrew. Tel-Aviv, 1985.

———. *State and Society in Mid-nineteenth Century Egypt*, Cambridge, 1990.

De Tressan, Pierre. *Relation nouvelle et exacte d'un voyage de la Terre sainte*. Paris, 1688.

Tucker, Judith. *Women in Nineteenth-Century Egypt*. Cambridge, 1985.

Verniero, Pietro de Montepiloso. *Croniche ovvero annali di Terra Santa*. Publicate par P. Golubovich, Firenze, 1929–1936.

Von Grünebaum, Gustav E. "The Structure of the Muslim Town." In idem (ed.), *Islam: Essays in the Nature and Growth of a Cultural Tradition*. London, 1965, pp. 141–58.

Von Hammer-Purgstall, J. *Geschichte des Osmanischen Reiches*. Pest, 1827–35.

Wallerstein, Immanuel. "The Ottoman Empire and the Capitalist World Economy: Some Questions for Research." *Review* 2.3 (1979): 389–401.

———. "The Rise and Future Demise of the Capitalist World System: Concepts for Comparative Analysis." *Comparative Studies in Society and History* 16.4 (1974).

Weber, Max. *The City*. London, 1958.

Wickham, Chris. "The Uniqueness of the East." In Jean Baechler, John A. Hall and Michael Mann (eds.), *Europe and the Rise of Capitalism*. Oxford, 1988.

Wood, A. C. *A History of the Levant Company.* Oxford, 1935.

Ya'ari, Avraham. *Masā' Meshūlam mi-Voltera le-Eretz Yisra'el bishnat 5241 (1481)* (The travels of Meshulam of Voltera in Palestine in 1481). Hebrew. Jerusalem, 1949.

———. *Mas'ōt Eretz Yisra'el* (Travels in Palestine). Hebrew. Ramat-Gan, 1976.

Ze'evi, D. "Ha'avdūt ba-imperya ha-'othmānit ba-me'ā ha-19—Hēbetīm ḥevratiyyīm u-mishpaiyyīm (Slavery in the Ottoman Empire in the 19th Century—Social and Judicial Aspects). Hebrew. Unpublished M.A. thesis, Tel Aviv University, 1985.

Name Index

Abu-Lughod, Janet, 16–17, 199n28
Abou el-Haj, Rifaat, 62–64
Aḥmad ibn Riḍwān, 53, 71
ʿAlam al-Dīn Sulaymān (maghribi sūfi), 72
D'Arvieux, Laurent, 174, 175, 176
al-ʿAlami, ʿAbd ql-Qadir, 72–73, 75
al-ʿAlami, muḥammad, 22
ʿAssāf Farrūkh, 58

Baer, Gabriel, 129
Bahrām Pasha (Kara Shahin Mustafa's son), 52
Barbir, Karl, 66, 76
Barkan, Ömer Lutfi, 129, 135–136
Baron, Beth, 235n58
Bayezit, 40
Bowen, H., 64
Braude, Benjamin, 167
Braudel, Fernand, 108–109, 199n22

Chartier, Roger, 186
Cohen, Amnon, 23, 103

Ḍahir al-ʿUmar, 114, 194
al-Dajjāni Abu al-Fatḥ, 25
Darnton, Robert, 79

Ebusuud Şeyhülislam Efendi (famous mufti), 131
Eickelman, Dale, 16, 25–26, 91, 109, 119, 185, 201n55

Fakhr al-Dīn al-Mʿani (the second), 4, 20–21, 40–41, 43, 45, 49, 57, 101, 165, 170, 174, 194
Faroqhi, Suraya, 17–18, 135–136, 184
Farrūkh Bey (governor of Jerusalem), 96, 208n46
Findley, Carter, 54

Geertz, Clifford, 110
Gerber, Haim, 95, 185
Gibb, H.A.R., 64
Von Grünebaum, Gustav, 15–16

Hasan Pasha Riḍwān, 55
Hattox, Ralph, 29
Haseki Sultan (Khasiki), 4
Heyd, Uriel, 93, 95, 98, 102, 205n7
Hourani, Albert, 16, 64–66, 84
Ḥusayn Pasha Riḍwān, 71, 208n43
al-Ḥusayni ʿAbd al-Qādir, 74–75

Ibn Khaldun, 92–93, 109
Ibn Mashīsh (famous saint), 72
Ibn Ṭulūn, 2
İnlacik, Halil, 65, 66, 121
İslamoğlu-Inan, Huri, 152, 169, 226n29

Janbulad (the rebel), 43
al-Jazzar, 194
Jennings, Ronald C., 185

al-Khāsikiyya, 4
Kara Shahīn Muṣṭafa Pasha (Riḍwān's father), 53
Keyder, Çağlar, 152, 169, 226n29
Kha'ir (Hayir) bey, 1
Khāsiki Hurrem Sultan (Roxellana), 13, 27, 199

Subject and Term Index